Killing Me Softly

Killing Me Softly With His Song

Lyric - Norman Gimbel   Music - Charles Fox

I heard he sang a good song, I heard he had a style and so I came to see him and listen for a while and there he was this young boy a stranger to my eyes. Strumming my pain with his fingers singing my life with his words killing me softly with his song killing me softly with his song telling my whole life with his words killing me softly with his song

Killing Me Softly

My Life in Music

Charles Fox

Foreword by Roberta Flack

THE SCARECROW PRESS, INC.

Lanham • Toronto • Plymouth, UK

2010

Published by Scarecrow Press, Inc.
A wholly owned subsidiary of The Rowman & Littlefield Publishing Group, Inc.
4501 Forbes Boulevard, Suite 200, Lanham, Maryland 20706
http://www.scarecrowpress.com

Estover Road, Plymouth PL6 7PY, United Kingdom

British Library Cataloguing in Publication Information Available

Library of Congress Cataloging-in-Publication Data

Fox, Charles, 1940–
  Killing me softly : my life in music / Charles Fox.
    p. cm.
  Includes index.
  ISBN 978-0-8108-6991-2 (hardback : alk. paper) — ISBN 978-0-8108-6992-9 (ebook)
  1. Fox, Charles, 1940– 2. Composers—United States—Biography. I. Title.
  ML410.F793A3 2010
  780.92—dc22
  [B]   2010006259

♾ ™ The paper used in this publication meets the minimum requirements of
American National Standard for Information Sciences—Permanence of Paper
for Printed Library Materials, ANSI/NISO Z39.48-1992.

Printed in the United States of America

For Joan, and the journey we traveled together hand in hand.

Contents

Foreword

$\mathcal{T}$his book is a very interesting tale of Charles Fox's pursuit of music. All of us who travel this same path know the story well—that is what makes us unique; that is what makes us different. Those who stand on the outside, looking "in" at the lives of musical geniuses like Charles Fox, will wonder with amazement at the discovery of the phrase "Killing Me Softly with His Song." It is in the book.

I have always maintained that the greatest musicians, historically, are surrounded by an aura of innocence: Mozart, Donny Hathaway, Chopin, Stevie Wonder, Beethoven, Johnny Cash, Puccini, Verdi, Charles Fox . . . a very broad group of artists, a very long list, all of whom share a common thread in that they seem completely unaware of the depth of their greatness and the extent to which their work, their music, their musical thought affects the lives of everyone.

When Charles Fox gets a call from a very young Steven Spielberg telling him that he hears "Killing Me Softly" on every station of his radio, every day, all day, and how much he loves the song, Fox is curious. First of all, he does not know this young director until someone schools him a little later on. His response is pure honesty, and of course, he'd be happy to do anything—score any film with Steven Spielberg. For he too is amazed that every time he gets into his car, every radio button he presses is playing this same song.

I had been to California to record a television tribute to Duke Ellington, "Duke Ellington, We Love You Madly," produced by Quincy Jones. I was full of incredible, overwhelming excitement, grinning from ear to ear. I finished that project, which had given me the privilege of singing, by myself, Duke's songs, as well as the honor of performing songs with Peggy Lee, Sarah Vaughan, and Aretha Franklin. How absolutely thrilling. Nothing could

ix

possibly match that excitement, or so I thought, until I boarded the plane heading back to New York and chose an audio program to listen to which featured "Killing Me Softly."

The title, of course, smacked me in the face. I immediately pulled out some scratch paper, made musical staves, and began jotting down the melody that I heard. I continued replaying the song, at least eight to ten times, until the plane landed. When I landed, I immediately called Quincy at his house and asked him how to meet Charles Fox.

Two days later, I had the music. I took my band to Kingston, Jamaica: Richard Tee on keyboards, Ralph McDonald on percussion, Eric Gale, guitar. We sailed into Bob Marley's studio, Tuff Gong, to rehearse the song and possibly record it. Wow! What memories!

Fast forward to the Greek Theater, on tour with Quincy. "Q" asked me to do an encore. "I've already done one—the only one we prepared." "Well, do another one, do something else" he replied. I told him that I had this song, "Killing Me Softly," and he said okay. The band looked at me like I was crazy. We started and everything fell into place. When we finished, the audience screamed. Q then came over to me, put his hand on my shoulder and said, "Do not perform that song again until you release it."

I am happy to say, as a perennial student of music, that of the hundred or so versions that I have been fortunate enough to hear around the world over the years, including that of the Fugees, I can tell that my recording of Charles Fox's beautiful song made an impact. Indeed, Lauren Hill, of the Fugees, told me that when her mother was carrying her as a baby, she played my recording of the song all of the time. And, in fact, Lauren insisted that I be a part of the video of their recorded version of the song—what an honor for me.

Charles Fox, write me another one. . . .

—Roberta Flack, musician

Acknowledgments

$\mathcal{T}$his book started out as a collection of letters that I wrote home to my family in the Bronx when I was a student in Paris. My mother saved those letters in a shoebox that we found many years later, in a dresser drawer in her bedroom in her apartment in the Bronx shortly before she died.

I have to thank the following people for giving importance to those letters and for their encouragement in turning them into this book:

My daughter, Lisa, for painstakingly collecting those letters and making four copies that filled two large loose-leaf books each. My son Robbie for being the first one to discover the letters in my mother's apartment and read them and later on mentioning them to his agent as a possible source for a memoir. My son David, who read many of the letters, who thought they were inspirational and encouraged me to write my story. My assistant, Will Collyer, who has more important work to do as a talented actor, performer, and composer in his own right, but who transcribed all the letters into the computer as well as the entire book, which I wrote in longhand on yellow legal pads, and in general for being a great sounding board to many thoughts along the way. My literary agency, beginning with Bob Rosen of RLR Agency, who found out about the letters from my son's agent, and called me to ask me if he could read the letters. My first reaction was that they were too personal and I didn't think that they would be of any interest to anyone outside of my family. He persevered, and I sent the letters to him. Bob called me after reading them and told me that there is a book here that he would get published if I would fill the book out with the rest of my story, before and after my life in Paris. Along the way, Bob responded to the development of the book in stages, as an editor would, with encouragement and challenges that helped improve the book immeasurably. My agent at RLR, Scott Gould, who believed in the book and found a welcoming home for it with Scarecrow Press. Stephen Ryan at Scarecrow Press for his believing in the book. Roberta Flack, a great and inspired artist, who responded, "I would love to" when I asked her if she would write a foreword to the book. Finally, to my wife, Joan, who is a part of everything I do, and to my grandchildren, Josh, Olivia, Jack, Ava, Jordan, and the twins, Brandon and Benjamin, as they are the ultimate joy and reason for preserving my story.

Introduction

Early in the year 2004, I received a call from Hal David, one of the great lyricists and the chairman of the Songwriters Hall of Fame. Hal and I had written many songs together and have been friends for a long time. He said he was happy to be bringing me the good news that I had been voted in to be inducted into the Songwriters Hall of Fame that year, to join an illustrious group of three hundred or so songwriters who have created the songs that reflect on every generation, beginning with Francis Scott Key, who gave us our National Anthem in 1776. This is the organization that honors the songwriters who have given the world the songs we sing.

I was so fortunate to be among the few songwriters who would be inducted that year. I really had no expectation of receiving that joyful call. I was thrilled and of course, felt greatly honored, and with that, my mind naturally drifted back to certain events in my life that might have led to that moment.

Several months later, following an afternoon rehearsal for the Songwriters Hall of Fame show in New York, I was sitting in a nearly empty ballroom at the Marriott Marquis Hotel, and chatting with Roberta Flack, who would be presenting the award to me that night. She had just finished the sound check and rehearsal for her performance of "Killing Me Softly," which she had discovered one day while she was on an American Airlines flight between Los Angeles and New York, and was listening to a preprogrammed album that contained our first recording of that song. At one point in our conversation, I said to Roberta, "How lucky for me that you found that song," and Roberta, who is a beautiful and spiritual person, said, "No, the song found me."

That's how it's been for me, often, in my life in music—a series of experiences and events, many that produced opportunities and occasional successes greater than I could ever have imagined, and many that never led to anything despite my best efforts. However, I never stop feeling grateful for what I'm privileged to do in my life. Looking back, all in all, it's been nothing short of miraculous.

As a young eighteen-year-old hopeful musician trying to find my way in the world of music, quite by accident, I first heard the name of the teacher who would ultimately be the greatest influence in my life and give me the tools and inspiration that I carry with me to this day, nearly a half century later: Nadia Boulanger.

I came to France for that summer of 1959, enrolled in the conservatory in the Palace of Fontainebleau, where Nadia Boulanger was the director. Music was all that I had ever considered as a career, but I was completely without focus. After my first private lesson with Mademoiselle Boulanger, I knew that composing would be my life's work. She was seventy-two years old and took me under her wing and said that she would like me to continue studying with her in Paris after the summer. For the next two years I saw her every week for private lessons, composition analysis class, keyboard harmony class, and occasional concerts and formal dinners in her elegant apartment on the Rue Ballu.

I never paid her for a lesson. She knew I couldn't afford it, and she was always more concerned for my well-being—that I had enough to eat. It was not a scholarship by any means. She was a dedicated teacher, the most renowned and influential music composition teacher of the twentieth century, and certainly for me, the most inspirational. And I was hungry to learn and experience all that was available to me. It was as simple as that. She said to me that one day, if I was able to, I could help someone else in return. That's a legacy that stays with you for life.

During my two years in Paris, I wrote very detailed letters home to my family who were eager to hear every word of my experiences. The center section of this memoir contains many of those letters in truncated form. My mother had preserved them in a shoebox in a dresser drawer in her bedroom in the Bronx. I discovered them only shortly before she died. They were the basis for writing this book. I surrounded those letters with my early student years in music and followed with my professional life since my return from France as a student, when I was twenty.

Since that time, I have composed the music for more than one hundred motion pictures and television films, as well as many long-running TV series. I've written hundreds of songs in collaboration with some of the great lyricists of the twentieth century, in addition to ballets and concert works for large orchestra, chamber groups, and solo instruments. I've had the pleasure of conducting symphony orchestras in many countries in the world recording or performing my music.

For this book, I've chosen to tell the stories that had the greatest influence on me in my life in music, and those that I felt would shed light on the journey of a contemporary American composer. I've had such a varied life in music, but the one journey I never before dreamed of taking was to write about those experiences.

Prelude: The Bronx, 1958

$\mathscr{I}$n all respects but one, that cold winter's night was like every other. It was not long after my eighteenth birthday, and I was returning home in the very late hours of the night—or early morning hours, depending on which side of the clock you lived your life—from a job playing the piano in a Latin dance band. At that hour there was never a parking space to be found close to the apartment house that I lived in with my family, and I had to park my father's car several blocks away, and then make my way in the chilly morning air, bundled up against the wind as I walked the rest of the way home on the empty Bronx streets. That particular night, I met my piano teacher, whom I began taking piano lessons with when I was nine. She was out walking her dog at that hour, and we stopped to talk in front of my apartment house, where she lived as well.

She asked me what I was planning to do with my life. As I had no clear-cut plans or direction, I really had no answer except that music was all I was interested in as a career. She asked me about enrolling in a conservatory, and I told her my feelings about not wanting to be in a formal educational system. She had another thought. "There is a great teacher in Paris who has taught many, if not generations of American composers." What did I think of going to Paris to study? Paris sounded so unreal, so far away, and dream-like for someone who hadn't even ventured to Brooklyn yet. During my high school days, my friend Steve Frankel and I would sometimes go down to the pier in the harbor on the west side, just to see the huge ships that would be in dock, and dream out loud of the prospect of one day seeing the world. So I responded immediately and happily to that thought. That was the first moment that I heard the name of the woman who would become my beloved teacher

1

and mentor, and who would give me the tools and courage and inspiration to last a lifetime, Nadia Boulanger.

My piano teacher, Nura Yurberg, told me about Fontainebleau, and the summer school there where Mlle Boulanger taught. "Who knows?" she said. "If she likes you and you want to stay in Paris, this could be very important to you." I told her that it sounded wonderful, but I was sure that my parents couldn't afford to send me to this school even for the summer. She said, "Don't worry, I'll speak to your parents and tell them how much this could mean to your future. Now you'll have to hurry and get an application to the school, which starts in just a few months from now. You'll need letters of recommendation." I mentioned my composition teacher from the High School of Music & Art, Mr. Mark Lawner. She said, "That's good, but you'll probably need a least two letters. Why not write to several well-known musicians in New York and ask if they'll give you an interview? A letter from someone like Leonard Bernstein or Thomas Schippers or Aaron Copland would surely get you accepted."

I don't really know what Mrs. Yurberg said to my parents to convince them that they should find a way to send me to Paris. My father was a window cleaner, and there wasn't a lot of extra money to go around. I do know that it took their unwavering belief in me and unending support of my interests and dreams. Or maybe they believed in the music bump story. When I was born, my mother's doctor noticed a bump on the back of my head after he delivered me and supposedly pointed to the bump and proclaimed it to be a music bump, that I was destined to become a musician. . . . So the story goes.

Leonard Bernstein and Aaron Copland sent back nice letters that they were not able to meet me. I appreciated that they took the time even to reply to me. However, I did get a letter from Thomas Schippers's assistant that he would be happy to see me, and that I should call to arrange for an appointment. Thomas Schippers was the principal guest conductor of the Metropolitan Opera Orchestra at that time, and like Leonard Bernstein, when he burst onto the scene, he was considered a wunderkind for his conducting achievements at a very young age. Of all the people I wrote to, he was the only person who agreed to meet with me.

He had a beautiful, statuesque assistant working for him whose name I somehow never forgot, Raymonda Orselli. I met her only that day of my meeting with Mr. Schippers at his apartment, but I always remember her kindness. The elevator door opened on the floor of Thomas Schippers's apartment on Park Avenue, and as I had trouble finding his apartment house and was a few minutes late, she was there as the elevator door opened to rush me into the apartment saying, "You're a little bit late; it's okay but we must hurry."

Thomas Schippers was very friendly and gracious, and greeted me warmly. I played my scherzo for clarinet and piano for him. I played a composition for string quartet. He commented on my enthusiasm in trying to show all four string parts by playing two or three of them and singing the other lines, jumping back and forth between the musical lines that needed to be brought out. He said he was interested in my career and subsequently wrote a brief but lovely note on my behalf to the Fontainebleau School and Nadia Boulanger. Armed with my two letters of recommendation, I sent off the application to the school and soon afterward received my letter of acceptance.

Looking back, that's when everything came into focus in my life. It seems, in retrospect, that everything in my life prior to going to Paris was only to prepare me for those two years.

❦

I started taking piano lessons when I was around nine years old. Most of my friends did as well, but unlike them, I really liked practicing and playing my pieces. I remember running home after school excitedly to work on a piece that I was learning. I couldn't hear the sounds the notes made in my head until my fingers played them, so every step my fingers took was a surprise to my ears. In every other way, my day was just like all of my friends'—sports, television (when we finally got one), books, comic books, and homework. When I learned to play well enough, I would sometimes accompany my father playing his mandolin. It was always good for a little extra allowance.

My piano teacher was a woman who lived in our apartment house. Aside from having been my first and only piano teacher, she would also be the person who years later would provide me with the thought that would be the turning point in my life. Nura Yurberg taught at the New York College of Music, but I merely took the elevator to the fifth floor for my lessons, with two dollars neatly folded in my shirt pocket. She was a lovely woman with a warm smile. The worst I remember her ever commenting on my playing was, "Oh come on, you can do better than that!" Although I studied privately with her, Mrs. Yurberg did include me in musical adventures with her other students, who were older than me. I gave recitals from time to time along with her other students. Those days were days of dread and fear, the day of the recital, but somehow I always managed to get over my fright in time to play. I saw my first opera with my teacher and her other students when she took us to the City Center Opera to see Prokofiev's *Love for Three Oranges*. It was so tuneful and spirited and so much fun and made such a great impression on me that it was a perfect first opera to see. Another time she took us to NBC Studios at Rockefeller Center to see a radio broadcast, complete with music and sound effects people filling in the necessary sounds to make the program believable to the listening audience in radioland. After the show, we were taken to a television studio, where each of us was interviewed briefly on closed-circuit television that could be seen only in the building. I remember the interviewer asking me what I wanted to be when I grew up. I answered with the only thing that I could think of at that moment, "A pianist." Mrs. Yurberg ultimately prepared me for my auditions for the High School of Music & Art, and the High School of Performing Arts. I was accepted to both schools and chose Music & Art because it offered more of an academic background as well as a thorough background in music.

Music & Art made an instant impression on me. The students filtered in from all five boroughs and were accepted to the school on the basis of musical ability or artistic ability for the fine arts program. A whole new world opened up for me. Here there were students like myself, who actually liked practicing their instruments. All the piano students at Music & Art had to learn a second instrument as there were four symphony orchestras and four symphonic wind orchestras to fill. I was given the choice of a bassoon or flute, and I chose the bassoon, which I played during my four years at M & A.

As a freshman at age fourteen, I met students my age who were very gifted classical and jazz musicians. There were jazz players who seemed to play as well as the great jazz musicians of the day. My friend Mike Gold, who was a great influence on me, played the clarinet, and you'd think it was Benny Goodman playing. A moment later he played the alto sax, and he sounded like Charlie Parker. There were drummers and pianists and other wind players to match. There were jam sessions going on in practice rooms during the school hours and after school. I was immediately influenced by my classmates and decided that jazz, which sounded so cool and inventive to me, was going to be my life. I watched my new friends play the piano and studied their fingers to see how they made those chords that sounded so fresh. I started listening to jazz on the radio and bought every record I could afford. I tried to emulate at the piano what I heard on records. Monk, Dizzy, Coltrane, Gerry Mulligan, the Modern Jazz Quartet, and Dave Brubeck. I had given up my piano lessons by this time, but practiced hour after hour, trying to improvise and find the chords that I heard the jazz greats play. Sometimes I would turn down the lights in our living room trying to create a jazz club atmosphere. Suddenly I was not asked by my parents to play Mozart or "Malagueña," as all they heard from the piano was some attempt to play a kind of music that they knew nothing about and really didn't like. That suited me very well, as I felt that it was satisfying some inner need to discover something for myself, almost like a rite of passage. I went to parties with my classmates where people would congregate around the piano and play nothing but jazz. At the same time, along with my friends from school, we would often go to Greenwich Village on weekends to hear jazz being played at some of the clubs like the Blue Note or the Village Vanguard. Rock and roll was all over the radio, and there were doo-wah groups on every street corner in Manhattan (in Music & Art there were doo-wah groups practicing on every floor of our building), but I had no interest in any of that. Jazz was all that interested me.

When I was fifteen, I formed my first band, a dance band, and we rehearsed all day on Saturdays and on an occasional afternoon after school. Four fifteen-year-olds playing the trumpet, sax, piano, and drums, and we all took it very seriously. Every now and then we'd pool our money and take the train together to 48th Street to Manny's Music Store and buy a stock arrangement or two of some standard songs, then we'd hurry back to Donnie's basement to rehearse the new numbers and see how they sounded. We all got goose bumps with the harmonies between the trumpet and sax, and we all smiled uncontrollably when the beat we played produced a sensation of being perfectly in sync with one another. We all shared the dream of getting a job in the Catskills and going away for the summer and becoming professional musicians.

When we felt we were sounding enough like a professional band, I started going downtown after school and knocking on the doors of the small-time theatrical agencies that represented the talent in the Catskills. Abe Blyman agreed to come to a rehearsal and listen to us play. His wasn't William Morris or a major agency, but Abe Blyman knew the Catskills. I think that he stood less than five feet tall in his highest heeled shoes. He was probably no more than fifty years old, but I remember him as seeming to be much older. He was very thin and wore striped dress shirts with a loosely tied tie and suspenders and spoke with a thick Jewish accent. They all did, the small-time booking agents that kept the Catskills supplied with all kinds of talent. He put us through the customary routines. "Let's hear a cha-cha, a waltz, a Foxtrot, a Lindy. Can you sight-read music? Can you cut a show?" (That's the vernacular for "can you accompany an act?") Twenty minutes later he gave us the supreme compliment. "All right boys, I'll see what I can do to get you a job for the summer."

Suddenly this band of fifteen-year-old musicians had professional representation. We had an agent. I had spent many summers of my youth with my parents in the Catskill mountains, but this summer of 1955 was going to be the first summer of my independence, of my adult life. The time to start to test dreams, and an agent held the key to that opportunity.

One day I got a call from Abe Blyman that the owner of a little hotel, the Melbourne Lake Hotel in Parksville, New York, was coming into town to audition bands for the summer, and he had set up an audition for us. We rented a rehearsal room downtown, on 8th Avenue, and we arrived long before our appointed hour to set up and do a little practicing before the owner showed up. At the exact hour that our audition was scheduled for, Abe Blyman walked in with the owner, who looked and spoke a lot like Abe Blyman himself except that he was much heavier.

Without any fanfare, the owner said, "Let's hear you play something." Then we went into a similar routine as we had when we played for Abe Blyman. "How about a Foxtrot, a rumba, a hora." Horas were the key to it. If you could sound good on a hora with a clarinet wailing a Jewish melody at the top of his register, with the band keeping a good steady beat, you were practically in. The owner must have thought that we were acceptable, and we were offered the job for the summer on the spot. The only problem was that he wanted a three-piece band for sixty dollars a week in total. We were of course a four-piece band, but our shrewd agent tried to talk the owner in to taking all four players for the same sixty dollars. Fifteen dollars a week per musician. The owner really wasn't sure. For him it meant an extra bed to house us, and more food to feed us. He thought about it long and hard. Abe Blyman pressed. We stood by anxiously. The owner was still quietly considering the options. For us it wasn't about the money. We just wanted to stay together as a band. Four musicians, four sets of dreams. Finally, the owner said yes. We had a job. Playing music. Entertaining. All our work and efforts, rehearsals all day on Saturdays and after school during the week occasionally, paid off. The sweet sounds of an alto saxophone and trumpet with the tight, glorious harmonies they made on stock arrangements of "Dream" and "Miami Beach Rumba" were enough to make us all jump out of our skins. Especially when they were played in tune. We really worked hard as a unit to play together. We did, and we loved it.

So there we were, professionals. If we had dreamed about being sailors, the gangplank of our ship was being hauled up into the hull as we were setting sail to a foreign shore. If we had dreamed about being writers, we just got our first acceptance letter from *Harper's* magazine. And if we had studied to become lawyers, we just passed the bar. Sweet. . . . The world was ours.

At the beginning of that summer, 1955, my father driving his first car, a new Bermuda blue Ford Fairlane, drove me to Parksville, NY, along with one of the other musicians in the band, Sol Motola, the trumpet player. As we approached the hotel, which was very modest even by the standards of the smaller hotels at that time, Sol and I could hear music being played in the casino. This casino was not like the casino we picture today in Las Vegas with a big showroom, but very much like many others in the Catskills at that time. A big wooden room with knotty pine paneling, empty except for wooden folding chairs and a makeshift stage. That was where the entertainment would take place for the summer. It was our workplace, our arena to be heard, our chance to be recognized for all our work and efforts. Sol and I asked my father to stop the car in front of the casino, and we leaped out to discover where the music was coming from. To our amazement, it was our band, if you could call a clarinetist and a drummer a band. When Phil and Donnie arrived at the hotel a little earlier than us that day, the hotel guests were so happy to have live musicians that they begged them to start playing. So what if they were missing some key ingredients? A piano? A trumpet? Sure it'll be better when we have a whole band, but who cares? Let's have music. Donnie and Phil were so anxious to please that they set up their instruments and began playing horas. Just a clarinet and a drum, but the music got the guests up dancing and clapping. Well, when Sol and I saw this, I excitedly took out our musical arrangements, Sol his trumpet, we set up the music stands, and in a minute we were a band, playing our hearts out and excited to be heard. The guests loved it and showered us with applause. We were smiling ear to ear. We finally played for an audience. We didn't play for too long. After a short set we packed up our instruments and music and headed to find the bungalow that would house our sleeping accommodations for the summer. I asked my father what he thought of the band, as he had never heard us play before, and in his ever-encouraging voice he said, "Pretty good, and I'm sure it'll get better." But we had the summer to learn and improve. After all, that's what the Catskills were all about for a young performer of any kind. A chance to learn. A chance to get started. And they paid you accordingly.

The Melbourne Lake Hotel was too small and too inexpensively run to hire new talent each week to perform, so they had the same performers for the whole summer, who provided all the entertainment. Harry Steinman was an old-time Jewish vaudeville comedian and Yiddish Theatre actor. He put on shows featuring the singing of Velma Revell along with his own, and together they performed his versions of Yiddish Theatre classics. He played parts mostly featuring a schleppy ne'er-do-well, in colorful, checked, baggy pants and funny little Pinky Lee hats, and actually used pancake makeup and lipstick. This was a world gone by even in 1955, but the audience loved it. Our band played for Harry and Velma during the musical numbers, and I would usually underscore the dramatic scenes with a piano solo, using some familiar Jewish melodies, or simply by making them up. It was probably similar to accompanying a silent film, and many of the scenes they performed were silent. It was a great training ground for becoming a professional musician, and it led to a very successful and satisfying summer.

Summer of 1955, Melbourne Lake Hotel. (From left to right) Phil Aster, Sol Motola, Velma Revel, Harry Steinman, Donnie Schenkler, and Charles. *Courtesy of the author.*

We had plenty of free time during the day, and the hotel needed extra staff for certain things, so we all took additional jobs to make a few more dollars. I became a bus boy. That meant from 7:00 AM to 8:00 PM I got to watch the same people fill up three times a day on an inordinate amount of food. By the time you finished cleaning up the dining room after the breakfast hour and resetting the tables, it was time to open the doors for the guests to have their lunch. It seemed to me that these people did nothing but eat all day, and then it was time for dinner. As bus boys, we had to take the order for the next day's meals for each guest, because the hotel didn't prepare a lot of extra food that could go to waste, so the guest who had just consumed an unbelievable amount of food would now have to consider what he wanted to gorge himself on the following day.

Every Sunday was payday for the band. Abe Blyman showed up religiously for this event and waited patiently on a couch in the hotel lobby, where his feet didn't reach the floor, to collect his commission. A dollar fifty per musician, and he always thanked us. Some business.

Something interesting and wonderful happened that summer that planted the seeds for future summers and beyond. Two musicians who were about to become high school seniors, and two years older than us, came to visit our Melbourne Lake Hotel. I knew one of them, a very fine trumpet player who's name was Joel Greenwald and who was also a student at the High School of Music & Art. The other musician was a pianist, and both of them were working at one of the really big hotels in the Catskills, the Nemerson Hotel in South Fallsburgh, with Randy Carlos's well-known Latin band. This was big time from my perspective. It seems that both musicians had gotten started professionally at this same Melbourne Lake Hotel two years earlier than we did. Now, only two years later, they were working at what seemed to me to be the tops, the pinnacle, the Mt. Parnassus of hotels. They invited our band to come over to their hotel that night after we finished playing, to see the Randy Carlos band play. The biggest hotels in the Catskills all employed several bands including a Latin band, which was the rage at that time. It is again today, many years later, but now the music is called salsa, even though it has hardly changed all these years. When we arrived at the Nemerson Hotel that night having finished our work, and heard the exciting sounds of mambo and cha-cha, with two trumpets playing in delicious harmony, with driving conga drums, timbales, and Randy Carlos's smooth electric guitar, with a million people on the dance floor, and young, sexy women moving seductively to the hot rhythms, and cool guys sweeping them off their feet, it was unimaginable for us. This was exciting. This was something to aspire to. To be part of. It immediately became my next dream. Everything I would do in music for the next year or two would be to prepare for this next step. Mambo and cha-cha became my life. I listened many times over to every record I could afford to buy. I studied the music and loved every minute of it. I started to write a book of arrangements for my own Latin band. Two trumpets and rhythm section, just like Randy's band. I must have written fifty arrangements.

That first summer in a band, independent and away from home, gave us the taste of what life could be like after graduation from high school, which was still several years away. But that was the start of it all for me. After that summer, there were other summers with other bands in the Catskills, graduation from high school, music composition studies in Paris, composing scores for many motion pictures and television shows, performances of my music on records, in the theater, on the ballet stage, and in the concert hall. Along the way, I was even the pianist in Randy Carlos's band for about a year. I've conducted symphony orchestras performing my music in New York, Los Angeles, London, Caracas, Budapest, Prague, Warsaw, Israel, and Tokyo, but I don't recall, to my memory, hearing any sounds sweeter than the music we played, and the harmonies that that trumpet and that saxophone produced, that summer of 1955, when I was fifteen.

But I'm getting way ahead in my story.

Sometime during the next school year, Randy Carlos had a hit record. At least it was a hit record in our world. The song was an instrumental called

"Smoke," and it played on all the jukeboxes where my friends and I spent many hours after school, sipping Cokes. It was "Happy Days," it really was. As it happened, that same trumpet player with Randy's band, Joel Greenwald, was the leader of our jazz band at the High School of Music & Art. He told me one day that if I wrote an arrangement for that band consisting of five saxes, four trumpets, and four trombones plus a rhythm section, that he would play it during one of their regular rehearsals. I happily wrote an arrangement of the Nairobi theme, which Ernie Kovacs used on his late-night TV series to accompany three guys dressed as apes, who usually would do nothing more than pass children's blocks from one side of a table to the other. At that time, it was a riot. When I heard that big jazz band playing my arrangement, it was another life-changing experience. I couldn't believe the sounds that I had written. The chills stayed with me forever.

The first person who impacted my life as a composer was my composition teacher in high school, Mark Lawner. I had a dismal record in high school for my academic subjects, indeed even in some of my music classes. I wasn't interested in my classes and did only the minimal amount of work to get by. However, I loved reading books and would stay up half the night reading to educate myself in the world of literature, and would be sleepy all through my classes the next day. It took only one teacher to turn that around for me and allow me to open up another side that sparked to the creative process and to learning about what went into musical composition. Before that I had the worst sort of pedagogue with an orchestration teacher whose identity I won't mention because his negative impact had no influence on my life whatsoever, but it serves as a constant reminder to me of the importance one must place on dealing with young impressionable minds that need nurturing and encouragement.

Mr. Lawner was the antithesis of that. He was a man with genuine warmth and a friendly smile. He was a composer who had published piano pieces that I knew of, but it was his understanding of music and his ability to communicate it that suddenly made me hungry to learn more. He regarded my musical creativity as something to be developed and cared for. I guess I must have known instinctively how important his class would be for me, because I forged a letter of recommendation to get into it. To be accepted into that class required a letter of recommendation from the orchestration teacher in the school, as orchestration was a prerequisite to the composition class, which was a very small class, and very difficult to get into. I knew that I couldn't get such a letter, so I wrote one myself, addressed it to Mr. Lawner, and signed my orchestration teacher's name. I felt that that was the least that teacher could do for me even though he didn't know it. I was accepted to the class and started to learn about musical forms and counterpoint and thematic development, and suddenly everything was ablaze with interest for me. It was like taking apart a watch and finally learning how it works, or seeing the engineering plans for a bridge to understand how both ends of the bridge could meet in the middle over the water. There were techniques used to develop motifs, and counterpoint to create individual voices, and harmonic structure to give it form. Under his tutelage, my first complete free composition for that class, a scherzo for clarinet and piano, was performed at the school's semiannual concert. It was one of the most exciting things to happen to me during those four years in Music & Art, to sit in the audience and listen to my piece being performed. I was so genuinely excited that I made sure that everyone around me knew that I was the Charles Fox whose music was being performed. "That's me, Charles Fox, that's my music," I announced to all within earshot, as the piece was being performed. I don't think that it was a lack of modesty on my part, but borne of a tremendous excitement in hearing my music being performed. There are moments that stand out in one's life that are incomparable; that was one of them for me. Years later I established a scholarship, a prize for a composition in that school, which now is known as the LaGuardia High School of the Arts, with the sole stipulation that the chosen composition each year should be performed at the semiannual concert. I wanted every hopeful composer to have the same thrill and encouragement that I experienced.

At the end of the school year my name was on the school's honor roll for having gotten an A in that class, along with the other A students in the school. I really enjoyed the irony of that.

❧

During the year following my graduation from high school, I continued to study composition privately with Mr. Lawner. That winter I worked in a Latin band in Lakewood, New Jersey, but once a week I religiously boarded a bus at 6:00 AM for the two-hour ride back to New York for my lessons. He remained my friend and mentor and even invited me to play golf with him and his wife. And Mr. Lawner wrote one of the two letters of recommendation that I needed to be accepted to Fontainebleau to study with Nadia Boulanger. He and his wife were traveling in Europe that summer of my first year in Fontainebleau, and they came to visit me. They took me out to dinner, and he told me how excited he was for me to continue my musical education with Boulanger, and he wanted me to keep in touch and tell him all about it. Many years later I invited him and his wife to the Brooklyn Academy of Music to see the San Francisco Ballet performing my first ballet, *A Song for Dead Warriors*. I'm not sure who was feeling more proud, him or me.

The next year in high school, my junior year, I began studying privately with Lennie Tristano, the great jazz pianist from Chicago. I had become familiar with his records during the previous summer, and learned that he gave private lessons. Lennie was unique in the world of jazz and was one of the great innovators. He had a recording studio in his home where he could record layer upon layer of his playing to produce a contrapuntal tapestry to his music.

I didn't know he was blind until I stood at his doorway in Flushing, Queens, for the first time. He opened the door to his house, which he shared with his brother, who was a psychiatrist. (Sometimes, through the walls, I'd hear an outburst from one of Lennie's brother's patients who was in a therapy session in the next room.) I held out my hand to shake his, and he stared right past me and said, "Who's there?" It shocked me only because I'd had no idea that he couldn't see. I studied with Lennie for that whole school year, and his music and teaching remained an influence on me.

After my lessons, it was already dark. I waited at the bus stop for the bus ride back to the Flushing train station. It was a long subway ride from there to mid-Manhattan and then a longer subway ride back to the Bronx. After that, a mile walk home. When I was waiting for the bus near Lennie's house, it seemed to me to be practically the end of the earth, as I would have nearly a two-hour trip ahead to get home. Years later, when I met my future wife, Joan, I realized that she lived only a few blocks from that bus stop and might have passed by and noticed me sitting and waiting for the next bus while she walked by with her friends. I'd love to be able to look down from a long-past sky and see if that might have happened.

I studied orchestration in high school that same year with Richard Benda, who was not a regular teacher in the school but came in once a week for a sort of master class in orchestration. I continued studying privately with him when the course was finished. He also taught composition with the method devised by Schillinger, whom he studied with, as George Gershwin did. The compositional part of his teachings proved totally useless to me because it was based on a rigid set of mathematical principles, and the development of musical material was achieved by learning to use permutations of musical elements rather than learning to develop musical material through harmony and counterpoint and by studying the works and musical forms of the masters. But Richard Benda introduced me to opera and to writing for the orchestra, and for that I'll always be grateful. He believed that in order to learn to write for the orchestra, in addition to learning the technical capabilities of the instruments, one must get close to an orchestra and watch how the string players attack their instruments with their bows and make mental notes of how each use of the bow makes the instrument sound. He said to study and remember the sound of two flutes playing together and two flutes plus a clarinet, a clarinet and oboe, and to make mental notes of these combinations and train myself to hear them and remember them, so that I could draw from that.

In order to get close to an orchestra he suggested I go to the Metropolitan Opera, the original Met, on 38th Street and 8th Avenue. That was a truly beautiful-sounding and magnificent-looking opera house, rich with history. Among myriad important events there, Puccini came for the (American) premiere of *Girl of the Golden West* with Toscanini conducting and Caruso singing. It was tragic that it was ever torn down. The Met had standing room sections in a U shape surrounding the whole orchestra section of the theater. If I arrived early enough, for two dollars I could stand right behind the double basses on the left side of the orchestra pit, leaning on a railing so close to the musicians that I could practically touch the double bassists. I went often, perhaps once or twice a week, to study and learn the orchestra, and along the way, I developed a life-long love of opera. Puccini's melodies soared through my head long after I left the opera house.

I discovered the Donnell Public Library on 54th Street, commonly known as the Music Library, and went there often to study the musical scores for the operas I'd seen. I couldn't understand how the understated orchestrations of Puccini's operas could sound so rich and wonderful in the theater. I had to know what was in them. I sat there for hours listening and studying, and I was able to borrow the scores and even take the record albums home to listen. I was like a kid in a candy store at the Donnell.

I turned eighteen in the fall of the year after my graduation from high school and spent that birthday in Birdland, "the jazz corner of the world" as it was known. After years of looking forward to being old enough to get into the jazz clubs I felt as though I had arrived, and the world of jazz was mine as I could now get into Birdland and sit by the railing that separated the band from the gallery of listeners to the left of the stage. If I was lucky enough, I could sit directly to the left of the pianist, who normally faced the back of the band stand, with his back to the front of the audience, and I could study his playing, being only inches from the keyboard. Of course, when Count Basie or Stan Kenton and other pianist band leaders played, the piano was in front and turned around, as it normally would be.

Shortly after that, I took a job with a Latin quartet at the Fairmont Hotel in Lakewood, New Jersey, one of the larger hotels in that area. I had no clear-cut direction for my future or even the possibilities, but during that period I continued taking composition lessons with Mark Lawner each week in New York, and I came back to Lakewood the next day, refreshed from the day off and from the exhilaration of my lesson. When that job ended and I was back in New York for the rest of the winter, and now being eighteen years old, for the first time I could use my father's car at night to get to the various clubs and dances, to my work in bands. My brother Manny would also use the car for his needs, and between my father, who was up at 5:00 AM every morning to go to work, and my brother and me, the car was in use practically twenty-four hours a day.

One particular night, coming home from a job in the very late hours of the night, I met my piano teacher. She was out walking her dog at that hour, and we stopped to talk in front of the apartment house where she lived as well.

That night, and that chance meeting, changed my life.

Not too long after that, I was on a chartered flight to Paris, along with other students who would be attending the Conservatoire de Musique, in Fontainebleau, France, for the summer. As I sat on that propeller-driven plane, with several stops ahead for refueling before we arrived in Paris, I had no thought of what to expect from this venture, and certainly no way of knowing the effect that it would have on my future, and in fact, on my whole life.

Letters from Paris, 1959–1961

After a long flight from New York that included stops for refueling in Gander, Newfoundland, and Shannon, Ireland, our plane approached Orly Airport flying directly over Paris at a low enough altitude that the city filled my window that I was looking out from. The tiled rooftops seemed to cover the city in a blanket of orange and red. It was my first glimpse of anything in a foreign country.

In my mind, I had always envisioned romantic but stereotypical views of Paris and Parisians that were almost caricature-like hand-drawn scenes of smiling waiters wearing white aprons, Frenchmen in berets, and gendarmes in their uniforms directing traffic, and all sporting mustaches while being accompanied by the music from Gershwin's *American in Paris*. And certainly there were plenty of gendarmes in uniform, and men with mustaches everywhere, but it struck me immediately that it was all real, and here I was in this scene which I had long pictured in my mind. The streets of Paris were filled with people strolling leisurely or walking purposefully, next to the honking cars and taxis and workmen's trucks, all in a race to get somewhere. But there were beautiful wide-open boulevards ringed with trees, and magnificent pala-tial buildings housing the art treasures and the official government buildings of the capital of France. And everywhere, there was the presence of a glorious past. And with its parks on seemingly every corner and the Seine carving its way picturesquely through its center, Paris was the most beautiful city I could ever imagine.

My seatmate on the plane and I decided to cut down our expenses by sharing a room in a hotel during the week in Paris before school started in Fontainebleau. A number of us on the plane followed someone's recom-mendation to stay in an area where the hotels would be more reasonable. At that time in Paris, everything was reasonable, and much less expensive than in New York, especially if you had American dollars. We all stayed close together, and we became fast friends.

Before coming to Paris, and during my school years, I had studied some Spanish in junior high school, then Italian and German at the High School of Music & Art, as I was erroneously put into a language for voice class, which was for voice students to learn to sing opera. I sang in that class as it was expected of me, along with the other students, who were voice students, but no one questioned my vocal capabilities or the fact that I was accepted to the school as a pianist. After two years spent singing in various languages, I was being advanced to a French class, when I finally had the courage to question why I was being moved from one language class to another and even had to sing in each language as well. When I learned that I was in this class in error, I was given the opportunity to choose which language I'd like to continue with, and I chose Italian. As a result, when I arrived in Paris, I didn't speak a word of French.

My parents had maintained a kosher house all my years growing up, and during those years it never occurred to me that I might try any food that wasn't kosher, even out of the house. A hot dog at a New York Giants baseball game or a hamburger at a luncheonette after a movie had no appeal to me even though my friends seemed to enjoy them very much. As a result, I was very unadventurous and squeamish as far as trying new foods, so venturing out onto the streets of Paris, and being in restaurants featuring dishes with names like *porc*, *mouton*, and *lapin* (rabbit), and having no communication ability with the waiters made for a very enlightening experience. I discovered right away that one could find steak on almost any menu, and as it was the only word I recognized on most menus, that's what I ordered for every meal during my first week in Paris. One day I ordered the steak "tartare" thinking that that was some kind of steak sauce, and that, I was willing to try. Of course I didn't realize that I had ordered raw chopped steak, and when I asked for it to be cooked "well done" (I had quickly learned to say "*bien cuit*" in French), it got a huge laugh from the waiter and everyone at my table. I was totally perplexed as to why they were laughing until someone explained; then I could laugh as well.

June 25
Dear Family,
   Well I've spent my first full day in Paris and all I can say is that I'm tired. We walked from 12:00 in the afternoon till 9:00 in the evening. From the southernmost tip of Paris where we live, across the Seine, past the Louvre, the Tuilleries,

opera and as far as the Conservatoire. The Conservatoire is indeed one of the filthiest buildings I've seen in Paris. I went inside and went to the secretary of the school. After a long conversation with a man who spoke <u>no</u> English, I managed to find out that the next school year begins in October. He gave me some papers having information concerning admission to the school, which I will have to translate with the help of a dictionary that I bought.

As for my diet, do not be too concerned, for an excellent steak dinner is about $1.00. I have not yet tried any French food.

Do not write me yet; I will be in Paris till the 30th of this month and then in Fontainebleau. The address there is:

Palace of Fontainebleau
Fontainebleau, S. M.
France

Love,
Charles

June 30

Dear Family,

This is my first evening at Fontainebleau, and I know that I can expect a truly happy summer. The dormitories for the men are the most luxurious I have ever seen. I share a large room with two other fellows, one a violinist who studies at Juilliard, and the other has not arrived yet. Our room has all new and modern furniture and is brightly colored. We have two large windows, one overlooking the main street and the other, the large garden which is part of the dormitories. There is a high brick wall covered with ivy which surrounds the building and adds to the privacy of the building.

I'm sure that it will be very hard to leave Fontainebleau in September, because the surroundings are the most pleasant I've ever known. Six of us have already rented bicycles for the summer, which cost us eight dollars. Since we arrived at 2 PM this afternoon, we have ridden around the countryside, through the forests, and the palace. It is just wonderful.

The town is small but it has just about anything one would want, including a theater, movie house, music store, and of course, sidewalk cafés. Let me not forget to mention the pastry shops, whose goods cannot be surpassed by any American pastries. Fontainebleau also has a riding stable, and you can ride through the woods for about a dollar an hour. It even has a golf course.

As for the school, I have been inside but it will not start till tomorrow when at 9:00 we will be welcomed by Mlle Boulanger.

As you can see, I am having a wonderful time, but of course I miss home a little. Do write and tell me how things are.

Love,
Charles

Our school was in the right wing of the Palace of Fontainebleau, which was built by François the first in the sixteenth century and used as a summer palace by Napoleon. It's a magnificent structure which sits in an immense cobblestoned courtyard leading to the familiar and regal horseshoe staircase, and to the main entrance. Surrounding the palace were beautiful formal gardens and a man-made lake that had a little island in the middle which held Napoleon's son's playhouse. Swans and peacocks were everywhere.

Fontainebleau is a peaceful little town nestled in the vast forest surrounding it. My new friends and I easily acclimated ourselves to it by renting bicycles for the summer, and immediately began exploring the forests, the canals, and the neighboring towns of Moret and Barbizon, which lent its name to a school of painting that preceded the impressionist movement.

Everything was new to me, beginning with the dormitory life. The students were mostly college graduate school students and music teachers and professional instrumentalists in addition to composition students from conservatories in the U.S. and other countries. Fontainebleau also had a school of architecture, so there were architecture students from around the U.S. and from foreign countries as well. It was an easy environment to make friends, and we soon became a close-knit family, all of us filled with the excitement of being in Fontainebleau, and for the music students, the anticipation of Nadia Boulanger's arrival.

July 4
Dear Family,
Life here at Fontainebleau is wonderful, and I'm enjoying it more every day. I don't think that I've told you about

Mlle Boulanger. She is the most exciting and thoroughly alive person I've ever met. She is such a dramatic woman in a subtle way, that at times I find myself practically in tears. I actually look forward to my classes with her. Work is becoming very difficult and I don't have much time to myself. That's the reason that I haven't written in the past few days.

I've signed up for practically every music class that I could. They include: Composition, Harmony, and Conducting with Mlle Boulanger. Solfeggio with another woman and a basic French course. I'm even in the vocal ensemble, and we will be singing a Bach cantata. Of course, each class, though free, requires that you buy some material.

So far I have bought a large notebook and two scores for composition. I have ordered two books for Solfeggio and a score for Conducting. Also, a score for the vocal ensemble.

I'm sorry to be spending money as I am but it really is quite necessary.

I don't mean to alarm you but I only have $20 left.

I'll give you an example of the work at school. In the late afternoon yesterday, Boulanger told us to write two chorales, a few sets of themes using different kinds of cadences—and analyze a Bach prelude thoroughly. We had to hand it in the first thing this Saturday morning. That was for the class composition lesson and wasn't very hard to do. But today I have my first private lesson with her, and I am told that I will be up to the top of my head in work. Other composition students who've had their private lessons already were told to write a suite for orchestra or a string quartet with a quintet of woodwinds, and were told they had one week to do it. Besides that you have all your other work to do.

We have already had a cocktail party in one of the beautiful gardens at the palace, and I am told that during the summer Mlle Boulanger invites music students to her home for dinner, and that is something because at the same time she invites the leading musicians of the world who happen to be in Paris, such as Stravinsky and Benjamin Britten, who have already attended her dinner parties.

I don't plan to go to Paris much on weekends because I am too happy here.

Love, Charles

July 7
Dear Family,

I'm sorry that I haven't written these past few days but I have been kept very busy.

Saturday I had my first private lesson with Mlle Boulanger, and it was a great experience to be in private with her for an hour. She studied my string quartet and said I had a lot of original ideas. But of course my lack of training was obvious also. I told her that I had definitely decided upon music as my life's work, and she said she was happy for that. I also told her that I should like to stay in Paris after the summer and study with her, even enter the Conservatoire perhaps. She said that the Conservatoire is run on a complete scholarship basis and it is therefore extremely difficult to pass the entrance exam. It is almost positive that I could not pass the exam this year, but if I worked with her for a year first, I probably could. She made it clear that if I did enter the Conservatoire, I would first have 4, 5, or 6 years of hard work ahead of me. Of course that would prepare me well for my future in music.

She suggested that I begin right at the beginning of traditional harmony with her. I can think of no better teacher to begin with.

The first day of school, we had an exam in ear training to see at what level we were. Out of the five classes ranging from advanced ear training to beginning or elementary ear training, I was put in the 3rd class. I was satisfied though, considering that most of the students have had their conservatory training already. During my private lesson Mlle Boulanger said that as long as I was able to get into class 2, by the end of two months if I work hard, I should be put into a higher class. On the following day, after my ear training class the teacher told me that I was ready for class 2. I was anxious to tell Mlle Boulanger, but she had already been told of it, and during the intermission of the master class with Robert Casadesus she came over to congratulate me. She said that as long as I have talent and the ability to progress rapidly, she is sure that my musical efforts will not be in vain. But there is so much work to do.

Let me know how you all are.

Love,
Charles

July 11, 1959
Dear Family,

This morning I had a very inspiring lesson with Mlle Boulanger. She had been told by Mlle Dieudonné (my Solfeggio teacher) that I had an excellent ear, and said that means a lot to my future. An hour alone with her is a very precious one, and I remember every word she said. She saw my piece for clarinet and piano today and had some favorable as well as unfavorable comments about specific things. After that she said she would like me to write a piece for 7 flutes, trumpet, clarinet, and string quartet. I don't think she could have found an odder combination.

At the end of the lesson she spoke of my health and how I must always keep well. That I must stand up straight so that nothing will interfere with my breathing and that I should have a little exercise. Then she said, "I hope you don't mind an old woman giving you this advice, but you see, I am very much interested in you."

So I left her feeling very inspired and I went to play the piano for the two hours remaining until lunch.

Today is Saturday and I have the rest of today and tomorrow free. I will practice some more, begin my composition and work on my ear training.

I feel wonderful, and hope you do also.

Love,
Charles

Aside from being so involved with my classes and preparation for them, and with my chamber piece that Mlle Boulanger asked me to write, and in general enjoying the freedom of being on my own in a foreign country, my summer was preoccupied with the prospects of continuing my studies with Mlle Boulanger after the summer, in Paris. There was no uncertainty about my intent and desire to remain in Paris from the first meeting with Boulanger, only the uncertainty of whether it would be possible. I never had a moment's doubt that Mlle wanted me to continue with her after the summer, but I also knew of the hardship that would present to my parents financially.

The faith they had in me, to encourage my dreams in spite of the hardship it must have been for them, inspires me to this day.

July 23
Dear Family,

It is exactly one month since I left NY. It seems much longer though because I have gotten so used to the life here.

Tuesday night I had dinner with Mlle Boulanger. There were, at the dinner, 4 or 5 other students, some of the teachers here, and the performers from the afternoon concert. I did not, however, sit near Mlle Boulanger and didn't even speak to her.

This Saturday the people at my dinner table and I will drive to the town of Solesmes, which is about 300 miles away. There is an abbey in that town which has the most authentic Gregorian chant to be heard anywhere in the world. It will be a tremendous experience for me and one I am sure which I'll never forget. It is those same monks from the abbey in Solesmes that have made the accepted recordings of Gregorian chant. We have to leave at 4:00 in the morning in order to get there for the 10:00 Mass. After the Mass, we will have lunch with the monks who have invited us. Because we are going by car, it will cost very little. There is a chartered bus taking about 30 other students.

I bought a book of piano exercises this week in order to practice more systematically. It did not cost too much.

I'll write again soon.

Love,
Charles

July 29, 1959
Dear Family,

I have a lesson tomorrow morning with Mlle Boulanger and will show her the beginning of my piece for 7 flutes. Incidentally, it is coming along fine. At my lesson I will bring up the possibility again of my staying in Paris. Perhaps, at that time she will offer her good advice. In either case, tomorrow I will send for an application blank to the Juilliard and Eastman schools.

Keep well.

Love,
Charles

July 30, 1959

Dear Family,

I write to you today so that you may know what happened at my lesson.

Mlle Boulanger said that she also wants me to stay here in the fall. She felt that this was not enough time to write to her friends, but suggested something else. There is a wealthy patron of the school here, and that she would invite him to her cocktail party tomorrow so that she could speak to him about me. I have been invited to the same party, and it will give me a chance to speak to him myself. Perhaps things will work out well.

She is anxious for me to finish my new piece so that it may be performed at a concert in the near future.

I'll let you know what develops.

Love,
Charles

P.S. I have just had a long talk over coffee with a girl who has been in Paris for two years now. She came for the summer to Fontainebleau, and stayed on in Paris with Mlle Boulanger. This is her 3rd year at Fontainebleau.

I spoke with her about the possibility of my staying and what I would be doing if it should not materialize.

I thought you would like to know what I have learned.

There are single rooms with a good piano in it, at the American Pavilion of the Cité Universitaire. These are the students' quarters. The rooms are clean, well heated and have hot water and cost around $25 a month. The only thing is that I will have to secure a room soon or they will all be gone.

If you are enrolled in a school in Paris, you are given a card which enables you to eat in the student cafeteria. The food there generally consists of steak and potatoes, and a meal costs around 25 cents. The student card also enables you to get a discount on opera and concert tickets as well as on books and music. Standing room at the opera is only 75 cents.

So as you can see, it will not require too much money to stay here.

Mlle Boulanger knows of my financial status, and I was told that she would probably charge me much less. I imagine *that if I am able to get enough money to live with, she will then speak to me about the cost of lessons. Wendy, the girl whom I spoke of, said that Mlle Boulanger generally charges 6000 Fr., which is about $12.00. She would though, if she saw fit, charge just enough so that the lessons are not completely free. That would amount to about 500 francs or so, which is approximately $1.00. She has already expressed her interest in me, so the cost of a lesson may be that little. I would also take private lessons in solfeggio with Mlle Dieudonné, which would not amount to much.*

In order to get a student card, I would enroll in a school, the name of which I've forgotten, and take private lessons in French. The price of this is only around $25 for the year.

I hope I am able to stay so that I can take advantage of studying with Mlle Boulanger.

Love,
Charles

Aug. 9, 1959
Dear Family,

It is Sunday night and I have decided to write you before I go to bed. I hope that tomorrow I will find a letter from you in the mailbox. I cannot remember when I received your last letter. I realize that you are all very busy, as I am, but I am not that busy that I don't get lonely every so often.

Progress on my piece is coming fine. It is nearly completed and will be performed in a week or so.

Mlle Boulanger has returned from Switzerland and the home of Yehudi Menuhin, and it will be a full week again. Cocktail parties on Monday and Thursday, concerts on Tuesday and Friday, and Boulanger's master classes on "Musical Language."

One would expect that because of her week's absence, we would just miss our lessons with her. But no, she has doubled her schedule this week and will make up every lesson. From 7:00 AM to 11:00 PM she will have not more than 2 hours to herself.

I spent the day today working on my composition. It is a step forward for me because I have not written the piece at a piano. This means that my orchestral conception is more exact and I can write much faster.

I don't recall if I told you or not but I have sent letters to Juilliard, Eastman, and Curtis, asking for applications. Of course there is a fee of around $15 to $20 that must accompany each application, so let me know what you would suggest in reference to this. Perhaps it won't even be worth the price of the application.

I hope that you have not forgotten me or that you are not angry with me for the handling of my finances. In either case, at least let me know.

Love,
Charles

Mlle Boulanger, Master Class in the Salle Jeu de Paume. *Courtesy of the author.*

Aug. 15, 1959
Dear Family,

   I'm writing you this letter on the train coming home from Paris. I'll tell you my reason for going in today, but first I'll inform you of this week's events.

   Mlle Boulanger came back from Switzerland, and it became another busy week. As I expected, she did not find a sponsor for me. At my lesson I spoke with her about staying in Paris, on a more definitive basis. She said that just to live in Paris I would have to figure on a minimum of $160 a month, to live well but have very little for concerts and books, etc. She said that if I could get $200 a month I would have no worries. I told her that the very most I could get from home would be $100 a month, and I know how difficult even that would be for you.

   So then we figured on a budget of $100. Anyway, I could possibly get along with that sum, but I would have to be very careful. Then I told her that we forgot to include the cost of lessons. To that she replied, "I did not think to mention it because we must make sure that you will have enough to eat."

   She would not talk any more of that, and I assume that she would not take money from me unless I could really afford it. I think she is seriously concerned with my future from what she has said to me. She said that she spoke to the president of Fontainebleau about me, in order that I may get a scholarship to return to Fontainebleau next year. She has been a source of inspiration for me, and I'm sure that its effects will last at least for the rest of my life. She said she would be happy for me to stay in her house, but she already has 4 people living there and would not know where to put another.

   So today I went to the Cité Universitaire in Paris to see about getting a room. The director of the American Pavilion was not there, so I will have to call him on Tuesday. The Cité is the residence of most foreign as well as French students in Paris, and it is truly magnificent. The Cité occupies nearly a square kilometer and is a city by itself. It is fully equipped with a hospital, post office, and even a swimming pool. I'm glad I went in because now I am absolutely certain that I would like to stay. I realize that you could not really afford it, and if you just say no, I will understand perfectly. I don't have to tell you what this means to me, but if I must come home, my interest in music will surely not die out. I am first beginning to realize what it means to me.

But I must know either way what I will do. By the time that you receive this letter and I receive your answer, it will be probably 10 days, and I only have 14 more at school. Perhaps you could send me a telegram, which costs between $2 and $3. I am really sorry to inconvenience you so, but I am so nervous because I don't know in what direction I must plan. . . . If I stay I must sell my plane ticket immediately and make reservations at the Cité Universitaire.

I received a letter from Juilliard this week, and they said that although it's too late to file an application, they will make an exception and give me some sort of exam before Sept. 15. But I must know if I am coming home, so that I can write to them and make an appointment.

I have been so busy these past weeks that I cannot even find time to write to you much. Even this letter which I began on Saturday has taken me till today (Monday) to complete.

Needless to say, my new composition has been taking most of my time. I hurriedly finished it, and made revisions (although there are still more I would like to make but have not the time), and then had to copy the 12 parts. It will be performed sometime next week, and I have much to do before then. I have scheduled the first rehearsal for tomorrow, and I'm looking forward to it as it will be the first time that I will conduct.

I noticed on the bulletin board that this coming week I am scheduled for 4 lessons with Mlle Boulanger. Not that I don't love my lessons with her, but I don't know what I can show her in one week that would require four hours. Anyway, I'm sure I will enjoy it.

Please hurry and let me know what I should do. And again, do not feel bad if you are not able to keep me here, because my conviction is so great now that I will make the most of wherever I am.

I received the money—Thank you.

Keep well,

Love,
Charles

Aug. 20, 1959
Dear Family,

I had my second rehearsal of my piece today, and Mlle Boulanger was there. Although it lacks a lot of rehearsal, she assures me that it will go very well when it is performed next Wednesday the 26th.

Yesterday, I went into Paris again to the Cité Universitaire. I found out that you have to be 21 years old and have a B.A. or its equivalent in order to be accepted to the Cité. Well I told Mlle Boulanger today; she said she will write a letter to the director of the American Pavilion, but she doubted whether it would do any good. She said that if that did not work, perhaps she could get me a diploma from the École Normale de Musique so that I could get into the Cité! She is thoroughly opposed to the importance placed on a diploma, and feels that in this case she would be more right than wrong. Perhaps it may not work though.

Things are fine and I'm looking forward to a prolific winter.

Love,
Charles

Aug. 21, 1959
Dear Family,

I received your telegram this morning and I can't tell you how happy it made me.

$150 a month is more than generous and I thank you, but I will try to get along on $100. I am grateful for the opportunity you have given me, and if I can manage on less money, I would certainly do so and not add to your burden. My plane ticket was sold today, and I will receive $150 for it. Mlle Boulanger suggests that I put that money away so that no matter what happens I can always come home. Of course the money I pegged for transportation was very little, and $150 is not really enough to come home on, except on a chartered flight. But it looks as though I'll probably be here through next summer, and at this time next year I should be able to get a ticket home for the same amount that I got for this.

During the winter I will apply to the Curtis Music School for the following year, and I'm sure there will be no difficulty in

Mlle Boulanger's class at Fontainebleau, 1959. Mlle is at the piano on left edge of frame; Charles stands behind the piano, with Alex Panama to the right of him. *Courtesy of the author.*

being accepted. Curtis, like the Paris Conservatory, offers a full scholarship to all of its students.

As soon as I find out exactly what my expenses will be, I'll let you know.

I miss you all, but I'm sure that this year will prove to be one which could only do me good.

Keep well,

Love, Charles

P.S. Mlle Boulanger is very happy for me and said that now we can get into the real work.

Aug. 27, 1959
Dear Family,

I'm sorry that I haven't written all week, but this is the last week of school and there has been so much to do.

Yesterday was the concert, the program of which I have included in the envelope, and there was much preparation for that. At the last minute I had to learn how to conduct all the rhythms which I used in my piece.

I was extremely nervous until I walked out on stage and was more involved with producing a good performance. The musicians played very well, and the composition was received enthusiastically. It was a pleasure though to have it behind me.

Jean Casadesus told me afterward that he tried to have us play it again, but the Faure Requiem was to be presented next and the concert had already run into the dinner hour. It was very inspiring to have gotten so much praise as I did because I really did not expect it.

I'll tell you something which I know will make you very happy, but I wish that you would not repeat it because it would embarrass me for having told you. The Allegretto section of the piece is based upon a simple (C) major triad with a very ordinary rhythmic movement. After a rehearsal of the piece on the morning of the concert, I left the hall and was later told by a few of the students what Mlle Boulanger's reaction to the piece was. She said that she could not understand why it was such a good piece when it is based on so simple an idea. She could not explain it and doubted whether I could but that it just sounds right. She said to them that I am a born composer. Please do not think me conceited for telling you what even I should not know, but if I can't tell my family, who can I tell, and it has made me so happy. Actually, I just can't believe that this is all true.

As silly as it may seem, Mlle Boulanger even complimented me as a conductor.

Mlle Boulanger said that she received an answer from the director of the American Pavilion at the Cité, and she would not permit it. She said she would write a letter to the prince of Monaco for me (Rainier), whom she knows very well. If he will accept me in the Monacan Pavilion, the director of the American Pavilion will have to agree.

In the meantime I can live very well in a hotel which costs about a dollar a night.

After the concert yesterday I was among those invited to dine with Mlle Boulanger. This time, however, I was seated directly to her left. Of course I couldn't eat nor drink much and had to get a sandwich later. After the meal we all sat and talked for an hour, and I couldn't even smoke. It's hard to tell whether it was an honor for me or a punishment.

Charles conducting first performance of *Introduction and Allegretto*. Mlle Boulanger first row left side, middle seat. Mlle Dieudonné to her right, one row back on the aisle. *Courtesy of the author.*

Today there was a cocktail party at the home of a viscount of something or other. There were princes of someplace in at tendance as well. It has gotten so that I do not feel strange talking to a future king. The viscount lives during the summer in Fontainebleau, in a house which was owned and lived in by Madame Pompadour. His gardens are just magnificent. The house is where Pres. Eisenhower stayed during the American occupation of France.

I had two more lessons with Mlle Boulanger this week. That makes 5 lessons in 2 weeks.

I enjoy your letters. Do not write to me at Fontainebleau any more.

Love,
Charles

Aug. 28,1959
Dear Family,

Now, as the summer is almost over, I have more time to write to you.

In the late afternoon today we had our final concert of the season. I came to the concert in a short sleeve shirt and chinos

*because it was so warm. I sat down and when I looked at
the program I noticed that the final number was the Cantata
No. 4 by Bach. I realized that I was singing in the chorus and
had forgotten about the performance, so I ran home to get
dressed. The performance turned out magnificently well and
left us all with the realization that a wonderful summer had
come to an end. There are still classes until the 31st, but many
of the students left today.*

*For me it has been a summer which made me realize how
much music means to me. I made many wonderful friends,
especially with Mlle Boulanger, whom I truly love. . . . Thank
you for making this possible for me.*

*I'm sure that Mrs. Yurberg is hoping that I am able to stay
in Paris. I have not forgotten all that she's done for me. Please
give her my regards and say that I will write soon now that I
have some time.*

Love,
Charles

After the summer, with all of my classmates having returned home on
the chartered flight, I found myself completely alone in Paris, not speaking
more than a few words of French, and having just enough money to get by if
I was careful. Still, I was very secure that this was my path, and I never had
a moment's doubt about my decision to remain in Paris. I simply went about
making my plans and searched for a permanent place to live, in order to be
settled by the time Mlle Boulanger returned from a month-long vacation.

During that period, I lived in a small hotel on the Boulevard Saint-
Germain, directly next to Café Flore, and across the street from Deux Maggots,
and without knowing it, I was in the very heart of the Latin Quarter. My room
was on the fourth floor, and there was no elevator in the hotel. It cost about
a dollar seventy a night, and there was a single bathroom on the floor, down
the hall from my room. During the day, I explored Paris and found my way to
establishing a life there by searching for a permanent place to live and by enrolling in the Alliance Française to study French. At night, I'd sit in the Café Flore
and nurse a *café* while fully immersed in reading *Crime and Punishment*. When I
finished reading for the night, I'd go back up to my room. I was unfamiliar with
the lighting system in many apartment houses and inexpensive hotels, where
there was a button by the entranceway that would turn the lights on, and to
conserve energy, they were timed to go off automatically after a minute or so.
I would enter the hotel, which had no desk clerk, just a concierge whose door

was closed and who was long asleep, I assumed. I was under the spell of the psychologically murderous mind of Raskolnikov and was always relieved when I found the button to light the hallways. I climbed the four flights of stairs and inevitably the lights went out before I reached my room, and sometimes even before I reached the fourth floor itself. Not being familiar with the lighting system, I was certain that the old miserable concierge was waiting in her apartment for me to return and would shut the lights out after I began walking up the stairs. I always got a twinge of fright when the lights went out and I had to feel my way in the dark. When I finally made my way to the bathroom on the fourth floor, I'd turn those lights on and leave them on all night, as they were not on a timer and could easily light my way back to my room. Every morning after I had left these lights on, the concierge would approach me and reprimand me for leaving the bathroom lights on all night, or at least that's what I got from her tone of voice and the words *lumière* and *toilette* being in the same sentence. I'm sure she must have explained the lighting system, but I wasn't able to decipher her words. However, I was not about to be bullied, and said in words in English, that equally were not understood by her, that if she didn't shut the lights off until I got to my room, then I wouldn't have to leave the lights on in the bathroom. That went on night after night and morning after morning until I found a room to rent as a permanent residence.

Sept. 2, 1959
Dear Family,
　　I arrived in Paris yesterday and all is well.
　　Strange as it may seem, I don't feel as though I am so far away from home. You are all on my mind so much, it is as if you were here with me. Of course I won't be home for a year, but it is hard for me to imagine what a year away from you is like.
　　I hope that you do not worry about where I am living, you know that I can take care of myself.
　　Paris is a wonderful city, and I feel at home in it already.
　　Keep well and write.

Love,
Charles

Sept. 6, 1959
Dear Family,
　　As you can see by the date, the Fontainebleau plane leaves tonight for the U.S. I've already said goodbye to my friends and

I guess it means that the summer is over. And it was a wonderful summer.

I have already enrolled in the Alliance Française to study French. There is a class five days a week for 1 hour and 45 minutes each day, and the price is only $6.00 a month. Actually it is that cheap for me because I picked the most undesirable hours for the class out of the given times during the day. That is, the lunch hour. I don't mind though, for I will have lunch at 11:30. Anyway, I start tomorrow and hope that by the end of this year I will know French well enough to read books in this language. Even now, the harmony book that I use with Mlle Boulanger is in French, but it is very difficult to understand, and at that, I'm sure that I am missing quite a bit.

It dawned on me before that out of a city as large as Paris, I know just two people. It's a strange feeling. But at least you can be sure that I'll get a lot of work done this year.

I am living well and feel fine. I'm a little lonely but that is to be expected. Keep well.

Love,
Charles

Sept. 10, 1959
Dear Family,

I like to take advantage of the free time I have by writing you more often. I know that you are happy to receive letters from me because I know how your letters make me feel.

I was to the opera last night and it was truly wonderful to hear a symphonic orchestra again after listening only to chamber music all summer. It was especially exciting to me to hear an opera again, as you know how I feel about that medium. The Damnation of Faust is a magnificent work, and I am looking forward to hearing it again.

The Paris Opera does not have a standing room as I had thought, but the most inexpensive seats are well worth the money. The equivalent in American money for the price which I paid for my seat is 70 cents. When I asked the woman at the box office for the 350 franc seats, she said, "Ah! Paradise."

Do not worry if I have a beer every so often, I have a liter (more than a quart) of milk every day with my meals. Before

I go up for the evening I take some fruit with me to my room.
Fresh fruit in Paris is wonderful.
    Give my regards to the family.

Love,
Charles

I spent a good part of each day searching for a place to live that was within my budget and where I was allowed to bring in a rental piano. I went to my French class at the Alliance Française every day, which was not far from my hotel. I was also living close to the American Cultural Center, where I could go and listen to records and read newspapers and magazines in English.

I knew that Mlle Boulanger lived in the Place Clichy area in the more northern part of the city. That part of Paris was in the heart of the Moulin Rouge area known for the nightlife, and the infamous Rue Pigalle, and *les femmes de la nuit.* The irony of my teacher living in this area didn't strike me until I had lived there for a while.

Sept. 18, 1959
Dear Family,
    I am very happy to tell you now that I have at last found a room which will serve as my permanent address for the whole year. It is a large, pleasant, and comfortable room in a good section of Paris, just 5 Metro stations from the opera and American Express. The room is one of three in an apartment which belongs to a middle-aged woman. Of course one advantage in living in an apartment is the kitchen, which will reduce my expenses for breakfast, coffee, and noshes greatly. The best advantage of this room is that it is large enough for a piano to be brought in, and the woman seems pleased with having a musician for a resident.
    The woman leaves for work at 8:00 AM and returns at 7 PM, which allows me to have complete privacy for the whole day.
    The apartment is equipped with a shower, which is a luxury in France, although it's in the kitchen, so I can only use it when I am alone in the house. The hotel where I am living now not only is without a shower, but without a bath in the entire building.
    The room has cross-ventilation and a large heater, which means that I will be very comfortable throughout the seasons.

And the price for the room is 14,000 francs a month all inclusive. This is just short of $30.00 in U.S. money.

The woman told me of a student cafeteria not far away, and I immediately went to see it. Its prices are comparable to those at the Cité. 200 fr. (40 cents) per meal now, and 100 fr. (20 cents) beginning Oct 1st. The restaurant is about 6 blocks from the apartment.

You can see that I'm being very careful with the way I'm spending your money. I try not to overlook a single financial matter, although I don't base my life upon it. It's merely a matter of knowing what I want, and being able to do it with what money I have.

Keep well.

Love,
Charles

Sept. 21, 1959
Dear Family,

I have now been in this new room for two or three days, and am very pleased with it. In a day or two I will have the piano here, and I'll be able to begin to catch up on my work. I could have had the piano here already, but the woman from the American Embassy is looking for the best deal for me. She has really been very helpful.

While living in the hotel my mind was not free and clear enough to work on a composition, but since I moved here I've begun work on the quartet.

I was to the opera this evening and saw Strauss's <u>Rosenkavalier</u>. At the opera I met Dr. Steigman, who is now retired, but formerly was the principal at Music & Art. He didn't remember my face or name although he felt he should have. In either case I'm sure that he doesn't remember the circumstances under which we had become acquainted. He said he was impressed when I told him my reasons for being here, and felt that I should let M & A know what I am doing, from time to time. With that he wished me luck and we parted. I always have and still do respect the man.

About the clothes.

First of all, Paris has a much evener climate than NY. The summers are cooler, and the winter not as cold. You say *that in NY it's cold; here it's still comparatively hot and I'm still wearing short sleeve shirts.*

I do not care to own another suit now, and as for sweaters, I have two. This summer, the black sweater wore through on the elbows, but I had patches of material (quite in style) put on and it's fine.

I would be much happier if you would take whatever money you have for my clothes, and buy clothes for yourselves.

I have been eating in the student cafeteria that I told you about. The meals cost 40 cents apiece and are not bad at all.

Keep well.

Love,
Charles

My new address is:

c/o Madame Boursier
31 Rue des Batignolles
Paris, XVIIe, France

Once I was situated at my permanent address, I was able to get back to composing and my work that I was preparing for Mlle Boulanger. My landlady, Mme Boursier, worked all day, so I had the apartment to myself with no outside disturbances, and now instead of having to take a metro to the American Express to check for mail, the mail was slipped under the apartment door in the morning by the concierge, who lived downstairs. My first act every morning was to go to the front door and check. If there was a letter from home, my day was off to a good start. I know how many times I would read a letter from home, and how uplifted it made me feel, so I can only imagine what my letters home meant to my family.

I lived in a quiet, working-class neighborhood, and as it turned out, it was only a few blocks from my teacher. It was only a short walk as well to one of the most beautiful parks in Paris, Park Monceau, which unfortunately for most tourists is off their normal beaten path, but became a regular part of my daily life.

My apartment was on the fourth floor, and there was no elevator in the building. There were only two small apartments on each floor. Our neighbors on the fourth floor were the Cormier family, with two daughters, about eighteen and ten years old. One day, as I was leaving the apartment, I passed Mme Cormier and my landlady, Mme Boursier, who were chatting in the tiny hallway between apartments. Mme Boursier spoke about as much English as I did French at that time, but Mme Cormier was somewhat more fluent in English. Her family could hear my piano through the walls, and my immediate concern about this was quickly assuaged when she said they liked living next door to a musician, and asked if I would consider giving piano lessons to her younger daughter. I thought of several reasons why I could not: Namely, I had no experience as a teacher, and I couldn't communicate with her daughter in French. At that point she introduced me to her eighteen-year-old daughter, a beautiful girl around my age who said that she would help me to learn French. With that I quickly changed my mind and agreed to teach the younger girl.

> *Sept. 30, 1959*
> *Dear Family,*
>   *My landlady is really quite nice, although I try to avoid her as much as possible. She wants to buy another lamp for my room, and I'm to meet her tomorrow so that I can pick out what I like. She even made me a chocolate pudding last week.*
>   *Keep well.*
>
> > > *Love,*
> > > *Charles*

I discovered that Mme Boursier and Mme Cormier would meet regularly for an impromptu get-together in the tiny hallway separating our two apartments. They were both very friendly women with ready smiles who always greeted me warmly and showed concern for me in a motherly way. One day I returned home to find them chatting away on the fourth floor landing. They noticed that I wasn't looking very well and asked me what the problem was. I had an earache that day, and I guess my face reflected it. In French, there is no single word for earache, or headache or toothache for that matter, so when I tried to describe my problem, I translated the words literally, "*I have a pain in my ear.*" But French does not necessarily translate English expressions literally. In French, if you wanted to say you were in love, you would say the literal equivalent of, "I have a pain in my heart," "*J'ai une peine de coeur.*" So, when I told these two women that I had a pain in my ear, "*J'ai une peine dans mon oreille,*" they roared with laughter because it made no sense, and probably sounded very funny to their ears. Then they explained why they were laughing and I was able to join them in laughter. But I'm sure my face was a little red as I went into my room and shut the door.

Oct. 2, 1959
Dear Family,

You've never said anything, but I guess you have much difficulty reading my writing. Mlle Boulanger said that my musical handwriting is also terrible. When speaking of that to me, she would always point to Stravinsky's manuscripts, which are always immaculate. She suggested that I write music always with a pen, and should there be a need for erasing, copy the page over. As much as I should like to produce decent looking 1st manuscripts, I'm afraid I'd never finish one page of music if I did that. She never admonishes my doodles on my manuscripts. I think she even kind of likes them. Except some instances, when there was a little design of four rows of two circles in juxtaposition, placed on a stave that wasn't in use. But she has very poor eyesight, and when she came across the page it was on, she looked at me with a very surprised look and said, did you mean that? Evidently understanding it as being part of the music. I explained and we both laughed. Now in reflection, I wonder how that doodle sounded musically, against what was meant to be heard.

Write soon.

Love,
Charles

Oct. 4, 1959
Dear Family,

I guess it's a little bit late but let me wish you a Happy New Year. I had planned to go to a synagogue here for the holidays, but I found out this evening that today was the last day of Rosh Hashanah. I will go though for Yom Kippur. I don't know why, but I have a feeling that I'll enjoy it.

I couldn't see _Tosca_ today because I was invited, by mail, by the girl I know from Fontainebleau to attend a party this afternoon. There was no way of getting in touch with the girl in time to refuse the invitation, so I was sort of obligated to go. It was not far from my house though, and I stayed there long enough to finish a glass of wine, and excused myself. I came home and got quite a bit of work done. I'm sorry I missed _Tosca_ though, for they do Puccini's works so infrequently, and you know how much I love his music.

I must tell you of my landlady's thoughtfulness (or over-thoughtfulness). She brought another chair in my room today thinking it would aid to my comfort in the room. Now I have a large double bed, which would do well in itself for my work, a chair for the piano, one for the desk, and one on either side of the fireplace. Perhaps she thinks I plan to throw a party!! I have also in my room, besides a desk, a large round table and two night stands. Of course I don't mind it, but it is rather funny.

I think of all of you very much and enjoy your letters.

Love,
Charles

Oct. 9, 1959
Dear Family,

I was to a party last night given by the girl whom I know from Fontainebleau. She and her three friends moved into an apartment off the Champs Élysées, and gave a small house-warming. It had been more than a month that I hadn't spent an evening with friends, so I enjoyed it.

Love,
Charles

My good friends in Paris were also students of Mlle Boulanger. Alex Panama had attended Juilliard before coming to Paris. He came from a wealthy family who owned a coffee plantation in El Salvador. He was a serious musician, and although we came from completely different backgrounds, we became very good friends. He always said that one day, there would be a revolution in his country because there was no middle class, and there was always such a divide between those who had means and the very poor. That certainly predicted the disastrous times that befell that country in the eighties. We would sometimes go to the Champs Elysées together to meet girls. If we saw two attractive girls walking together, Alex, who spoke French fluently, would always leave it up to me to make the introductions with the girls in my broken French. By the time I would confound them with my verbiage, they were already laughing, and the ice had been broken.

My friend Bernardo Gonzales Sanchez was from Cuba. He too came from a very wealthy family and had tutors in four languages when he was very young. His father was the minister of commerce under Batista. Bernardo was traveling around Europe after his graduation from Michigan Law School when Castro came into power, and Bernardo was cut off from his family and country and financial support. He decided to finally study the piano, which he was always denied being able to do while he was growing up. Now that his life had suddenly changed, he devoted himself to the piano, and within two years he performed the Ravel G Major Concerto with an orchestra in Paris. He had all this pent-up talent that he was finally able to let loose. He remained studying with Boulanger long after I left Paris.

Tom Weaver was a fine violinist who had studied at Juilliard and came to Paris to study with Nathan Milstein and for a short period of time with Boulanger. My friend Gerri Ostrove continued with Boulanger after Fontainebleau, as I had done. She had an apartment with three other girls near the Arc de Triomphe, and we all became good friends, and their apartment was a center for a lot of free time away from my work. Clara Hoover was another good friend who had a luxurious apartment by our standards, and she too was part of our small circle of "*étrangers*" (foreigners) living in Paris.

Oct. 13, 1959
Dear Family,

I hope you enjoyed your day in shul yesterday. I went to one that's probably the largest in Paris. It seemed strange to see in Paris a mob in yarmulkes standing in front of the shul. Inside was pretty much the same as Eames Pl. but not really. I guess it's just that they're both shuls. I don't think that this synagogue, though orthodox, is as orthodox as we are used to. Inside they charged 50 francs for a paper yarmulke. I, of course, had money, but I thought you weren't allowed to carry money on Yom Kippur. The Jewish families seem to be similar though. Boys with their new suits, and women with new hats and dresses, everybody wishing everybody else a good year. I stood in the back I guess for well over an hour. Naturally it brought back so many happy memories. When I come home next Sept. I'll be happy to go to shul again with all of you. Perhaps there are customs and ceremonies which the Jewish religion upholds which I cannot agree to practice, but I want you to know that I'm proud to be a Jew. I think perhaps in time my feeling towards it will grow, although I'm not forcing it, it's just a newly discovered, unexplainable belonging and feeling part of a religion.

Tomorrow I will give a lesson after my French class, and then see Mlle Boulanger. I'll write soon.

Love,
Charles

Oct. 15, 1959
Dear Family,

Today is a beautiful day. The weather has still not given any signs that winter is approaching.

I feel wonderful, healthy, and am happy especially because Mlle Boulanger returned yesterday and I saw her then. She looks just wonderful after taking a vacation. Her vacation consists of only judging contests, giving lectures, conducting a little, teaching, and meeting hundreds of people. But it did seem to do her much good.

I was of course excited about seeing her again. Her maid ushered me into the room where Mlle Boulanger was with a group of students and friends. After her warm greeting she said she was worried about me because she had not heard from me sooner, none of her other students knew where I was, and she didn't know what became of me. I didn't know what to say because I've just been sitting around waiting for her. We all talked for a while, she told me to come back Saturday at 1:00 for my lesson, and I left.

What I saw of her apartment is magnificent. In the living room she has 2 large pianos, and a comparatively large <u>pipe</u> organ. There were so many thousands of books pertaining to music, and books of music, that I thought perhaps I had walked into Durand Publishing or Carl Fischer's. She has the most beautifully bound editions of complete works of even the most obscure composers. Most of them have her name or initials in gold on the cover. Evidently they are mostly all gifts.

Aside from my weekly private lessons there are Wednesday class lessons, which I imagine are similar to the Comp. class lessons at Fontainebleau. This summer in that class we studied the Bartok 5th string quartet, the Mozart D maj. quintet, <u>The Abduction from the Seraglio</u>, and Stravinsky's <u>Rake's Progress</u>. So you see how much we can accomplish in this class alone in a year.

Know that as long as I will be seeing her twice a week I'll never be lonely.

Love,
Charles

Oct. 18, 1959
Dear Family,

I had my lesson with Mlle Boulanger Sat. afternoon. Just being with her, as I've told you before, is a wonderful experience. So I've begun work on the Dubois harmony book, which I started to work with at Fontainebleau, but put it aside at that time for composition. There is much work for me to do for my next lesson, especially since I have to translate the book as I go along. But I will manage well; of course it takes much longer. She also suggested that I never let my studies interfere with my own composing and that I must write every day, even if it's just a matter of taking notes for a future purpose. By way of this she admonished Prokofiev's occasional lack of discretion in adding musical segments of his works which were evidently not suitable. I hadn't noticed but I will make a point to remember.

Of course most of the time, great music was not written spontaneously, but the master craftsmen can manage to make it sound spontaneous. Mlle Boulanger suggested that I also should study with Mlle Dieudonné, who is a professor at the Paris Conservatoire, but was the solfeggio teacher at Fontainebleau. So I intend to study ear training with her.

Mlle Boulanger also suggested that I actually do enroll in the Ecole Normale de Musique, for a number of reasons. First of all I will save 6000 francs ($12.00) a month for my meals, as the school costs 5,000 ($10.00) francs a month, it will mean a slight savings. But by entering I will be able to attend Mlle Boulanger's Keyboard Harmony Class, which is very important for me. So altogether I will have 3 classes a week with Mlle Boulanger. Or possibly more if the Keyboard class meets more than once a week. So her lessons, along with Mlle Dieudonné's lessons, my daily classes at the Alliance Française, and my own practicing, reading, and composing will really keep me very busy.

I will manage, though, always to keep writing to you as often as I have. Sometimes I carry a letter for you in my pocket for a day or so forgetting to send it. So if you don't receive a letter when you expect it, know that it is for that reason. I'm sorry for it, but you know me.

Enjoy yourselves and keep well.

Love,
Charles

Tues., Oct. 20
Dear Family,

My studies go along, there is more work for me to do but less to talk about.

I am well and content.

Mlle Boulanger doesn't want me to spend too much time on my harmony exercises, but that I must is inevitable. Of course the translating itself takes a good deal of time. Also, the way I am preparing my harmony is according to standards way above any of the U.S. conservatories. Most of those schools use the Piston book or something else on that order. It is a fine book, but the Dubois book that I'm using is much stricter. When Piston says in regards to 5ths and octaves, avoid parallelisms and consecutive 5ths and octaves when possible, Dubois has many rules pertaining to just when you may use consecutive 5ths and octaves. And the rules are different depending on between which voices the 5ths and octaves occur. Also I have to do my harmony on 4 staves so that each voice can be regarded more easily and you think in terms of 4 voices and not the harmony resultant of the same. Also, each voice is written in the clef best suited for its range. The four clefs being the soprano clef, contralto, tenor, and bass.

It is of course much more work but it suits me better because it becomes a real challenge. Be well.

Love,
Charles

Sun., Oct. 25
Dear Family,

Well I had a lovely weekend, and hope you all enjoyed it as well.

I had my lesson on Sat. and just after it went on an errand for Mlle Boulanger which took the better part of that afternoon. But it was a beautiful day and I had a chance to explore a part of Paris to which I had never been before, so the day was not a loss. That evening I saw _Tosca_ at the Opéra Comique.

This afternoon I attended a concert with Byron Janus. Rachmaninoff's 3rd was performed, and although I don't particularly care for that concerto, it was a very filling performance. Also played was _Roman Carnivale Overture_, Stravinsky's suite *from Petruchka, and a boring symphony by a Frenchman who was present to take his bows.*

It had been quite a while since I had seen a symphonic orchestra by itself. (Not part of an opera co.)

Some time ago I told you how little Paris had to offer in the way of concerts. I see now that I was badly mistaken, but at that time the season had not started yet. As a matter of fact they have a great amount of concerts and recitals. I'm going this week to another symphonic concert and also to a concert given by Rubinstein.

Yesterday was the 24th, and it was exactly 4 months since I left. Time certainly has flown by because it doesn't seem as though I've been away more than a few weeks.

I've finally gotten into my string quartet, although progress is slow.

Take care and give my love to the family.

Love,
Charles

Wed., Oct. 27
Dear Family,

At my last lesson, Mlle B gave me an envelope with a few pages in it that described her Wed. comp. class, which I've already told you of. Anyway, it lists all the works to be studied until June. It also says that the price of the course is 15,000 fr., about $30.00. Next to that sentence there is a note written by Mlle B. which says, "As settled between us." Aside from that line, the whole outline was a mimeographed copy. I'm not sure just what she meant by that and if she wrote that on all the copies to her students. I haven't paid at all for my lessons, and I don't think I'll have to, but I certainly don't want to take advantage. But the class is very important to me, so I'll enroll in either case, and as I said, manage without additional help.

Keep well.

Love,
Charles

I turned nineteen years old a few days later, and along with a birthday card from my parents was a check for fifty dollars. That allowed me to buy a radio for my room. I found one that had shortwave capabilities as well, and suddenly I had music in my room. It's amazing to think how much of a difference that made, but I was able to pick up broadcasts from everywhere in Europe including Russia, the BBC in London, as well as Radio Free Europe. I bought the *London Times* on Sundays, and I could check the radio schedule and plan to listen to certain performances as they were broadcast on BBC. Sometimes a concert being performed in Paris was being broadcast live on the radio, and I would plan to be home to listen. It was wonderful to have music in my room, and it made such a difference to me.

Fri., Oct. 30
Dear Family,
Your letter reached me yesterday, the day before my birthday. You gift was very generous as well as thoughtful.
Well I guess I'm getting pretty old, being 19 and all. In a few years I'll be too old to turn over garbage cans.
Bonsoir ma chère famille, et merci.

Love,
Charles

Tues., Nov. 3
Dear Family,
I had a very enjoyable day today, and now before I go to bed, there is time to talk about it.
I had my lesson today at 6:45 as I received another letter this week changing my lesson to that time. Mlle Boulanger excused herself for changing my time so much.
I think you'll be happy to know the following: At the beginning of my lesson I asked her if she would wait until I received this month's check from you, before paying her the $30. But she said that she didn't want any money from me. I offered to pay her at least part of the money, but she said that when someday I'll have a lot of money, she will then accept it.
Needless to say that not having to pay does ease my burden. She is so wonderful, but that term doesn't really describe her. I think you understand how I feel.
The lesson was, as usual. . . . She found mistakes on my corrections of my mistakes. Don't be alarmed, if I didn't have so many mistakes, there would be no sense in my studying

harmony. Then again, most of the time, what I do wrong may not actually be a mistake (technically), but there were better solutions to the problems. And sometimes she'll find an exercise which turned out extremely well. She'll look at me with a happy glow surrounding her and tell me so. And I feel as though I've accomplished something to speak of. . . . It's silly, but actual.

Today, though, I did an unforgivable thing—parallel octaves. Her reaction to this was completely unique. She began stamping her feet, and banging her fists on the piano and my head! Oh very lightly but with gusto. When she finished this, she said that for a regular mistake I have just to pay 10,000 francs, but for this I deserve a spanking.

Please don't think that she was really angry or excited, because it was done completely with gaiety. But know that my lessons are <u>never</u> without humor, excitement, tension, and most of all, life.

So this week I'll be busy with my 3rd set of corrections, as well as with advancing in my harmony book. I could tell you much more about just that one lesson with her, but I must get to bed soon. I left her feeling completely free of everything but that which has true value, had my dinner, and went to a concert.

I was to a unique concert and worthwhile mentioning.

Darius Milhaud conducted a program of his own works. For me, it was sort of an introduction to his music.

Milhaud walks almost pitifully with the aid of 2 canes. He conducted from a chair.

The first number, his 8th symphony, was for the most part exciting and masterful. His double piano concerto with orch. was played by Vronsky and Babin. (Well-known male-female piano team.) Next was a concertante, I believe, for bassoon, trpt, horn, double bass, and orch. Both of the latter two were light in flavor, and I didn't particularly care for them because the composer seemed to lose himself in his musical humor and became incoherent. His use of the percussion is particularly strange. I think he tries to imitate melodies with such instruments as the snare drum.

All of the slow movements of those 3 works were not only beautiful but rich in sobriety and understanding. A pleasure to hear.

The final piece was a work for chorus and orch. This was completely inspired writing. (I mean inspired in the sense of from the music itself and not outside experiences.) I must finish now—

So you see I enjoyed myself today.

Keep well and together.

Love,
Charles

Fri., Nov. 6
Dear Family,

Just returned from a concert of contemporary works. I met a great many of Mlle Boulanger's students there although they weren't as lucky as I. They came to the concert without tickets, but hoping to buy them there. The performance was sold out, which I think is close to miraculous. I got a ticket early this week.

If you're not interested in hearing about the performances I attend, I won't write about them. In the meantime I'll describe this one.

The last number on the program was Bartok's <u>Miraculous Mandarin</u>, which seemed, in comparison to the other works on the program, mildly dissonant.

Stravinsky's <u>Chant du Rossignol</u> and Schoenberg's <u>Variations</u> Opus 31 were given excellent performances this evening. As for the compositions I have nothing to say.

There was a work by a 35-year-old Italian, Berio I think. In the program notes it said that the composer intended (for best performance) to have the orch. divided into 5 sections, each placed in a different part of the theater. The difficulty in doing that is obvious, but they had one section in the back of the theater, and 4 on stage.

The music itself is difficult to explain, but if I compare it to the Pointillism school of painting you might get an idea . . . dots and dashes of color as opposed to strokes. In itself it was a fine composition and the work of a mature composer. I doubt though the permanent value of this <u>kind</u> of music for a number of reasons.

Variation is one of the most important elements of composition. This kind of composition limits greatly (as I'll explain) the resources for variation. Harmonic variation is not possible as long as music is still mostly written in the 12 tone system.

We are at the end of the rope in that respect. Orch. variation is also greatly limited because in order to get that smattering of sound, effect, notes are tossed back and forth between the instruments right from the beginning. The same holds I think for variations in register, as extremes in register are also used without spare. Melody is unrecognizable, variation of it. . . .

In summary, the piece was boring, the sound interesting, the total musical effect, natural.

My <u>real</u> complaint as you see is with the means and not the results. What was more interesting was the audience's reaction. The composer had to be called I don't know how many times to acknowledge the thundering applause and shouts of bravo. That was wonderful. People want to acknowledge their contemporaries' works as a valid expression of the times. . . . There is still hope for the composer. Perhaps more so than ever.

So . . . how is my cat?

Love,
Charles

Mlle Boulanger's assistant, Mlle Annette Dieudonné, was a superb teacher in her own right and taught at the Conservatoire as well as the Ecole Normale de Musique. I had to enroll in that school in order to study with her and to be able to take Mlle Boulanger's keyboard harmony class. My lessons with Mlle Dieudonné, however, were strictly technical: solfeggio and ear training. She too was a disciplinarian but without the outbursts. She had students ranging in age from five years old to conservatoire-age students. She was a lovely woman with a genuinely warm smile, and I always enjoyed being with her. She seemed to be around the same age, perhaps a bit younger than Mlle Boulanger, who was seventy-two years old the summer of my arrival in France.

Fri., Nov. 13
Dear Family,

I went for the first time yesterday (in Paris) for a lesson with Mlle Dieudonné in solfeggio (ear training). Aside from an American girl, also a student of Mlle B., the six or so other students are French. You'll probably laugh when I tell you that the French students appear to be around ten years old. That in itself wouldn't be too bad if I could keep up with them. I'm happy anyway for there being at least one American in the class. Better for the morale. . . .

Halfway through the lesson a few more students came in, which made me completely disgusted because they could not have been more than 5 years old. They weren't part of the class though. It shows you the difference between U.S. and French training.

I'm not seriously annoyed but rather think the situation very funny. What I am concentrating on now is learning the 7 clefs well enough so that I will be able to transpose piano music easily, and then get into score reading at the piano. Aside from the clef business, the class has nothing else to offer me. I do pretty well in dictation, and for that reason, I'll have to change to a class which will be a little above my head.

Love,
Charles

Wed., Nov. 18
Dear Family,

It is late Wednesday night and I am tired, but I write now so that you will not be without a letter from me for more than 3 days.

I am learning so much about what it means to be a musician. Of what one has to have mastered to be considered a musician. The description of that above would take me a year of letters, so I won't begin to say much.

Mlle Boulanger has two students who are very young children named Giovanni and Paolo, who live with her and are the sons of her servants, Giuseppe and Zitta. One of the boys entered the room in which I was having my lesson yesterday. For what reason I can't be certain, but Mlle played notes all over the piano to which the boy immediately responded by identifying them. He could seemingly pick out all the notes of a tone cluster played with an open hand. He easily read my harmony exercises written in 4 clef . . . 7 years old!

Technique involves time. I have much ahead of me and little behind.

So I am now on my 4th week of harmony corrections. Mlle admitted that she criticizes things now which she didn't last week because it is only slowly and thoroughly that one can progress.

First let me extend her regards and sincere thanks for yours.

I had a lovely evening having dinner with a friend in a very pleasant restaurant off the Champs Élysées. It cost about $1.00 but it's good for the morale to get away from the studies for restaurants once in a while.

After a leisurely dinner, we visited our friends who live near the Arc de Triomphe, the girls whom I've mentioned once before. They've invited me over for a Thanksgiving dinner. Holidays seem so remote to me, I had forgotten that Thanksgiving even existed. Today I went to the Alliance Française to find out that it was closed because it is Armistice Day.

We left the girls at 12:45 but the trains had already stopped running. Subways here run only until 1:00 AM. So I walked home. It didn't take more than an hour, and it was pleasant.

Love,
Charles

Thurs., Nov. 19
Dear Family,

My lesson Tues. was very inspiring. I prepared quite a bit for the lesson, and as a result, Mlle B. only got around to checking less than half of what I prepared. That leaves an easier week of work this week because I can do much new work, instead of spending a great deal of time on corrections.

Correcting is more difficult because there are few alternatives. Mlle B. had an inimitable way of describing a student making first exercises as opposed to when he is making his corrections on the same. In the former, you get the impression of a real "happy-go-lucky," writing anything without much discretion. (Of course this is far from true, but in comparison to the latter, it may be considered so.) Her imitation of a happy-go-lucky is what is inimitable, but I was reminded of Marcel Marceau and the "loose" appearance of his body. She also added all kinds of "squeaks" and other sounds, which are always a pleasure to hear from her.

The making of corrections is quite the opposite.

I'm afraid I'll never be able to properly describe Mlle. I can only enjoy now, and remember later.

My quartet has been at a standstill. The second theme is the cause of it. Last week I showed my progress to Mlle, and she said the 2nd theme couldn't remain as it is. This Tuesday I told her I would drop that theme out completely and replace it with one which would not cause so much difficulty. She told me a story, have no time to relate it now, but the meaning was: A woman she knows well, who is deaf, dumb, and blind. Aside from things this woman has done which would seem miraculous, she has made her family (husband and children) happy for 40-some-odd-years.

Then Mlle said that I have already created something (the 2nd theme) and if that creation is even as difficult to work with as being deaf, dumb and blind, then it is still possible to do something wonderful with it.

It was for me a wonderful lesson in musical economy. I immediately thought of Bartok's 5th string quartet in which the musical economy is brilliant. Mlle then reminded me of the opening theme of the <u>Eroica</u>, which if you did not know what Beethoven would do with it, you'd think it offered nothing.

Meanwhile, your son, inspired, is still struggling and has yet to find a solution. And it is not until I do that I can complete the exposition and begin the development.

I have been enjoying the tobacco very much.

Love,
Charles

Wed., Nov. 25
Dear Family,

My French, by the way, seems to be improving. I have a few friends who speak only French, and we get along pretty well. (Well, at least they don't laugh at my attempts.)

I keep confusing my solfeggio teacher, Mlle Dieudonné, who speaks English with a very heavy accent. Now, I am quite used to French accents, but at Fontainebleau it seemed very funny to hear things like "Zis is zee la."

So, being in a class with French students, I always refer to notes, time values, etc. in their French terms. Except of course when I don't know, or forget to use French terms and rely upon Mlle Dieudonné's English. The note "C" is pronounced the same as the French "si," which is actually "B" in our language.

Mlle always has to ask me what language I'm speaking. And of late, Mlle Boulanger also.

Love,
Charles

Thurs., Dec. 3
Dear Family,

Mlle Boulanger had to cancel my lesson this week because of a composer who visits her once a year and occupies her time for a full day. It happened that he came on the same day as my lesson. The day before that, though, she found that she had an hour in which to make up my lesson. I haven't a phone, so she sent Alex Panama to my house to tell me. He got Rue des Batignolles confused with Blvd. des B. and never found me. But I saw her the next day for the Comp. class. It is anyway very unusual for her to have an hour completely free. For all I know, she may have wanted to see me at 7:00 in the morning or 11:00 in the evening.

Our class this week was (and for the next 2 weeks will be) devoted to Stravinsky's <u>Canticum Sacrum</u>. I had analyzed 2 pages of it in preparation, and although it is very little, I was satisfied at having done that much. The class was a pleasure.

After, Alex P. and I worked on dictation in my room. We've arranged to meet twice a week for that purpose. And when you spend even just a few hours 2x a week in taking dictation, it greatly improves your ear. So he gives me (3 part) dictation and I, him. We worked on that for about 3 hours and then read through double piano music for another 2 until it was too late to play. It was about 10:30 when I ate that evening. Had a pizza near the Etoile (Arc de Triomphe) and together visited friends.

I guess I forgot to tell you about the Ecole Normale. The first week Mlle suggested that I take her keyboard harmony course. The next week I told her I would like to and nothing further was ever said. I passed it off anyway because I'm really not prepared for such a course with her. It involves, among other things, transposition at the piano and orch. score reading at the piano. There are five or six students, and the class meets in Mlle B.'s apt. for a 4-hour continuous class. But Alex feels that I would be able to keep up, and I plan to mention it to Mlle on Tuesday. Also that I'd like to study piano here.

It's very thoughtful of you to want to buy a gift for Mlle Boulanger, but it's entirely unnecessary. She doesn't want thanks for what she's done for me. I love music, my studies give me great pleasure, and my composition, joy. That's the only thanks she wants.

And consider for a moment (just for the fun of it) what you could possibly give her anyway.

Ma chere famille.

Love,
Charles

Wed., Dec. 9
Dear Family,

Mlle sort of made up for last week's lesson that I missed by making the one I had today nearly 2 hours long. I avoided talking about anything which would be sure to divert her attention from my harmony. Of course—sometimes she goes off on her own, but that's unavoidable. But you see, an hour with her passes so quickly, and sometimes she's only able to see half of my work. So today I was turning pages quickly so that she would check as much as possible.

I think that this coming week, I should make the last of my corrections on my exercises from Oct. (Corrections are made on small pieces of paper [to suit individual corrections] and are scotch-taped over the original version.) Some of my whole sheets of manuscript paper are as thick as a little book. Mlle said that I'll soon be up with another student, who's been working on one exercise since August.

But if anything, it's a healthy sign, because if I had to make no corrections or very few (generally), it would mean either that I know harmony and composition and orchestration perfectly (which is silly) or that I am capable of attaining only so much musicianship.

You see, silly, dull, and seemingly meaningless exercises in harmony are the basis for understanding the comparative values in composition.

After all, composition cannot really be taught. A composer has just so much and so little he is able to say regardless of his background, environment, or intelligence.

All his studies can lead him to the point where, within what he is capable of doing, to use good, sincere, and sound judgment. That's all.

And you take these little figured basses of 8 bars, with two phrases, even using only root position chords. They're compositions in themselves. But don't think that many teachers are able to make you aware of this, if they are aware themselves. Fin.

I'm sure you're all bored by now.

I was to a concert last night of contemporary music. Remember that I spoke once before of a concert I was at, which performed works of contemporary "pointillistic" "masters"? This was the same except it was for chamber combinations.

These concerts disturb me beyond words. If I could, I would not go at all, but I must go. I never thought I could actually feel disgust at serious attempts to create, but I do now.

I attend these concerts and will still, whenever I am able. There's no doubt in my mind that one day this music will come into prominence. It will, along with all the electrical devices which will change man's life. My sincerest feelings are that music will destroy itself.

Will write soon.

Love,
Charles

Sun., Dec. 13
Dear Family,

I've put my quartet aside for the time being, to write a few pieces for harp. A girl whom I see often and is also a student of Mlle B. spent a couple of hours Friday evening showing Alex and me the principles of the harp. She is by the way an excellent harpist, and studies at the Conservatoire. She's here on a Fulbright.

The harp is difficult to write for because it is completely different from all other instruments. That is, the "double action" harp. The chromatic harp is written for as piano music, but is used very little. The harp is not nearly as difficult to write <u>well</u> for as the violin, but to learn originally requires a good deal of time. I bought the scores to Ravel's <u>Introduction</u>

and Allegro and the orchestral version of *Tombeau of Couperin*, both of which use the harp. After studying those scores, I have some more questions to ask Ruth, but I've also begun work on a piece.

I would like this year to learn to write for the organ as well.

Alex and I went at 5:00 AM one morning to the "market." Actually, it was 5:00 after the *Late Late* show. I had never been there before, and that hour in the morning is the best time to go.

The market seems to occupy at least a square mile of space, and early in the morning the retailers from Paris and surrounding towns buy their daily supply of all fresh foods. Aside from the people who have business at the market, it is where people congregate who have closed all the nightclubs and cafés in Paris. Also tourists of course. We went to one of the more famous restaurants there. This area is noted for its onion soup. I won't begin to describe it, but I look forward to having some again.

The restaurant has a wonderful atmosphere at that hour. Outside, the workers beginning their day, and inside, the "party-goers" finishing it. And with a accordionist playing and singing French songs, it is anyway typical. I bought the music to Stravinsky's piano sonata.

Also saw a Stravinsky festival Thurs. with *Le Sacre*, *Petrouchka*, and *Jeu de Cartes*.

Well, c'est tout!

Love,
Charles

Sun., Dec. 20
Dear Family,

I was mistaken about terms in something that I once said. Perfect pitch is the immediate recognition of sounds <u>without</u> relating it to another sound. I know people who are able to identify all notes immediately if given a starting note. I have memorized "A" and am able to figure out all intervals, slowly. You can't imagine how much a regular amount of dictation has helped me. Also, I decided to work on Sundays, which means 3 times a week, aside from my class with Mlle Dieudonné. We have been doing 3-part dictation, and now also one voice, which is very difficult for me, but it's getting much better. When 15 or 16 notes are played in rapid suc-

cession, which are not related to a key, it's too hard to try to remember the line, so it's necessary to work only by interval. And of course if you can't recognize the intervals immediately and have to think, then notes are still going by and you're bound to get lost. But I find that sometimes I recognize notes not by interval but by themselves. Anyway, my ear is definitely improving.

The harp can be a beautiful instrument and very effective in an orch. or ensemble, but a lousy instrument to write a solo work for. I won't bother telling you why, but it has been giving me a great deal of trouble in writing for it. On the other hand it's a challenge to write a good idiomatic piece and still write notes that please me. I'm having a lot of fun with it and will finish my first piece in a day or so.

C'est la vie.

Keep well and write.

Love,
Charles

Sat., Dec. 26
Dear Family,

Today is Hanukkah I think. Not much I can do about it but decided to have lunch at the kosher delicatessen. I'm still at the restaurant working on my coffee, but thought I'd write to you now.

It's been a busy Christmas for me but not in the usual way. Christmas in Paris is very different from that in NY. No Santa Clauses or bells (or snow!) but parties similar but better than on New Year's Eve. So that's how I've spent my time this week, Réveillon(ing).

Mlle had a party yesterday aft. and I brought her flowers. I was very surprised to receive a gift from her because she generally doesn't give presents to her students. Anyway it was a very large manuscript book, which I can always use, and she put a little inscription on it, so it was a nice gift. When she gave me the present I kissed her hand. I'm getting so damn European. But I'm sure I must have broken her hand in doing so.

I showed Mlle my piece for the harp at my last lesson, and she seemed to feel sorry for Ruth (the harpist), who will probably have to take dancing lessons to be able to manipulate the pedals fast enough. I intended the piece to be very difficult to play; it was the least I could do to get even with an instrument that is so difficult to write for.

I have recently become a member of the leisure class here. I now ride 1st class on the Metro. A ride costs 9¢, 3¢ more than 2nd class, but I don't use more than 10 tickets a week so I am happy to do it. You know what the rush hour is like on the Metros in NY; imagine you were able to ride all the time in an empty car, even during the rush hours. It's the same here.

I think I'm going to stay away from work on my quartet, and write something for the harpsichord. In the quartet, I got myself into a harmony rut and wasn't able to move without going against myself. The harp piece is the most dissonant of all my pieces, but the sound in general pleases me.

Take care. Happy Hanukkah.

Love,
Charles

Mon., Dec. 28
Dear Family,

It's practically 1960 and for me, time to consider next year. Juilliard is out. That's definite! In fact, schools and degrees don't interest me at all. Specific teachers? Yes! Piston would be fine, but he's at Harvard and doesn't teach privately. I'm not sure whether Milhaud will be in San Francisco or Paris next year. Studying with Copland would not be a bad idea especially since he lives close enough to NY for me to live at home.

What I'm considering for next year is that I definitely want to study conducting. Jean Morel at Juilliard is a fine teacher and conductor, but again, that probably would mean taking the other stuff Juilliard has to offer. To study with Bernstein would also be a good idea, but in either case, I want to decide first what I want to do, and then work on doing it. I don't care to stick my nose into everybody's door to see who wants me. I'm probably in a good enough position to do what I like, within reason. But bear this in mind, jumping around from teacher to teacher every year is not healthy. At best, it can give me a smattering of knowledge.

There is of course another possibility for next year, but I don't know whether it has entered your minds yet. That I'll come home after the summer, spending 2 months with you, and returning to Paris to finish studying harmony. Incidentally, any of the above would have to involve a scholarship.

Let me know how you feel about all this, and I promise to take it well into consideration.

Love,
Charles

Jan. 1, 1960
Well my Dear Family,

Just a quickie to wish you a Happy New Year. Here we are well into the 4th hour of the new year, but in New York it is around 10 PM, 1959.

For me it was the quietest NY Eve I've spent in about 5 years, accustomed as I've been to drunks, yelling, and mambo music. This evening, only a quiet party at Mlle Boulanger's.

This morning at 7:00 AM I found myself at Orly Field awaiting the arrival of people I'd never met. They are friends of Mlle B.'s, and she was unable to meet them herself, and asked me to meet and welcome them. I couldn't very well refuse although I knew it involved staying up all night. I spoke with the people for a few minutes at the airport, gave them gifts from Mlle and received some for her and went home to bed. When I saw Mlle this evening I told her that I enjoyed doing the service. After all, what could I say, that I was very tired and would rather have been home in bed? She returned by saying that I could have the pleasure in the future if the situation should present itself again.

Oh, a couple of days ago I was to a party given by Mlle Dieudonné. That was amusing enough to tell you about. The party was to begin at 4:30. I had thought it was for 2:30. I had difficulty finding her house and so I arrived at 4:00, and when I saw that there wasn't anyone but Mlle home, immediately offered my apologies to her. She said, "Nonsense," that someone has to be first at parties, so I left well enough alone. We talked for about an hour before anyone else arrived. Not many people came altogether, and she insisted that those of us who were there finish all the food she prepared. I can't remember how many pieces of cake and glasses of punch I had, but I could hardly eat dinner that day.

For Christmas I brought Mlle Boulanger 10 flowers, not roses, but to me they looked like roses. They were wrapped as flowers generally are, and Mlle accepted them and handed them to Giuseppe to take care of them. But her house has always many flowers, especially that day.

So, I thought it would be pretty much the same with Mlle Dieudonné and decided to economize by buying only 6 flowers. Mlle D. had of course no flowers at all and immediately gave her personal attention to their care. But at least the store included lots of ferns!!

My once loyal suit is slowly deserting me. It may be necessary to buy another this spring to remain in the top ten.

To a wonderful year for all of us.

Love,
Charles

Thurs., Jan. 7th
Dear Family,

Well, I've finally entered Mlle B.'s keyboard harmony class at the Ecole Normale. The reason that she hasn't mentioned it before is because she thought I couldn't afford it. It's something like $12.00 a month but all $50.00 payable at the beginning of the term. Today was my first day with that class, and what a class it is! I really have no business being in it now because she has only 6 or 7 of her best students taking the class and really puts them through hell.

I suppose she'll be pretty lenient with me for a couple of months. Even so, she yelled at me today louder than she ever has before. It's frightening until you get used to it. But anyway in comparison to the others, she was at worst patting my hand. It's for the best, I suppose, and don't think it's unbearable, but it is certainly not pleasant.

I was playing the most simple of figured basses today, but I had never done them before so it's quite difficult. It was difficult enough for me to keep track of 4 voices with correct voice leading, but she kept yelling to play more legato, with more feeling, etc. But mainly she insists that no matter what happens, not to stop. It's really difficult to keep your mind during all this, but I'm sure that by the time I leave Paris I'll have a good keyboard technique.

The class begins at 9:00 AM and is 4 hours without a stop. By the 4th hour everyone is practically falling out of their chairs and watching the clock. At 2:00 today I had a solfeggio lesson for 2 hrs, and at 5:00 I gave a piano lesson. That was really too much for one day, so I made arrangements to have my solfegg. lesson on Mondays.

My piece for harp is finished, and I expect to have a performance of it here in the spring.

I'm really happy that you've understood so well my plans for continuing my studies. I really did decide some time ago that I must remain in Paris for more than one year, and as long as you agree, I'll make it my business to be able to stay.

Technique is a funny thing. It's only important when you don't have it, but when you do, well, it's something that you never think about.

Tiens, je n'ai rien de plus à dire, maintenant.

Be well and happy.

Love,
Charles

Friday , Jan. 15
Dear Family,

Wednesday, Mlle Boulanger asked me for the first time to transpose at the piano. She first explained a few principals to me and then put one of Schubert's songs in front of me and asked me to transpose the piano part while the others in the class sang the melody. It didn't sound a hell of a lot like Schubert, but anyway it was a beginning for me.

There is no guesswork in transposing. You simply make use of different clefs and raise or lower certain alterations of notes depending on what the distance is between the new and old keys. So I've begun for the time being transposing only down a 2nd. That involves reading the treble clef as if it were the tenor clef, and the bass as if it were the alto clef, with alterations of course. It will take a long time and a lot of work until I am able to sit down and play any piece in any key, but for the time being I'm happy to begin at the beginning and look to the future.

And you don't know how much pleasure it gives me to work on transposition. It's something that I never dreamed (before I came here) was possible for me to do. So I practice now transposing Schubert songs, Mozart sonatas, and easy but more dissonant works. Very very slowly of course, but as I say, it is the beginning.

You know that if I do leave Paris with the technique I hope to have, I'll probably be able to make a living in NY only with serious music. Accompanying for instance. Or what I would really find enjoyment in is playing harpsichord in a Baroque ensemble. For that I must acquire a good technique in reading continuo, or figured bass. The harpsichord part in an ensemble during the Baroque period was not written on 2 staves. What was written was a bass line (generally the same as the cello) with numbers on top of the line which represented the chords.

I'll continue another time.

Love,
Charles

Thurs., Jan. 28
Dear Family,

Last Thurs. after I finished writing to you, I had a class with Mlle Boulanger. I transposed for her for the first time. I think I did quite well considering the pressure and the fact that I had been practicing transposition for only a week. Nevertheless, she saw that although the notes were not perfectly correct, that it is a matter of time and practice until technique in transposition will no longer be a problem. She was yelling because my legato wasn't legato enough and things like that. But you see, already I'm able to do things that I never dreamed I would be.

I expect that tomorrow's class will be mostly orch. score reading at the piano. Souhaitez moi bon chance!

Tues. I was to another Pierre Boulez (contemporary musique) concert. Perhaps at the next one in May, we'll have a greater number of people opposed to these unmusical sounds, and we'll be able to cause a real fiasco. And Boulez audiences in Paris and Germany are the most open minded anywhere. Varese's "Improvisations" was perhaps the mildest of all the works on the program, and I'm certain that a performance of it even in NY would not bring many followers to say the least.

A couple of the pieces were repeated which brought scattered shouts of "Pity," "Have mercy," etc. from the audience. I must admit that I booed occasionally myself. But I sincerely believe that if this music will be accepted by a great many people in a future era, it will have to fight very much before that. And until I feel that there is no longer a need for harmony in music or for a more or less constant sound, I will be among those fighting against it. But I must first be absolutely sure of what it is that I oppose.

This Friday I'll be at an unimportant recital of a pianist, and Sun. a concert conducted by Hindemith. Sat., I'll be at the rehearsal of the same. And one day next week, I hope to meet Mr. Hindemith at Mlle Boulanger's apt.

Love,
Charles

Mon., Feb. 1
Dear Family,

My quartet, which is progressing very slowly, takes most of my time. It was necessary to work on it completely at the piano because there were too many wrong sounds as a result of not referring to the piano. But to change those notes which didn't please me did take me quite a bit of time, and I sometimes spent 5 or so hours on a single measure. As for what I've already written, there is just one phrase which I've been unable thus far to orchestrate with the best results. It will prove to mean a decision which will take the side of orchestration or composition. Very simply, this part of which I speak will suffer orchestration-wise if I decide to keep a certain note. If I change that note to suit proper orch., the difference will be very slight, but not as pleasing. And sometimes I think how silly it is that I can spend as much time on a decision involving so small a musical fragment that it will pass in a fraction of a second. The completed 1st movement will be quite long. I am nearing the end of the development section and have already 13 pages of music. And I plan, in the coda, to write a fugue. I'm in no hurry though and will let things take their natural course.

[I shaved my beard off!!] BUT, I feel as though I am deprived of a hiding place and will, <u>to begin with</u>, let my moustache grow. Would you like a picture first?

Love,
Charles

Mon., Feb. 15
Dear Family,

Glad that you're having some warm weather. It's never as cold here as NY, but it's still not spring either. Spring in Paris promises to be all that it is supposed to be. Even now you can sense on a sunny day, the excitement in the air and the feeling of spring, although it's still a month away. Alex said in April and May, Mlle Boulanger gets less results from her students than at any other time. And that aside from a few hours of work in the morning, and again towards evening, it's very difficult to work.

I think that for the spring, I will supplement a few things to my wardrobe. . . . Wardrobe . . . Hah! Of my white shirts, all but two have frayed collars, so I'll probably buy two more, a pair of shoes, and I guess that's all. Please don't think this is outside the realm of my monthly allowance. It is not.

Keep well,

Love,
Charles

Sat., Feb. 25
Dear Family,

This morning Mlle had us playing canons from Bach's <u>Musical Offering</u>. It was not all as easy as just reading, for the canons themselves were not written. I did one quite well and sort of amazed myself. (But not all of course.) There was written a single line, and the canon was this line played exactly by two voices but one beginning with the last note and working backwards until the first. (Are you getting the picture? I'm certain not the effect though.) At the beginning it wasn't too difficult, but as the two voices passed each other so did my eyes begin to get cockeyed. At one point I disgustedly threw up my hands and said that I was completely lost. After all, my 2 hands were crossed, I was reading one line going in opposite directions, and unless you are perfectly sure of yourself all is lost. But Mlle consoled me and I managed to finish.

Other little games involved reading clefs upside-down, backwards, beginning a measure after a first voice, and playing in two keys at the same time. Lots of fun but 4 hours worth . . . ppphhheeeew.

I'm going to see <u>Tosca</u> again tomorrow . . . just for the fun of it.

Love,
Charles

Sun., Feb. 28
Dear Family,
    Today appeared to be the first day of spring. It was a pleasure just to walk around Paris. Alex and I managed to do some dictation in the early afternoon, but that was my day's work. And I also spent the evening copying music.
    Next week we will begin making arrangements for our trip to Spain. Alex told Mlle that he planned to go, and she said that it was necessary to do no work at all for 10 days or so. He also said that he is trying to convince me to go, and she felt that Alex was right in wanting me to go also. You see if Mlle B. had said that we oughtn't to go, we would not. Of course we planned it so that as far as Mlle is concerned I am being more or less convinced that I should go. In my particular position it is better this way than if I just up and went without Mlle's approval.
    I've learned many ways to get around Mlle (when I find it necessary) without disobeying her. Her mind is always so active that child psychology generally works best. For example: At Fontainebleau she will never permit someone to postpone a lesson with her because that person wants to travel someplace. That is because most of Fontainebleau's students are not very serious and come only to get to Europe. There was one time when I wanted to go on the trip to Solesmes. (And did as it turned out.) It happened that my lesson was scheduled for the same day as the trip, and since most of the music students were also going, I wasn't able to get anyone to exchange lessons with me. So I went to Mlle and told her this, and she (knowing how profitable the trip is to a musician) said that I could go if I wanted to but she would not be able to make up the lesson that I would have missed. I promptly replied that my lesson was far more important than the trip and would gladly miss the latter. At that, she nearly pushed me onto the bus promising to make up the lesson. In fact the last 2 weeks I had 5 lessons.

I'm going to an interesting concert tomorrow. Orchestral works of Boulez, Stockhausen, and others. I can hardly wait for the booing.

At a performance of Tosca Friday I got annoyed enough to boo because of the audience's disgusting shouts of bravo when they really should have thrown tomatoes. The Parisian concert audience is the most indiscreet, idiotic, and misinformed imaginable. Puccini is corny enough and when performers add their own personal corn to it, well . . . it becomes monstrous. Worse is that the singers save their voices for the high notes so that unless you listen closely you hear nothing else. And furthermore, all Italian operas sound lousy in French, and French French horn players don't know what the French horn should sound like. What's more, whoever plans the week's events at the opera is out of his mind. Since Carmen had much success in its presentation, they do it 6 times a week with Rigoletto or Faust occasionally. Yeah. . . .

I'll write soon.

> *Love,*
> *Charles*

Thurs., March 3
Dear Family,

Heard some wonderful contemporary works this evening and will be at the opera tomorrow for a Ravel festival. I would like very much to go for a weekend to Frankfurt, Germany, to see their production of Lulu by Alban Berg.

I saw Wozzeck last year at the Met, but this is Berg's last and incomplete work and I would not hesitate to spend a day traveling in order to see a good performance of it . . . but it may not be possible.

Oh, listen to this. Yesterday I spent the whole afternoon with the conductor Igor Markevitch in his home, helping him to make changes in orchestration of Schubert's 3rd Symphony. He is leaving Sunday for the U.S. with the concert's Lamoreaux Orchestra. I imagine that very soon he will perform at Carnegie Hall and as well on television, so try not to miss it. Now that I have met him and have spoken with him at length, I am considering studying conducting with him next year if it is possible.

His changes in orchestration were interesting. I was not able to hear if they were effective or not, but on paper it seemed to do away with a cluttering of sound and add more depth to the essentials. . . . I do consider that a lot of Schubert's orchestration is cluttered, as is Schumann's, Brahms's, and Tchaikovsky's among others, but I don't know whether one has the right to change it. In either case, when you're as famous as Markevitch, you can get away with it. I remember reading that Toscanini added trumpets where they were not written in a Beethoven symphony, but crossed them out after having played it that way.

You know, when I realized what I was doing yesterday (making changes of notes on individual parts), I thought how amusing it would be to write a few notes (completely out of place) which would cause at least a major disturbance when performed. But have no fear, it was no more than a childish thought. Anyway do find out when they will be on television. Also at Markevitch's house was the concert master of the orchestra. When he told me that they were leaving Sunday for New York, I jokingly suggested that he take a package to you for me. He said that he would be happy to do so, but anyway I have nothing to send you.

At the end of this month I hope to meet the Russian composer Khachaturian.

C'est tout pour maintenant,

Love,
Charles

Wed., March 16
Dear Family,

Boulanger has just returned from Poland, and my classes will re-begin tomorrow. In a little while I have to go to the Trinité Church for a service commemorating the death of Mlle Boulanger's mother and sister. I understand that it's a yearly ritual which one is obligated to attend that has been asked to do so. Anyway the orchestra will play some music by Nadia and Lily.

Friday I was to a performance of Bartok's opera, <u>Bluebeard's Castle</u>. I went again on Sunday to see the same thing.

Some uses of the orchestra were so effective that I had to go again to make note of them.

You know, I really have to thank Mr. Benda for many things. It was he that suggested that I go to the opera to study Puccini's use of the strings, which resulted in many other things. Since then I have taken hundreds of mental notes of combinations of sounds and uses of instruments. That's really the only way to study orchestration.

I could talk more but I must not.

Love,
Charles

Tues., March 22
Dear Family,

It is only 9:00 in the morning and I have not begun my work yet, but I write now because I wasn't able yesterday and don't want you to worry.

Have a lesson with Mlle this afternoon.

Yesterday I went for the third day in a row to the Montmartre section of Paris. It's really lovely up there this time of the year. That area around the Sacré Coeur is the highest part of Paris, and one can see almost the entire city from there. As any tourist will tell you, that is the section of Paris where Utrillo spent most of his time painting pictures of Parisian scenes. And today there are generally hundreds of artists up there painting the same exact things even in the same style. Of course they're all lousy artists there, and tourists come up by the thousands with their push-button memory boxes, but it still remains one of the few parts of Paris which has not lost the turn of the century atmosphere. My real business there yesterday was at the music store. I finally bought the Vidal Basses, which is quite expensive ($12.00) but it was necessary for me to own.

From Montmartre I went to the Vogue record company, which deals with Seeco Records and is the same company that released La Plata's records. My aim in going was to see whether I couldn't get on a couple of recording dates and even write for the same, as a result of La Plata's records.

You have no idea of how excited they got there with me (an American cha-cha musician). You know how difficult A & R men were in NY. Well here, the first man I went to see called *up two men, and within 15 minutes they had come to his office to speak to me. One was an A & R man along with 2 other big shots from Vogue. Together they called immediately France's 2 leading Spanish bands, Jack Ary, and Benny Bennet, both of whom have record dates coming up and need tunes as well as a pianist. I have to go downstairs now to phone these 2 guys and won't know anything till then. In either case this will be good because recording work involves very little time.*

Excuse me I've got to go.

Love,
Charles

Mon., March 28
Dear Family,

You know, I don't really care to look as though I am a native of France, but with my beard, and my features, I've been told that I do. But I'll tell you, I like the idea of being an American and cling to my ivy league clothes. But as my wardrobe is being invaded little by little by foreign-made items, and my old clothes are "giving up the ghost," I have to depend on my American accent not to be taken for a Frenchman. But that will surely never change.

Will write peut-etre demain.

Love,
Charles

Tues., March 29
Dear Family,

I have just returned home after a lesson with Mlle. I'd like to work for a couple of hours on solfeggio before dinner, so I won't write much now.

After speaking with Mlle I know that I will be in Fontainebleau for the summer. The school itself does not (cannot) give scholarships, but the few students who are there on scholarships are the result of Mlle herself. So she said that she would not like for me to stop my studies for the summer, so that she will do all that she can for me.

As long as I won't have to spend extra for my food, I can put that money toward the school. So I may have to pay just $150 dollars or so all together for the summer.

Re next year: I told Mlle that you would probably be able to send me the same as you do presently, but that I'd like to get even a little scholarship to be able to at least pay for my lessons. But she again said that it's not necessary and my first obligation is to relieve you of the extra expense. . . . And that if one day I will have money, I can repay her, even if it's not to Mlle herself.

As of now though, I have nothing in sight except perhaps a French govt. grant. Mlle knows of the existence of a large Jewish organization in Chicago that helps students. But she doesn't know the name or the address. Maybe even the Zionist Organization has something.

Mlle was in a good mood and I had a quiet lesson. She gave me tickets to a concert this evening. Another in the très avant-garde series. This time I'll have a good seat though.

Take care.

> *Love,*
> *Charles*

Thurs., April 7
Dear Family,

Things seem to work out well because to my great delight, the Frankfurt Opera Company is coming to Paris and is bringing Lulu and also Mozart's Cosi fan Tutte. Since they will be performing in a regular theater and not the Opera House, each work will be given a full week's run, which will enable me to see each more than once. Also, Stravinsky's Sacre and Oedipus will be staged next month, so I am kind of happy to be here. And even things are looking up with the Paris company. Tomorrow I'll see Boris and next week Eugene Onegin.

After the recent changes in plans I had almost made another in deciding once more to take a vacation. Mlle Boulanger suggested that I do travel and had a wonderful proposal, which I turned down nevertheless. A rich family living in the country near Normandy on the west coast opened their mansion there to a few students (5) of Mlle. Not to make it a complete gift they asked that we pay for our meals and lodging 50¢ a day. I did accept to go but then refused because we were not to go until the 21st of April, which is really after the vacation, and it would have interfered with my lessons for a week. So anyway

I do not regret my decision, being quite happy in Paris at the moment. Also on the 25th of this month Von Karajan will conduct Beethoven's 9th Symphony at the opera and I would not consider missing it.

Have I told you that I shaved off the lower part of my beard leaving only a moustache? And now I am adding to that, so I'll have a "Three Musketeers" type moustache and think that I may be happy with it then. I'll send you a picture soon.

So much for music, I'm going to take a haircut.

Be well all.

Love,
Charles

Thurs., April 14
Dear Family,

I'm going to have dinner in a few minutes so I won't be able to write much now.

It's with great pleasure that I tell you now that after some 6 odd months I have finally completed the 1st movement of my string quartet. Though it is not actually finished (because there are still some wrong notes and things which have to be corrected) at least I have written a first and last measure with a lot in between. It is a little embarrassing to tell my friends that I've finished and then have to admit that it is only the 1st movement, but of course I have done some other things as well since Oct. There were several occasions when I put the piece completely aside for more than a month. And after that it's not so easy to re-begin work, especially when you can only afford 3 or 4 hours a day a few times a week. It is, though, a very long movement, perhaps even too long. I just timed it and hope that it won't really take that long because it comes out to 11 minutes. The second (slow) movement, which I wrote in NY, takes about 6 minutes, so those 2 movements alone are approximately as long as most whole quartets. I have the necessary onionskin paper already and will copy the score and individual parts out as soon as possible in order to have the 1st movement performed at Fontainebleau or perhaps sooner than that in Paris.

I will hold off with having the 2nd movement played until I write an additional 2 and can present a whole work. But before that I will begin another work for orchestra and chorus which will be written specifically to be performed at Fontainebleau this summer. Although I haven't yet begun that work I think that it will not give me much trouble, and if I can finish it before the summer I will spend the summer with the quartet again.

Be well.

Love,
Charles

Wed., May 4
Dear Family,

Enfin it is warm. Until today I've been wearing my heavy winter coat. It had been very warm at the end of March, but all through April it was still winter.

Mlle Boulanger gave us the keyboard class Sunday morning. We have another tomorrow morning. It was a wonderful class last week. We sight-read some of Max Reger's ugly music for piano and orchestra. At first, some of the members of the class were at the other piano, and some of us at the piano where Mlle was. But by the time that we had gone through a few concertos and I was then reading the Liszt concerto, all of us were at the other piano leaving Mlle alone at the first piano. Of course, sight-reading a concerto, especially the Liszt, is pretty impossible for me and the others; the only things we are obligated to do is not stop at all. Even that is not so difficult because of what I consider "the club around the piano." And it is exactly that. For example, while I am playing, the conducting student of Igor Markevitch conducts. Another points to each measure as we proceed. Everyone counts the beats and taps me on the shoulder at the same time, so it is hard to get lost. Anyway, whatever happens, Mlle blames the conductor, who no one sees. Mlle thought that my conducting at one point was "monstrous" and stood up to imitate me. From that you could gather that I conduct as if I were throwing a bowling ball and pushing a hockey puck with my foot at the same time.

I finished the Hindemith book this week. Now I will do it twice more before the summer and then put it aside for good.

That's all I have time for.

Love,
Charles

Thurs., May 12
Dear Family,

There doesn't seem to be much to write about, these days. Not that I'm doing less than before but I guess that I'm just getting pretty used to things around here and take them for granted. It doesn't seem so long ago when things were so new that I would take pictures of them or just stare. The Seine River is the one thing which I could never take for granted. Every time I'm there or even just pass by on a bus, I stop to think that I'm really in Paris. That's something which I still find hard to believe even after nearly a year. My life is so different from what it was at home, and yet I feel that I still am in and have never left New York.

Paris is so beautiful during the spring. It's almost unreal. And yet I can't help but anticipate the excitement of going back to New York, which will always be my home.

Love,
Charles

Fri., June 3
Dear Family,

Here we are into June already. Just a few weeks left until the summer. The year certainly has gone fast.

Mlle Boulanger was quite angry with me yesterday. I'm sure that I must be improving.

My little piano student stopped taking lessons permanently. Better that way because she never worked anyhow.

Forgive me if my regularity in writing to you seems to show that I'm not conscious of the days that pass in between letters. I really am not. I always think of you though.

Love,
Charles

Tues., June 7
Dear Family,

You may not have realized it, but until today I was not certain of going to Fontainebleau for the summer. Today, Mlle told me that she had arranged things definitely. I told her that I would be able to manage to give her $150 for the summer and possibly $200, although that would not leave me with very much. She said that perhaps I wouldn't have to pay more than a hundred, but I don't care to take advantage. After all, the cost is normally $600 for the summer. Anyway, I'm pretty happy.

I had a very good lesson today. I had 30 pages of harmony written for this lesson, and of what she was able to check in an hour many things were right. At one point she asked me if my harmony is coming along well. . . . From the look on her face I knew it was, so I said so and added that it was even beginning to be fun (a little bit). That made her so happy that she said, wait until you begin counterpoint and fugue. I'll never learn to keep my mouth shut!

Before today, I had never actually disagreed with anything Mlle said while speaking with her. But today she began talking about the great depression in Berg's _Lulu_ and _Wozzeck_. I can't recall exactly what she said, but she spoke admonishingly of those two works after having praised Stravinsky and Mozart in reference to music so correct that not one note of a piece could be changed, and that that is the difference between an ordinary good work and a masterpiece. So evidently she did not consider _Wozzeck_ and _Lulu_ more than an ordinary work. Then she looked at me and asked me if I _still_ liked those two operas, and I said yes immediately, adding that I'm not certain that the music is beautiful, but certainly wonderful. She said that anyway it may or may not be a masterpiece (the 2) but still Berg's seriousness is always related to morbidness, whereas Stravinsky and Mozart can sound very light and happy and have the greatest amount of seriousness. I said that the former fascinated me. Mlle then said that I may be right and she may be wrong, or visa versa, which means that she definitely disagreed with me. She dropped the subject, but it must have been on her mind because a few minutes later she said that that is similar with _Tristan_. But I never heard _Tristan_, so the conversation ended there.

I saw a beautiful opera this week, Pergolesi's _La Serva Padrona_ by an Italian group. I want very much to study the score because of its recitative. The more great music I hear, the more I am convinced of the beauty in clarity. Especially today when plain dissonance itself helps to cloud the total sound.

Anyway—

Mom, I think that if you should care to write her, Mlle B. would be very happy to hear from you. She often asks about all of you. If you would like to do that, let me know and I'll tell you her address.

Love,
Charles

Wed., June 15
Dear Family,

I hope that you're not angry with me for writing only once a week. I know how you want to hear from me as much as possible but every so often there seems to be no time for writing.

My French is coming along quite well. I'm still studying and enjoying doing so.

It's much better to have lessons with Mlle in French because she never gets so angry when she speaks French and even gives you answers to harmony problems. This week she gave me so many answers that my corrections for the week took no more than an hour.

I spent most of the afternoon yesterday with Jack Ary in his home. He is more or less France's Tito Puente. Malheureusement, I could not accept his very inviting offer to play in his band this summer down by the Mediterranean. Surprisingly, the job paid as much as the best hotels do in the Catskills. But I am writing some things for him anyway.

I purposely mentioned Puccini to Mlle to see her reactions. It was as I thought it would be. She did not react violently but did not seem very happy. I don't see how she can say that Verdi was such a great master and then make a face and say that Puccini was <u>also</u> a good composer.

Anyway, for Mlle, there has been really only one composer since Mozart, and that's Stravinsky.

I'm leaving off work on my cantata until July 1st, when I will know exactly what instruments I'll have and how good the instrumentalists are. Mlle told me that there will be at F. an excellent trombonist, which will greatly add to the fun of writing the piece. Also a percussionist who has only jazz drums here. But the string orch. will be no more than a violin, 2 violas, and 2 celli and no basses.

Of course I could (as so many composers do) just write music in piano score and orchestrate later, but I could never get myself to do that: To me, in my music, every note and every line must be conceived orchestrally, for if I do not hear an instrument then what I write must be wrong.

Love,
Charles

Going back to Fontainebleau for the summer was like going home. It was so beautiful and comfortable, and the air was like being in the country, and I knew most of the local shopkeepers and waiters in the little village as well as the staff at the palace.

But this year was different in that I didn't want to lose a moment in my preparations for my lessons and beginning a new composition for the instrumentalists who had come to Fontainebleau.

This summer I didn't live in the dormitory as I did the first year, but in a little house adjacent to the restaurant and behind heavy wooden gates, where we all took our meals, students and teachers and Mlle Boulanger alike.

Fontainebleau was also a summer school for architects, and they shared the dormitories where I had stayed the previous year. I would sometimes see them working on a project with several students surrounding the architectural plans that they were developing. I always envied seeing them working together. Composing is such a lonely profession.

Thurs., July 21
Dear Family,

The summer also seems to be going by quickly, and now it's just a matter of a few weeks until I'll be home. I think the Fontainebleau plane leaves on the 7th; I hope to be on it. If I can possibly manage it, I will remain in New York until my birthday. Aside from everything else, I do need a month's rest.

Mlle Boulanger said today that she expects me to enter a composition for the competition this summer. I thought I would orchestrate my piece for harp, but she wants me to write a new work. The deadline is August 4th so I do expect to be rather busy these next two weeks. Even at that, I don't see how I can finish it in time, but I'll try at least. I'm scoring it for all of the instruments we have this summer, which amounts to a fairly large chamber orchestra. Strings, woodwinds, & brass. I expect that my quartet will be performed on Aug. the 5th.

Probably also in Aug. I'll finally hear my clarinet sonata. I'll have tapes made of all these things for you to hear when I return.

Excuse me—I have no more time now.

Love,
Charles

Wed., Aug. 3
Dear Family,

Found out some interesting news this week. It seems that I am here at Fontainebleau this summer as a result of a scholarship given to me by a Mrs. Schulze from NY. Mlle Boulanger asked me to write her a note of thanks and invited me to dinner with her. I don't know why, But Mlle's small dinner parties approach being enjoyable. Now I am not so sure that I will have to pay F. anything, but perhaps.

My composition is due tomorrow. This night will certainly be a sleepless one, but even at that, I don't see how I can have it completely finished by then.

Will write soon.

Love,
Charles

Tues., Aug. 9
Dear Family,

Before leaving for Switzerland, Mlle Boulanger told me that she received Mom's letter. She was very happy to hear from you and enjoyed the letter so much. She asked me to tell you how sorry she is that she hasn't the time to write you immediately, but will when she is able.

I am also very happy that she did receive a letter from you, Mom. Mlle always asks about things at home.

My last lesson was late Saturday night. Everything is always so serious at night that what is said is always very meaningful. I showed her my new piece, which I managed to sketch out completely. But it is no more than a rather full sketch. I still have a couple of days in which to finish it completely. Then another day to copy out parts and rehearse it on Saturday. If I cannot do this, it will not be performed this summer. But I know that I could not let such an opportunity pass.

The quartet just began rehearsing my piece. I hope that it will please you when you finally hear it.

Well, be good.

Love,
Charles

Aug. 16
Dear Family,

For the first time in weeks I can sit down and write you an unhurried letter and not feel as though I'm wasting time. My new piece is finished, the parts copied out, and now I can relax. If I had a few more weeks, I would add to it, but it can pass as it is. I am scheduled to perform it on the 29th. The same week, the quartet will perform my string quartet, so this amounts to an important time for me. Have I ever mentioned the instruments that I scored for? 2 flutes, oboe, 2 clarinets, 2 trombones, and string orchestra. I'm certain that I'll learn a great deal from conducting it. Tomorrow I'll rest, perhaps even lie in the sun. Then after that it's back to harmony.

Be well.

Love,
Charles

Fri., Aug. 19
Dear Family,

Only two things on my mind these days: my new piece and "home." I really can't take my work very seriously, so I'll be more or less faking it for the next two weeks.

I rehearsed my <u>Intro and Allegretto</u> today for the first time. I'm seriously wondering if it can be ready for a performance a week from Monday. But it would not be so if musicians would learn to count! That's why Mlle's training is so necessary. At least I can read a piece from beginning to end without getting lost or stopping even if I don't hit one right note. But that way, 80% of the difficulty in sight-reading is mastered.

Tomorrow, I and the other composers who wrote for the competition are to play the works for Mlle B. I would be very frightened, except that I know that only Mlle will make the orch. respond to what's written. But I have learned something from today's rehearsal, and that is, to sound as I wrote it to sound, I will need a full string orchestra instead of just 8 or 10 strings all together. But for that, we will have to wait.

After having written 4 works since I left NY. I am beginning to realize principles in my own composition, i.e.: those things which I always love and accept, others which depend, and still others which I could never love and never accept. But obviously I am bound to change with time and experience.

Even now, though my music is filled with struggle, and unsureness, there is at least one part of each composition (perhaps only a measure or just a chord) which I know belongs to me, because I found it.

Love,
Charles

I returned home, and it was wonderful being back with my family and friends. I started playing in bands again, hoping to save enough money to return to Paris in two months. The comfort of being home soon wore off, and the reality of returning to my old life and being in my parents' house soon made me yearn to be back in Paris. And I was anxious to get back to my work with Boulanger.

I began to get caught up in a lifestyle that, in my mind, I had passed by living a whole different life as a student in a foreign country. The family dynamics and financial pressures that existed at home were getting to me, and I couldn't wait to get back to Paris.

I couldn't save enough money fast enough, so I borrowed two hundred dollars from a friend and bought a one-way ticket on the *Queen Elizabeth*. A week later I was back in Paris.

My second year away I didn't write home nearly as often as I did during the first year. It didn't seem as though anything was that new to write about, and I was immediately immersed in my work.

It was so comforting to be back in Paris on my own. This now felt like home to me. The city was as beautiful as ever, and I had friends to contact and I could speak the language. All the things I couldn't say when I had moved there the year before.

Tues., Nov. 8, 1960
Dear Family,

Arrived yesterday after dinner. Everything was pleasant enough on the voyage except for the constant rocking of the boat. We went through storms most of the trip, which on a boat is very conducive to sleeping, so that accounts for most of my activities during the past five days. My stomach was too upset for the most part to be able to work very much. But regardless, sailing is much more pleasing than flying as far as I'm concerned.

The hour that we landed in Paris was not very helpful because I wasn't able to reach any of my friends by telephone or otherwise, so I had to go to a hotel.

I'm writing now from Tom Weaver's room. What I plan to do is move into this building on another floor where there is a small but adequate room which will cost approximately $25. I plan at the moment to stay there no longer than a month, but immediately I must think of leaving the hotel, which I'll do tomorrow morning.

Tomorrow I'll get in touch with Mlle Boulanger.

Will write again soon.

Love,
Ch

I rented a room in the same house that my friend Tom Weaver lived in, as well as a Swiss girl. My room was a garret on the top floor with a slanted roof, rather small and claustrophobic. I had no room for a piano, so I used the piano that was in the living room of the house. Tom was a violinist and didn't need the piano to work, and the Swiss girl was an artist.

The house was owned by an elderly couple who slept separately in different parts of the house. In order to get to my room on the top floor, I had to walk through the old man's room as mine was reachable only through his. He was always asleep by the time I was ready to go up to my room for the night. As I entered his room quietly, so as not to wake him, he was fast asleep flat on his back, wearing a pointed sleep hat that flopped over, snoring with a loud whistling sound. I always felt like I was walking through the set of *Gianni Schicchi*, and I could hear Puccini's wonderful opening music to that opera in my mind as I passed by his bed on tiptoes.

Tues., Dec. 14
Dear Family,

It occurred to me that I have not heard from the conductor who is to do my flute piece in reference to his receiving the parts that I sent. Have you received the program for the concert yet?

I've not yet begun studying French again but will soon. I speak and understand the language pretty well now, but there is still so much that I don't know.

I don't think I told you how much the voyage on the boat pleased me. Aside from the fact that I did get seasick. To be on such a large and luxurious boat in the middle of an ocean was an unforgettable experience. One feels so completely free not being in any country. The feeling of freedom is wonderful, but yet I see that it doesn't compare with the feeling of being tied down and belonging. Of course, that is considering the latter is by choice. But nevertheless, freedom must come before or else the other will never be appreciated, and then the <u>true</u> freedom will never come. I've been hearing Schubert songs in my mind all evening. What a pleasureful change. Even for the first 2 weeks I was still hearing rock & roll and cha-cha.

I'm a little lonely but nevertheless, happy.

Love,
Ch

Tues., Dec. 20
Dear Family,

I know that in a day or two I will receive a letter from you with your reaction to the concert Sunday. I do hope that you enjoyed the performance. This is of course the first time you've heard any of my compositions, so that alone must have pleased you. As for myself, it was a nice feeling to be in Paris knowing that my piece was performed in NY.

I must admit that for a while I was confused as to whether or not I would have a performance as scheduled. After all, the conductor never wrote to me that he received the orch. parts, and you never mentioned a word of the performance either. In fact, it wasn't until Mon. when I saw a copy of Sunday's <u>NY Times</u> that I was sure at all. But in either case, on Sat. night, Tom, myself, and a Swiss girl who lives in the same house went for dinner to the Jewish delicatessen as a kind of celebration.

I have some recent, interesting news in reference to my harp piece. Ruth brought her copy of the piece to her teacher, who has kept it for himself for the past 2 months. Each week she asked him for it, and each week he said that he hadn't finished looking at it. Finally a few days ago he called Ruth to tell her how excited he was about the composition and asked to see me. Ruth's teacher is a world-famous harpist who teaches at the Conservatoire here in Paris. This afternoon Ruth and I went to Monsieur Jamet's home. She is studying the piece now for a performance this spring. They worked for nearly 2 hours just to get through it once, but of course, they stopped very often to ask me how I wanted certain things played.

Monsieur Jamet was evidently very interested in the composition and seemed very eager to suggest that I write a concerto for harp and orch. He said that I write very well for the harp, but that I should not hesitate to call on him if I ever have any questions about that instrument.

Perhaps one day I will write a concerto for the harp, but for the next 2 or 3 years at least, I have my mind set on other things.

You know, that as I get more and more out into the world and meet wonderful musicians on a kind of equal basis, the more I feel like a composer instead of a student. And it is a comforting feeling because I know that when I leave my studies in a few years, I will really feel as though I have a right to consider myself a composer.

In the meantime, I do harmony as though it were my profession. I feel that with time, everything will come as long as I do what I know is right.

My regards to the family.

Love,
Ch

Thurs., Dec. 29
Dear Family,

I received the program and your letter telling me of the performance. You know how happy I am that you have at least heard one of my compositions. For myself, it is only the composing which means anything, but it is for you that I would want to be successful.

There are so many pieces that I want to write that it is difficult to limit myself to writing them one at a time. But yet I must.

Before I continue about music, let me tell you of what I did over Christmas.

I know you'll wonder how, but Tom and I spent five days in England.

On Friday afternoon, after my lesson with Mlle we took the train to London. The trip took about 15 hours, but that included a 4-hour ferry ride across the Channel. Also the strike in Belgium held us up for a while.

I spent Christmas with a girl that I met on the <u>*Queen Eliz*</u>. *On the third day in London, Tom and I rented a 1960 Austin and began a 600-mile journey around England. We first went south to Brighton, which I suppose is Eng.'s Miami Beach. From there we went west to Portsmouth, Southampton, and Salisbury. There, on the Plains of Salisbury is Stonehenge, which has manmade rock formations over 3000 yrs. old. It was kind of interesting. We made our way north through Bath, Bristol, and Gloucester and finally up to Stratford-upon-Avon, where Shakespeare lived, as you know. We spent much time there. It's a lovely town and of course one which has devoted itself to the preservation of everything related in any way to Shakespeare. We were fortunate that the priest of the church where Will is buried gave us a personal tour of the building. I'll never forget that old priest who couldn't remember the word Christmas and kept referring to it as "this holiday that we're going through."*

Salisbury is also a wonderful town where most of the houses still are covered with thatched roofs.

London is much like NYC. I could say very much more about our trip, but I really haven't the time now.

Should you wonder about it, the whole trip from beginning to end cost me $50. I did enjoy it very much.

Mlle B. told me at my last lesson that I must write a piece for the competition in Monaco this year. She suggested in fact that I write a concerto for harp and orchestra. But, whereas I will write something for that competition, it will not be a harp concerto. She said that perhaps I will not win the competition, but if two members of the jury (which is composed of famous musicians) like my work, it will be worth it. I found out later that Mlle is one of the members of the jury.

But the deadline is March 1st, which leaves me just two months to complete a work for orchestra, which must be approximately 30 minutes in length.

I doubt that I will succeed but I will try. So— back to work. Be well.

Love,
Charles

Tues., Jan. 3, 1961
Dear Family,

As much as I thought that it would be a long time before I would write a concerto for harp, I am presently devoting all of my time to it.

The main reason for my decision to do so came as a result of Ruth's definitely promising me a performance of it next year in Baltimore. I guess with the Baltimore Philharmonic. Also, she felt that because Monsieur Jamet asked me to write the concerto, he might use it as the "morceau de concours," which means that it will be a requisite for all harpists at the Conservatoire. That would mean publication by Durand and at least a performance in Paris.

I'm scoring it for a large orchestra.

Will write again soon—

Love,
Charles,
Happy New Year

Mon., Jan.
Dear Family,

I'm sorry that you worried about me not being happy to be back in Paris. I must admit that for a while I had many things on my mind which did disturb me, but at least now all is completely normal. I do love Paris very much. The constant tension caused by money in NY does not for the moment permit me the freedom I need. I suppose that when I've finished my studies I will realize that I must work regardless of the surrounding. However for the moment the struggle is too great. I must overcome my own weakness, and I could only do that alone, although I would prefer not. You see, I'm fighting to find the truth in music. In my own music. The truth is what I make it <u>but only</u> if I am completely sure, and then no matter

*how many people say it is wrong, it's right. Sometimes I feel
as though I have the power to defy the whole world because of
the conviction pertaining to my music that comes when I am
really involved.*

*Music is so much more than inspiration, beautiful sounds,
organization of material, etc. etc. . . . . It is a world complete in
itself but accessible only to those who look to find it and understand it.*

*My harp concerto goes very well. It is all that I have my
mind on these days. I am working very hard in order to show
the whole first movement to Mlle B. Friday. But nevertheless, it
will be surprising if I can complete the work, copy it over, and
get it to Monaco by March 1st.*

*I have some other things to tell you about, but I must get
back to work now.*

*In a few days I will send you a tape of my piece for harp
solo. Perhaps you can make an acetate from it.*

Love,
Charles

Jan. 20
Dear Family,

*I have the tape recording of my piece for harp and will send
it in a few days. The performance is not technically perfect, but
considering how little time the harpist worked on the piece—it is
pretty good. Ruth and Monsieur Jamet both consider it one of
the most difficult pieces ever written for that instrument. On the
recording you will probably hear the pedals banging from time
to time as they're changed. The pedals for the most part must be
changed so rapidly that difficulty in covering up the noise as a
result must be helped by adding felt underneath.*

*I feel sure that that piece will be published either in France
or NY this year.*

*My concerto hasn't moved very much since my last letter.
I can't see how it will be possible to finish it in a month. But
Mlle B. is in Monaco until February, so I will have more time
to work on it. She gave me a present last week, a book of poems
by T. S. Elliot—put a lovely inscription on it—*

I must go.

Love,
Charles

Mon., Jan. 30
Dear Family,

Concerto! Concerto! Concerto! That's all I've been working on. I haven't even done any harmony or piano for the past two weeks. And even at that I've got very little written.

I struggled with a set of themes and spasmodic ideas for more than 2 weeks and then finally threw it all out and started again. Not that the sheet wasn't worth keeping, but those particular ideas just weren't ready to develop, although I certainly did try. But I think now that if I let them mature slowly in my mind, they will make a good basis for a fourth movement, which I did not plan to have before.

The second movement should go well by the time I get around to actually writing it. I know how that movement will begin and end—it's an allegretto with a light texture, so I expect that it will not give me much trouble. The only thing I know about the slow movement is that the concerto will need one! And the 1st movement is going very well, but so slowly.

Mlle has been in Monaco for two weeks, so for my next lesson on Friday I'll have to show her what I have done with the concerto. Especially since I've done nothing else.

I am happy to be writing a concerto for harp. When she asked me to write it, Mlle said it would be silly at this stage for me to write a symphony or something when everyone writes symphonies which never get performed. And there are so many good harpists around who perform regularly with orchestras, and who are starving for a new concerto.

The most recent concerto for harp that I've found is by Jolivet—the French composer who had a work performed on the same program as my flute piece—remember? That was written in 1952 and is a pretty lousy piece (as are most of his works, even though his is performed regularly in Paris). But his concerto is still better than one by Norman Dello Joio written in the 1930s.

I've heard some pieces for harp solo by Hindemith, Prokofiev, and Ben-Haim—an Israeli composer—but none of those men have written concertos.

Also, it interesting to note that there has never been (to my knowledge) a concerto for harp with a full orchestra—and probably for a very good reason—

I am using a full orch., but that leads to many complications which delay the progress of the work from time to time. The harp is a thin-sounding instrument and could get lost very easily with too much of an orchestral sound behind it. But that presents a challenge in orchestration which I happily accept.

Handel wrote a concerto for harp which I have not heard, and Mozart wrote one for harp and flute—I bought the score to the latter and have looked through only the 1st movement, which is rather boring although it must sound good—

I did hear another concerto by a rather unknown Spanish composer which is kind of light and charming but does not begin to explore the possibilities—

So that is more or less what the present situation is with harp concertos.

Although the idea of my finishing the piece within a month is practically 100% impossible, I do hope to have it finished by April 1st.

Mlle will be in the U.S. during the month of April—I think to give a lecture tour.

I think of you all the time.

Love, Charles

Wed., Feb. 8
Dear Family,

Well I finally moved into a new apartment and believe it or not, I've taken a whole apt. by myself. You see, I moved out of my old room about 5 or 6 days ago, not wanting to have to pay the rent for Feb. Since then I've been staying with a friend and spending most of my time looking for a place. While I had that to do, I couldn't work at all—and these days, even a moment is precious. So I found this apt. yesterday afternoon and moved in the evening. Listen to all the "modern" conveniences. Bedroom, dining room with piano, kitchen, and a bathroom complete with a bath. Perhaps this will be too much for me, but I really don't mind it. The apt. is completely furnished and very well too. The rent is $60 a month; have no fear because I know that I can get along quite well on the money you send. I probably will have to cut down on concerts and things like that, but it's worth it a hundred times over just to be able to work without any distractions—are you pleased?

So, I have not slept last night—the concerto must be ready by March 1st. Otherwise, I think Mlle will be pretty disappointed. But you know, writing fast because there is no time to lose is lousy—I wrote perhaps 5 or 10 pages last night but I did not have (nor do I now) any understanding of what I've written. I seem to have no direction at the moment. But Mlle feels that once I've completed the piece, I can even begin again if necessary—but at least I will be able to see the whole. I guess she's right, but when I have no love for my music even if it is to be changed, I don't understand why I even bother.

Anyway, perhaps today I will have a good day and then my whole opinion will be changed.

New address.

37 Rue Bobillot, Paris XIII

Love,
Charles

Tues., Feb. 21

Dear Family,

I'm sure that you'll be happy to know that I've finished the sketch for the first movement of the concerto. Eleven minutes of music on some 60 pages of score paper. It scares me when I multiply that by three or four!!

Of course even though I have the movement written from beginning to end, the orchestration is so incomplete that I still cannot tell how smoothly the whole thing will go.

I am beginning to feel that I have here a "basically" good movement. What I am thinking of doing after it is completely finished is tearing it up and saving only that which is really meant to be. Know that I will not permit it to be performed until I am more or less happy with it.

I'm glad that you liked my "dance" for harp—knowing that, I don't hesitate to say that you will like the concerto even more—I'd like to get all of my compositions on tape for you to hear, but it's so difficult when you have to deal with more than one musician—and seven at that!!!

Glad to hear that Bernard is coming along well in his Haftorah. After all, he's got 2 pretty good "haftorah" doers in our family to follow.

Pip pip.

Love,
Charles

Sun., Feb. 26
Dear Family,

I wish that I could tell you that the concerto will be finished by March 1st, but in fact, I am very far from being able to tell you that. For 2 or 3 days after I had completed the sketch for the 1st movement, I sat around and contemplated what I could do with it. Finally I decided that there was only one thing to do if I were to be sincere with myself—I threw away most of the whole thing—and more may go before I am finished. It may take months more to finish the whole work, but I decided that I was not going to pressure myself into writing what I was more or less indifferent to—after all, if I am a composer and am capable of discovering things in music, then I have an obligation to myself to do so.

If I were not forced into finishing those pieces in time for performance—both pieces that I wrote at Fontainebleau ('59–'60) would have been changed very much.

Now that I have missed the Monaco competition for this year, there is no need to hurry any more. Now I will let things take their natural course.

We are living in a world of mathematics today—music is so greatly affected by this that some compositions are based purely on mathematics. Some composers that I know have no idea of what their music sounds like until they hear it played. I know very few composers who work without systems. But the only good music employing systems that I know is good not because of, but <u>in spite of</u> the systems.

I understand very well the various tools with which my contemporaries work.

Schoenberg was working to achieve perfection in organization of materials—but he was a musician and had mastered the great works before him. When it came down to it he threw systems out and wrote contrary to that simply because it sounded better—

Music has not changed—nor has its function and purpose—Because we write music which is (considered) "dissonant" is not reason to believe that sounds may be taken for granted. When you hear a note which is unmistakably "wrong" in Mozart, do you not jump? We all do! And so do I jump when I hear a wrong note in the most modern music—Perhaps it is not so striking (if at all) to the unfamiliar ear—but I hear it and I protest—

For someone else I say that it's his business—for myself—I cannot permit it.

But there is so much more involved than just that—so very much more.

If it is not to write music that I sincerely love and feel the need to write, then why bother? I have nothing to fall back on—I don't need anything to fall back on. I am a composer and I will prove myself.

I miss you all.

Love,
Charles

March 21
Dear Family,

Well it's spring at last and Paris has begun to show it. It hasn't been terribly warm these past few days, but we haven't had a real winter's day for nearly 2 months.

I hope that you all had a wonderful time at the bar mitzvah.

Mlle Boulanger is leaving Fri. for Monaco, where she will spend a month judging the competition and I suppose relaxing a bit. She will not be in the States after all this year—I don't expect that I'll have a lesson now until the beginning of May. No complaints!!!

But next year promises to be fairly inactive as far as lessons are concerned. Mlle will spend one month in Russia and 3 months in the U.S.

You see she is supposed to conduct the NY Philharmonic in Feb. and then the Boston Symphony in April—She cannot fly, so returning to Paris by boat in between the two dates would be rather silly—I know that the date in NY cannot be changed, but she is trying to change the one in Boston. But if it will remain as it is, it would almost be worth it for me to return

to the States also for those three months and continue my les-
sons there—although I'm sure that she will be constantly sur-
rounded by "autograph hunters." Anyway—that whole thing
is pretty far-fetched.

Funny things are happening to her in her old age. Since
she accepted the NY date, she's been referring to Bernstein as
"Lennie."

She caught me with a funny question at my last lesson
which I suppose is not really funny but it did surprise me.
When I least expected it she asked me how long I was going to
stay in Paris. I could have answered immediately, but instead
I said, "Well" and then proceed to stare at the ceiling (I don't
know why), but finally I said that when I returned to Paris it
was with the intention of staying for 2 more years. Then I said,
"But" and stopped, and continued looking at the ceiling. After a
while I answered, "Yeah, that's it, 2 more years."

She answered only, "Ah, good" and wasn't surprised at
my hesitation. You know that she knows me pretty well. In
general a student-teacher relationship can be nice when they
get to know each other.

I remember when I was studying with Mr. Benda, every
so often he would stop short in the middle of a sentence and sit
absolutely motionless without saying a word for as much as 5
minutes sometimes. Finally he would continue exactly where
he left off as though he hadn't stopped at all. It was annoying
for me at first, but after a while when it came I just considered it
to be a "break" and lit up a cigarette. I never did figure out what
happened to Mr. Benda on those occasions, but I'm pretty sure
that he was a "dreamer" like most musicians that I know, and
every so often he would sink away without knowing it.

Mlle is not a "dreamer," and therefore her intuition is ter-
ribly lacking sometimes.

I'm sure that you'd be surprised at the meals that I make
for myself. It's funny how I'm so conscious of well-balanced
meals, healthy foods, etc. I used to imagine that when I would
be able to, I would eat only delicatessen. But I rarely have any.
I eat mostly—steaks, liver, chops of all kinds, potatoes, string
beans, peas, salads, cheese. I even make a casserole once in
a while. Of course I don't really know what I'm doing in the

kitchen, but it works! Really!! And it all started when I learned that all you have to do is throw things into pots, put them on the stove and wait. I feel very good!

Be well,

Love,
Charles

April 19
Dear Family,

I really cannot spend much time with this letter as I'm in the midst of work. Back to harmony again, but even that is not going too well. I've begun work on 9th chords, and I've found it not too easy to hear. Of course after spending more than a year on just triads, it took some time to begin to hear 7th chords well. But harmony doesn't really bother me. At least there I know that it's only a matter of time until a problem is worked out. But with the concerto, c'est une autre chose! I've been working on it as much as 8 or 9 hours a day when I've not been too discouraged. I think I've been making mental progress in realizing what is wrong. But as far as visual progress, I have about a hundred pages of notes plus 60 pages of the original sketch, and all I have kept is about 2 or 3 pages. Perhaps even that will go. I've been studying the works of Webern daily. He was a student (along with Alban Berg) of Schoenberg and was probably the first composer to employ a pointillistic technique. That same music which I was revolted by last year and now I'm coming to believe that it's the only music which can exist to grow. The thing that impresses me most with Webern is his master's touch of employing only that which is organic. It must be that he was trying to write music that could be free from those unwritten rules pertaining to all of the music until the 20th century and most during it. (Although his own rules govern his music more than I've ever seen with any other composer.) I understand well the need for this simpleness and purity of music, but looking at my concerto one would never know it. I look back at the pages I've written these past few months, and all I can find are notes that I don't really mean. Not wrong notes but inorganic. I turn the pages of my concerto and I see an orchestra before me. Looking closely at each orch. section I see notes hanging ungracefully from the instruments, hanging from the tuning pegs of the strings, the bottom of the bassoons and from the mouthpieces of the trumpets. And from the harp in front of the orchestra. Notes just hanging everywhere.

I don't know. I think the reason for it is not just this particular piece, but the whole style that I've always written in. I'd like to finish this work so that I can explore freely. I'm so tied down to tradition at this point that I can hardly make a move without first consulting Beethoven and Bartok especially. Until last summer I didn't even realize the influence that Bartok has on me. And now it's gotten to the point where I get out of bed in the middle of the night, rush to my bookshelf to get a Bartok score and see what he did!!

What I'm beginning to realize is how much courage (and I really mean courage) it takes to express oneself. This will be impossible for me to explain, but sometimes I reach a point where the music flows so well and so right that I just cannot write another note. I don't know, I think it's a kind of fear. I know that when that happens it must be followed through to the end or it is all wrong. The result is so obvious in listening to music. At times I can pinpoint it to the note and say, this is where the composer lost courage and proceeds to "bow out" showing perhaps at least a great technique. At least that is better than to be fooled by oneself into thinking that something exists which does not.

There are so many things involved in the game of writing music. It can be such fun, but at the same time (and for the most part now) such a struggle.

I received the $50 today.

> *Love,*
> *Charles*

Sun., May 19
Dear Family,

I'm sorry for putting off this letter for a few days but I've been waiting to find out definitely about some very good news, and I wanted to tell you about it only after I was certain.

The good news is that my composition for the harp of which you have the recording is going to be published here in

Paris by Le Duc publishers. Of course it doesn't mean as much as all that, but nevertheless it will be my first published work and will put me in a good position to get other works published and performed. And even for its own sake, it will be exciting to see one of my pieces in print. The man who is responsible for it is Mr. Jamet from the Conservatoire, whom I've already mentioned in an earlier letter. I can be certain of only very little since I have not spoken yet with the publishers nor Mr. Jamet for some time. But Ruth tells me that Mr. J. would like to make that piece the "morceau du concours" for the Conservatoire (perhaps in June, I don't know), which means that all the harpists at the Conservatoire will be obligated to learn and perform my piece for their "Prix," which is more or less equivalent to our "degrees" in the U.S.

So as I said, it doesn't mean too much, but perhaps with time and practice, work and love, everything will work out well.

The concerto??—ha!! My poor concerto. Existing only in my mind and in the future.

I haven't seen Mlle for more than a week. At that time, for my private lesson she really surprised me. I thought that I would put my scraps of paper in some sort of order and show her what I had done with the concerto. I had expected to be bored, but no, for 2 1/2 hours right through dinner time there was not a minute lost. Measure by measure and even note by note she approached it purely objectively. She proved herself to me to have such a keen understanding that now I really know for myself what a genius she is. When she finished with a page, I was hesitant to show her another for fear that she would not continue in that manner, but I was as well anxious for her to see more because she could put into words what I had only felt—and for the most part she was so right.

Finally, she told me (in effect) that I must <u>stop</u> studying harmony and concentrate on counterpoint. Why? Because harmony (that is, my study of it) is <u>ruining</u> my composition. She didn't say that but we both know it. I've become so involved with the smallest elements of my music that I've sort of lost track of the whole. As I've proven with my concerto, I no longer see just the effect of a section, but again, the relations between the smallest things.

Undoubtedly, if I am a composer, and I am capable of growing within myself, this will only bother me for an indefinite period, and when I come out of it, I will probably be better off for it. At the moment though, I'm afraid. If I begin studying counterpoint, will I get so involved that she will tell me in a year to stop that also? Who can say! But I must consider everything carefully before I continue blindly. Looking at her former pupils I see that Jean Françaix never came out of it. Nor has Aaron Copland really. Elliot Carter I guess has. As she told a friend of mine when he first came, "I cannot make you a composer. If you are one already, perhaps I will ruin you. All I can do is give you a technique."

You see that there's much more to this whole business than meets the eye. Now, I'm not certain as to whether I will begin counterpoint.

Harmony? I guess I feel qualified to teach harmony at Juilliard! But the issue is much more important than that. It's my future as a composer that I must consider.

I did not see Mlle last week, and I don't plan to this week. I will just write to her and tell her that I have nothing prepared.

Well, that's about all that I can tell you today. Perhaps by the end of the week I'll have decided what to do.

Don't worry or anything, but know that everything will work out for the best.

I think of you all very much.

Love,
Charles

It was a very turbulent time for me. I had come to a crossroads in my work. All the minute details that went into the structuring in my harmony exercises seemed to be keeping me from seeing a broader picture and were not allowing me to see past structural problems in my compositions. It got to the point where I'd jump out of bed in the middle of the night to study a score of Beethoven or Bartok and analyze how they got through a particular problem. All the attention to detail and technique was now starting to get in the way of my freedom as a composer. I knew it, and Mlle knew it. That's why she suggested that we leave harmony alone for a while and concentrate on counterpoint. I was very unsure of myself for the first time, and I was frightened to jump too quickly into the next phase of my work with Mlle, afraid that I'd compound the problem and I'd be in the same position with counterpoint as

I was now in with harmony. I had a growing feeling that I needed a break for a while before going ahead with my studies. And when I added up the time that Mlle Boulanger would be in Paris during the coming months, that too left me feeling very unsure of my immediate plans.

The conflict was growing within me, and for a while, it was all I could think about. I loved my teacher so much that it seemed preposterous that I was rationalizing why I should take a break from my studies. But the conflict was real, and I'd discuss it with Mlle, but she allowed me to come to terms with my needs without influencing me or pushing me one way or the other. She just let me know that she'd be there for me regardless of my immediate decisions.

June 5
Dear Family,
I really can't say yet what I will be doing this summer. Decisions still to make.

Most probably I will just remain in Paris with or without lessons as we will see. Against my better wishes, I forced myself to the last Wednesday class in order to speak with Mlle afterwards. She asked me what my plans were, and I said that I didn't know yet. She said that anyway she would see me when she returns from Eng. (She left the following day for 10 days.) That was the first time I had seen her in a month.

I don't know exactly what I'm doing yet. She will teach at Fontainebleau for about 6 weeks only because of concerts and other things. And of course she is so busy there that I would probably not have more than just a few lessons. In Sept. she goes to Russia and Oct. to Hungary and other places. That leaves just 3 months in between the time that she returns from the East till February, when she leaves for the States. All that means that I would have no more than 10 lessons or so for the next 7 months.

Anyway, I've been composing again, so I really haven't given much thought to my studies. Actually though, I've done little more than analyze the possibilities of a tone row—C'est-à-dire: an arrangement of all 12 notes of the chromatic scale. My analysis has been so far completely technical (mathematical if you like), the purpose of which is simply to organize all the elements of the "row." I've been working so far only on graph paper. I seem to discover things every day, but I'm still at a loss for understanding and applying them.

But all this is only a preparation to composing. I have no intention of systematizing my music, but rather organizing the means. In the end it's only the ear and heart which count.

Et bien, mes chers.

Be well.

Love,
Charles

June 9

Dear Mom and Dad,

First, I want to apologize for the other letter not arriving sooner. I've had so much on my mind these past few days that I misplaced the letter, and when I didn't see it, thought it was mailed.

I've already mentioned a few things that I've considered doing this summer, but now I have a decision which I think will make you very happy. I hope so because to wish for your happiness and to tell you of my great love and respect for you is all that I can give you for your anniversary.

I am free from my studies, and even if I shall continue them elsewhere, I am, above all, a composer now. What I will do for the summer is to come home to NY, to you. I know that I had not prepared you, but I wanted to be sure before I said anything. If you are happy, know that I am also. After all, I live a pretty lonely life here in Paris. If I could fly home once a month, I certainly would, but for the moment that's not practical.

Of course, now there's only the matter of the trip, but listen to what I have to say before you say "oiy, oiy, oiy." There is a student flight from Paris to New York in July and New York to Paris in September. The total price for the round trip is $115.00. But it must be paid immediately or as soon as possible to secure a reservation. I've already flown Air France, and their planes and service are wonderful . . . anyway . . .

If you want, send me the $150 for the month of July right away. With that $150 I'll buy my plane ticket and have a little extra for other expenses incurred on the trip. In August you will *not have to give me money because I will be working in N.Y. So actually, you save money by my coming home!*

I've received the $100 for this month, but the rest I'll need to live until I leave in the beginning of July.

Please either answer with a letter or send the money immediately. I realize that you may not have the $150, so in that case if you wanted, I could borrow the money from a friend here and pay him back before I leave. In that case all you'd have to do is to write and say that it's O.K.

I hope that everything is wonderful for your anniversary and that I'll be with you in few weeks.

Be well and happy.

Charles

Sat.

Dear Family,

I have only a moment to write as I am leaving in a few hours. Thank you for sending the $200 so fast. It really helped me out.

In my telegram to Arvito I said that I would return within 10 days. But as it turns out, that is not possible because of the great cost of flying by jet. The original plane that I had planned to take doesn't leave till June 30th, so I could not take advantage of the ridiculously cheap price.

Instead I am coming home by boat. But this way I will not arrive until the 26th as the boat takes 8 days. Please call Arvito and tell him that I will arrive the 26th and explain why.

I've been fortunate enough to again secure a single room on the boat, which is of course much more pleasant.

Anyway—the boat is the MS Aurelia and it is the Cogedar Line—Arrives in N.Y on the 26th, but for the exact hour and pier you will have to find out. Must pack—

See you soon.

Love,
Charles

After a lot of agonizing, I decided to take a break from my studies and accepted an offer from a friend, a Latin band leader, Arvito, to work with his band for the summer in the Catskill Mountains. I was happy to be returning to New York, and I fully expected to be back in Paris with Mlle Boulanger in the fall, and therefore left my winter clothes in my apartment.

❧

As it turned out, I never again returned to Paris as a student. My friend Tom Weaver took over my apartment and sent all my belongings back to me in a trunk. One year later however, I was married, and together with my wife, Joan, I traveled back to Paris. The highlight for me was in visiting Mlle Boulanger and introducing her to my bride. She was, as always, so happy for me.

Over the years, I returned to Paris often, and each time that I was there, I would stop at the little flower shop downstairs at 36 Rue Ballu and send flowers up to Mlle's apartment. One time I did that while Joan waited in a rented car in front of her house as I went in to purchase the flowers. While I was in the shop, Giuseppe (who along with his wife, Zitta, and their two children, Paolo and Giovanni, lived with Mlle, and together took care of Mlle and the apartment) passed by the shop. Giuseppe saw me and came in to greet me. He insisted that I bring the flowers myself up to Mlle. I protested that I could not disturb her and barge in unannounced while she was giving a lesson. He prevailed, and I rode the elevator once again to the third floor. Flowers in hand, I was greeted by Zitta, who was so happy to see me and asked me to wait as she brought the flowers directly to Mlle, seated at the piano as she always was. My heart raced as I could hear her voice turn gruff, coming through the walls, as it would when she was disturbed.

"*Qui est là?*" I heard. In a moment she was at the door, greeting me with kisses, holding my right hand tightly in both her hands. "But I'm so sorry that you catch me at a time that I cannot give you a proper greeting. How is your lovely wife? How are your children?" she asked. "How are you? Are you composing?"

That's all she ever wanted to know, if I was composing. Finally she said, "I must return, but please consider this a proper greeting," and she kissed me once more and left.

I was so energized and buoyant after my brief visit that I bounded down the three flights of stairs, out the door of the apartment house, and proceeded to walk about halfway up the block toward the Place Clichy, when I heard Joan's voice shouting my name. For the moment, I was transported back to my youth and momentarily forgot that my wife was waiting for me in the car, totally perplexed as to where I was going. That was the effect she had on me, and that would be, as it turned out, the last time I would see Mlle.

Over the years she would respond to every letter I sent with her words of love and wisdom and encouragement, and every letter started with "My Dear Charles" and ended with "Yours, faithfully, Nadia Boulanger."

In 1979 I was planning a visit to her to present her with a copy of the score for my first ballet, *A Song for Dead Warriors*, which had just premiered with the San Francisco Ballet, and which I dedicated to her. Unfortunately, she passed away only a few days before my arrival, at the age of ninety-three. I of course bought flowers in the flower shop downstairs, just as I always had, and brought them up to her apartment. Mlle Dieudonné was there to greet me along with Giuseppe and Zitta, and Mlle Dieudonné put my flowers in a vase on a mantel over the fireplace next to a photograph of my beloved teacher. We talked for a long time about "our dear lady," and then I left for Père Lachaise to visit her resting place.

Not a day goes by that I don't think about her and appreciate what she gave to me. Nothing less than a life in music. To this day, while I'm writing, if I hurriedly write a note and attach a stem that doesn't reach all the way to the note, I can hear her voice say to me gently, "But my dear, if it's an important note to write, why not take the time to have the stem reach all the way to the note?"

New York, 1961–1967

*W*e live our lives one day at a time, but we look back in chapters.

Looking back, the end of that chapter of my life was the start of one that was filled with all the uncertainty that accompanies the transition from student to professional, and from single to married with children, all the while searching for my place in the seemingly elusive world that I had chosen to be part of. Music was all that I knew, and all that I was prepared for, but my direction was far from clear although my dreams remained resolute. But beginnings are the hardest, and my interests in music were so varied that I was happy to be back in an atmosphere that I knew well.

I was suddenly back in the life I had known before I left for Paris, playing the piano in a Latin band in the Catskill Mountains. It was exciting and even refreshing to be in familiar, comfortable surroundings, playing with a group of musicians whom I had mostly known and enjoyed playing with and included some of my very good friends. Laurels Hotel and Country Club was a top-line hotel and an exciting place to be that summer, and playing with the Latin band was the center point of the excitement whenever we played, whether it was by the enormous pool during the daytime, with all the people dancing in pool attire, or at night, when we were in the main ballroom playing sedate cha-cha and bolero tempos before the shows, and hot, swinging mambos and pachangas into the late hours of the night. It was the antithesis of the lifestyle that I had known in Paris and was very welcome as an escape from the dilemma I had gone through in deciding to return for the summer. As of this point in time, I was still intending to return to Paris in the fall, and I kept my apartment and winter clothing there while my friend Tom Weaver took over the apartment during the period that I'd be gone.

At the beginning of the summer, one evening before dinner, as I was walking into the main dining room, my eye caught sight of the most beautiful girl, wearing a light blue evening dress, helping a child get ready to enter the children's dining room. I can still picture her beautiful face and the impression that it made on me when I first saw her. It really was love at first sight. My friend and roommate, trumpet player Marty Sheller, remembers me running into the room we shared, with me belting, "I'm in love, I'm in love," to which he told me to remain calm and take a deep breath. Still, I don't imagine that I could have had any thought at that moment that a little more than a year later we would travel to Paris together, as husband and wife. Joan Redman was eighteen and working as a children's counselor at Laurels Hotel that summer that I was twenty. Her friends told her that I must have been older because I had a moustache that made me look older, the remnant of the beard I had grown in Paris. When I heard that, I shaved the moustache off that day, but when we saw each other that evening, Joan didn't even notice the change.

Although we spent a lot of time together that summer, as we saw each other every day, ultimately, at the end of the summer we each went our separate ways without any expectation of a future together.

The months following that summer I was rather lost, a fish totally out of water. I had decided early on that it was not fair of me to continue having my parents support me—which was certainly difficult for them, although they never stressed that to me—and I decided not to return to Paris as a student. I moved back to my parents' apartment in the Bronx trying to plan my future, all the while continuing to play in bands, but it was the lowest point that I had ever known. I went to the Israeli consulate to see if they would consider helping me if I would move to Israel with the hope of composing music in that country. The consulate's response was that the Israeli government would give me a plane ticket but that I would have to work on a kibbutz for two years until I could speak enough Hebrew to be able to teach as a way to support myself while I composed music. As romantic as that sounded initially, it meant that I would be a farmer for two years, and then a teacher, and that was totally out of my realm of thinking. I didn't realize at that time that I must have been in a depressed state, as I had no direction and I was aware of it. My dreams of the future were on hold.

⁂

Sometime that fall, I joined the Randy Carlos Orchestra, which was a well-known Latin band that had made successful records. One night, we were playing at a club called the Magic Touch, on Long Island, when in walked Joan and several of her friends. She had heard that I was playing with Randy's band. We were in the middle of a number when I saw her walking in, and I remember her face, and how beautiful she looked, and her smile, as she saw me, trying not to look too impressed, but was unmistakably there because I was. My depression was already beginning to lift, as I could now partially identify the cause as being more than just the uncertainty of my musical future.

After that evening, we started seeing each other again, and all was right with the world when we were together. Later that year, during the winter, I was working at the Willows Hotel in Lakewood, New Jersey, with Randy's band, when Joan came to visit me. I was expecting her arrival that day when somebody at the front desk of the hotel told me that I had a visitor waiting for me, and I rushed back to the house where our band stayed, knowing that it would be her. When I saw her standing there, bundled up with a turtleneck sweater, looking so beautiful with a fresh and radiant look from the winter's chill, and having traveled for several hours just to be with me, I knew as well as she that we would have a future together.

In order to have some money saved before our wedding day, I took a job the following summer with a repertory theater, summer stock company in New Hampshire as the musical director of a five-piece orchestra. Our hopes were high as I left for New Hampshire but came crashing down when the ill-funded company did not get enough receipts at the box office to cover the salaries of the actors, let alone the musicians and stagehands, and we were all stranded without having been paid anything for all our work after one month. Joan came up to visit me, and we barely had enough money to get back to New York.

We were married in September, the following year after we met, and I was anxious to return to Paris with Joan, to show her the world I had known. We decided that with all of our wedding present money, we would travel throughout Europe until the money ran out. We sailed on the new French Line ship, the *France*, with money that I borrowed from my Paris friend Clara Hoover. We spent a wonderful week in Paris, with the highlight being for me to introduce my bride to my teacher. It was very important for me that they meet each other, and Mlle Boulanger loved Joan from that first meeting.

Mademoiselle always had an open house on Wednesday afternoons at her apartment for friends who were in Paris and who would like to drop in on her, unannounced. Other than that she was at the piano bench teaching from 7:00 AM to 10:00 PM or later if she was not attending a concert.

She was very formal, and extremely old-world, but I loved every minute that I spent with her. She was also joyous and a lot of fun to be with. She could even be silly. She would do imitations of composers, and students making the most unusual sounds that were meant to parody that person.

She sometimes was perplexed with Americans' habits. Chewing gum for instance. That was not at all a French thing to do. And worst of all, she once told me that from time to time she would find someone's gum stuck to the underside of her piano. It's still hard for me to imagine someone actually sticking their chewed gum to the underside of Nadia Boulanger's piano.

She would not look at one's harmony work if it was in pencil. She insisted that everything be in ink. Considering all the possibilities that were at hand, it was impossible to work in pen, so I had to do two versions of everything. In pencil to work out the problems, then in ink to show it to her.

Mlle was not just an extraordinary musician and a wonderful teacher; she had a great gift for understanding what makes music work and what moves it toward the inner depths of one's expression. She always referred to it as looking for the truth. That was all one could ever hope to achieve . . . the truth. The organization of notes and expression of them in such a way that it could not possibly be changed. If one could compare it, it would be similar to looking for the musical equivalent of the building blocks of life. And she brought with her to this rarified place an uncanny understanding and love for music, and as well, a virtual history of music. Her teacher was Fauré. Ravel was her classmate and friend at the Conservatoire. Her closest musical ally and friend was Stravinsky. He sent his son to study with her. Her master classes were with composers Poulenc and Jean Françaix, violinist Yehudi Menuhin, pianist Robert Casadesus, cellist Maurice Gendron, and vocalist Pierre Bernac at Fontainebleau, as well as Ravi Shankar, sitting on the floor of her apartment with his sitar along with his sitar-playing protégé and tabla player, explaining his music to us.

We left Paris and drove to Fontainebleau on our way to the south of France. Beautiful Fontainebleau, with its austere palace, the right wing of which housed the Conservatoire de Musique, my school, where I first met Mlle Boulanger. And the magnificent gardens behind the palace, and the private lake of the Emperor Napoleon, with its own little island in the middle, where his son would play with his governess. And the immense forest, where Joan and I picnicked along the canal in the shade of the trees, and the student's residence, where I lived during those summers. And the caretakers of the school, who were still there to welcome me back in late September, even though the summer session had ended. It was wonderful to be back, feeling very much at home, but now married, with my beautiful wife by my side.

From the south of France, we continued down the coast of Italy, visiting Puccini's house on the lake at Torre del Lago and spending a week in

Rome, where we had a chance audience with Pope John, for the price of a dollar for two tickets, along with fifty other people in the Vatican. We were in a rather large formal room, still not really believing that the tickets we purchased from someone on the street were not fakes, and that we were in the Vatican awaiting the Pope's entrance. But we were having a growing uncomfortable feeling as we were waiting of being a little out of place as we were certain that everyone else there was Catholic and would probably kneel at the sight of their Holy Father. We discussed what we would do. Joan covered her head with a handkerchief, and we decided that we would simply bow our heads out of respect. With that, the large double doors on one side of the room began to open, and the gentle "Papa" entered, carried aloft on a regal, golden-looking throne by eight personal attendants. As he entered, rather than kneeling or bowing, the people started shouting at the top of their voices, "*Viva il Papa! Viva il Papa!*" and applauding, and many whistled loudly, as though they were hailing a cab in New York, taking away any sense of solemnity or religious gravitas. He was carried through those large double doors into the room, all the while blessing the audience, of which we were thrilled to be a part, and a moment later the procession led out of the room on the same side that he entered, after having made a half-moon sort of path. Though Joan and I are Jewish, I always regarded Pope John's blessing as a good omen for our future together.

I was planning to get back to work on my harp concerto, which I had long abandoned, so we were hoping to find a place to spend a month. We drove south of Rome down the beautiful Amalfi coast and then discovered Positano. It was the most beautiful place we'd ever seen, and it was an ideal spot to spend a month. We fell in love instantly with Positano, where during our first night there, our hotel room looked out over the striking, picture-postcard-looking, white-and-pastel-colored homes, perched comfortably on the twin mountains that overlook the little village below on the beach. The little fishing boats were bobbing gently in the calm Ligurian sea, and we heard the music of an accordion player coming from the Buca de Baca restaurant on the beach below, completing this idyllic picture. The next day we met a charming character of a man, whose name was Charlie Cinque, whose mother had sent him to America during the war to avoid his being drafted into the Italian army. He spoke English perfectly, and he owned a large apartment that he agreed to rent to us, which was midway down the hill in front of the church. It was the same apartment that John Steinbeck had rented, and from which he wrote a book about Positano. One hundred twenty dollars for the month, and Positano was ours.

In front of our spacious balcony, the workers who carried the food and wine down the hill for the restaurants, and then returned with the empty bottles, used to stop for a brief respite and take their heavy load off their shoulders before continuing up or down the hill.

In this peaceful, beautiful, and serene atmosphere, I was completely free and content, and able to concentrate again on my concerto. I was up each morning with the dawn, and I would sit on the balcony sketching my music and enjoying the fresh morning air. At 9:00 AM I would walk up the hill with my briefcase containing my developing score to work at Charlie Cinque's mother's house just beyond the main road, the Amalfi Drive. Charlie's mother had a piano in her living room, and my arrangement with him was that I could use her piano after 9:00 in the morning. As I walked up the hill, I would pass the shopkeepers opening their stores, and they would greet me with, "*Buon giorno, signior compositore.*"

In 1962, Positano had not yet attracted many Americans, and it seemed that everyone in this little village knew about the young American honey-mooning couple, and the young composer who sat on his balcony at 6:00 AM every morning, writing music.

It was a very warm and welcoming atmosphere, and my score was thriving along with it. By the end of the morning I was finished with my work for the day, and Joan and I were free to explore and enjoy this most extraordinary place in the world. By the end of our month there, I had the first movement of my concerto finished, but we were barely ready to leave. We drove back to Paris, visiting Florence, the Swiss Lake District, the Austrian Alps, through Munich to Strasbourg, and finally after spending another week in Paris, back to Le Havre and to sail home on the USS *United States*, our two thousand dollars of wedding present money now well spent.

Some people, perhaps most, might feel that it was foolish to spend all of one's money on a three-month trip around Europe, but the memories that it left us with, and the time we had to get to know each other, free of all the surroundings of home, was the engine that was to propel us during the coming hardship years that we were to know, while we were struggling to get by. I have never regretted for one minute that we had nothing upon our return, because after that, everything that Joan and I did and accomplished we appreciated, and did together.

Until I arrived in France as a student, and more specifically, until I met Mlle Boulanger, I really did not know in what direction my music would take me. After my first private lesson with her, I was certain that all I aspired to do was to compose. Now that I had left my student days behind me and was married and, as we were shortly to learn, that Joan was pregnant, I had an immediate need to pursue a career that would afford me the opportunity to support my growing family and still pursue my personal dreams in music.

I loved jazz immediately after being introduced to it in high school. Jazz spoke to me of freedom from convention, freedom to explore, and of the possibilities of digging down into the core of one's being. It excited and moved me for its melodic and harmonic invention and the artistry that was everywhere evident. And it was cool. Cool to love it and be passionate about it. More than anything, I loved playing jazz, even though I was far from being ready to attack it professionally.

Latin music was a genuine passion for me. It still is. In recent years the name has changed to salsa, but the music has changed very little over the years. My attraction to Latin music was instant, and playing it came easily and naturally. Whether it's the infectious rhythms, the simple but consistent harmonic and melodic construction, or simply that it swings so intensely is not that clear or even necessary to understand. Playing in a Latin band is pure fun. When a good Latin band is in the "groove," there's no groove in any music that can compare. Its origins are similar to those in jazz in that the music basically grew out of the people singing their emotional expressions in the fields, but here their expressions and responses were to a consistent rhythm played by a number of conga and bongo drummers. Rhythms like the guaguanco and guajira, and the son, which derived from the people in the fields and in the country and in the cities, developed over the years in the dance halls and nightclubs into the mambo and cha-cha. It was basically an ethnic music to begin with, and as such, relies on a continuum of rhythmic drive that is so prevalent in much ethnic music. When a number of musicians are playing the same phrase repetitively, to the extent that they are all practically breathing together, there is an exhilarating feeling that they all share at that very moment. The groove can keep growing and getting more intense, and musicians and audience all share that moment.

I was considered by the Latin musicians and bandleaders of that day to be someone who played "*típico.*" In other words, I had the heart and soul of the "authentic" music in me, and I understood and felt the underlying clave rhythm, which is the cornerstone of that music. I appreciated being thought of that way, and was, in fact, proud of it. The rhythm section is the heart of Latin music, and my piano playing fit in with the others in that category. I played with some of the exciting bands of the day: Joe Quijano, Ray Barretto, Randy Carlos, Arvito, and Tito Puente at the Apollo Theater in Harlem. With Ray Barretto we performed often at the Palladium, the home of Latin music, and at Birdland, the "Jazz Corner of the World." I wrote songs and arrangements for those bands as well as others, and one of the personal moments that I savor is when the combined orchestras of Tito Puente and Charlie Palmieri, the great pianist, rehearsed at the Palladium and subsequently recorded a piece I wrote for them entitled "Africana."

❧

I had my own band for a while, adopting the name Carlos Zorro, which is literally my name translated into Spanish, thinking that I would be accepted even more in that field. I made several records, the first of which was with my own charanga band, in which I composed and arranged all the songs. Elliot Romero, one of the great Latin singers, wrote the Spanish lyrics and sang the solos. Johnny Pacheco, one of the genuine stars of Latin music, played the flute brilliantly for my record, and I used some of the other great Latin musicians such as Bobby Rodriguez, who was Tito Puente's long- time bass player, Frankie Malibe on conga, and Louis Ramirez on guiro. All stars in their own right. My brother Manny, who went on to great success as a Broadway producer with *Sophisticated Ladies* and to establish his own record label, arranged the funding for this album but never told me who invested in the record. Gema Records, a well-known Latin label, bought the rights to release and distribute the album. I didn't learn until much later that the secret investor for the record was none other than my father. Investing in a Spanish language dance record was not something that you'd normally expect from a Jewish window cleaner from the Bronx. It only reinforced to me the faith and commitment my father had in his sons.

Joe Quijano band; Charles at far right is at the drums because there was no room for a piano in the picture. *Courtesy of the author.*

There must have been some Latin blood in our family somewhere down the line because coincidentally, my younger brother, Bernard, who is a Broadway sound designer and engineer and inventor of many innovative electrical and sound equipment components, also started his career as the engineer for most of the great Latin records that the Fania label released in the sixties and seventies.

That charanga band record that I made in 1962 was rereleased on CD in 1999 by a Puerto Rican label, Disco Hit, and that is my only connection to the field today, except that I'm happy to have continuing friendships with some of those musicians. Latin music was for me one of those chapters in my life that although closed for many years still impacts my music and still makes me smile.

But for all the enjoyment I had in playing with those bands, I still couldn't earn enough money to support my family even though I seemed to have enough work. The Latin music business was on the low end of the professional musician ladder in New York, and the scales set by the Musician's Union could not produce a living wage. Most of my friends in Latin music had day jobs as well. My ambition was to earn one hundred dollars a week on a steady basis so we wouldn't have to worry about the rent or food.

⮞⮜

The first apartment that Joan and I rented was on Dartmouth St. in Forest Hills, a very nice and quiet area of Queens. One hundred and thirty dollars a month rent, and it was always a struggle. There were times when we would have to be rescued by Joan's or my parents with a ten or twenty dollar bill just to get by. There were other times when I would collect all the empty bottles in our apartment that had accumulated and for which you left a deposit in the market, to redeem them and have barely enough money for a little dinner. That part was not fun, but it also forces you to garner all your strength to move forward in your life because there's no relaxing at the wheel when lack of money is a constant companion.

Still, it was a far cry from the experiences that I had when I lived in Paris, for there, when I ran out of money, there was really nothing to eat. But there, at least, I was alone and didn't have to worry about a wife and child.

As detailed as I was to my parents in my letters home, there were aspects of my life in Paris that I didn't share with them. For one, I couldn't let them know that I wasn't always able to manage on the money they sent. I spared them from ever knowing that sometimes by the end of the month, until the next money order arrived, I had a day or two or even three without anything to eat when my money ran out. It would have anguished my parents to know this, and really I could have managed a little better. It didn't seem tragic as I wasn't alone. Some of my friends had the same problem. In the days of "l'ancien franc," the old franc, if you could borrow five hundred or one thousand francs, you could get by. Five hundred francs was a dollar, but sometimes even that wasn't possible. Most students in Paris didn't have a phone. It was too expensive and there was no one to call. If you wanted to get in touch with someone on a day that you didn't have class together, you simply went to that person's house, even it if was on the other side of Paris. Paris is not that large, and you can walk from one end of the city to the other in an hour and a half to two hours. And, of course, the metro could take you anywhere quickly for very little money (just a few sous).

One time when I hadn't eaten for a couple of days, I went to my friend Alex Panama's house to see if he had any money. He was happy to see me and said he was just sitting down to eat, would I like to join him? He had some extra cubes of sugar.

Another time, in a similar state of hunger, I went to my friend Clara Hoover's house, and I arrived just as she was just sitting down with some friends for a cup of coffee. "Would you like some coffee?" she asked.

"I would, thanks," I answered.

"What would you like in it?"

"A hamburger please." Everyone laughed, including me, but Clara knew that although that was meant to be funny and got a laugh, it was also truthful and serious. She then went into her kitchen and brought out enough food to get me over the hurdle. To this day, it pains me to see someone who is hungry. There's nothing romantic about being a student and starving in Paris, or anywhere else, for that matter. As an adult, I have always observed the Jewish High Holy Days but have never fasted on Yom Kippur. There were too many days when I fasted against my will for it to have any religious significance to me now.

My friend Bernardo Gonzales Sanchez, who was a fine musician and composer but had very little money to get by on, was once at a dinner party at Boulanger's house and found himself sitting next to Marc Chagall. Chagall, obviously having empathy for this young composer, took the fine linen napkin that was his during that dinner and did a drawing and signed it, and gave it to Bernardo, saying that he hoped this might help him. It might have, had he sold it, but Bernardo still has that napkin to this day. I'm not sure that Boulanger appreciated the loss of her dinner napkin though.

In my second year in Paris I was living on the Rue de Rome, near the Place d'Italie, toward the southern end of the city, and one day, I really needed to find something to eat. In desperation, I searched the kitchen for anything that might have helped me to get by. Luckily, or so I thought, I found a can of pumpkin pie mix, and after that some flour. Voilà! "I'll make a pumpkin pie!" How hard could that be? I followed the directions on the can. For the dough, all I had was flour, no butter, yeast or eggs. But at least I had tap water to mix with the flour. It was sort of gooey and didn't really bind well together, but after a while, it looked a lot like dough. Next, the pumpkin pie mix. The recipe on the can listed all sorts of ingredients to add to the pie mix. I had none of them except salt, so I added that. Then I kneaded the dough and formed the bottom crust in a pie pan that I found in a cabinet in the kitchen. I spread the pie filling evenly on the dough, and finally added strips of dough, criss-cross on top of the filling. It actually looked like a pie. I followed directions carefully to put the pie in the oven. I was so excited when it appeared ready and the crust had a nice color. As for the taste, it was so bitter and sour, probably because there was no sugar, or perhaps that can of pumpkin pie filling had lain at the bottom of the cabinet for too long from a previous renter, that as hungry as I was, it was still difficult to eat. But I forced myself to eat some of it. It was painful and awful, but it helped me to get by. It took me nearly forty years before I could get myself to try a real pumpkin pie. I was truly surprised that it tasted so good. It had remained an unpleasant memory for so long. I was finally able to move past it.

Joan never questioned me about my choice of professions. She accepted what I did at that point in time, and knew how much I liked playing and writing Latin music even though we were barely getting by. But she shared my dreams, and together, we knew that there would be many roads ahead. We had musician friends who played for weddings and bar mitzvahs, but I really had no interest in doing that, even though I could have earned more money in that field. I didn't enjoy playing that music, and I was concerned that it could have lulled me into accepting it as a career. I always knew that I'd have a limited career in Latin music, so it freed me to try to make headway in other areas. Joan and I have always been on the same side regarding my career, raising children, and general outlook on life. She's always been truly there for me with love and support at every turn. How lucky I've been to have her to share my life with.

However, I needed more than ever to make the crossover to American music and the pop market.

∽☙∽

The transition to the world of pop music to try to earn a living was not an easy one for me. Growing up in the fifties, I had a real disconnect with the popular records of the day. In the early sixties, before the Beatles, Paul Simon, Burt Bacharach, and Hal David, the pop records on the radio didn't interest me, musically speaking.

One of my very good friends since public school, Ed Newmark, who was a record producer and an executive with a record company, suggested to me that I could earn a living doing pop arrangements if I would learn what went into those records. I decided to put the classical music on WQXR that I was accustomed to listening to on hold, and the jazz and Latin stations that I loved as well, and I forced myself, sometimes painfully, to listen to the rock and roll and pop music stations so that I could learn and hopefully find a place for myself in that world. One might say that I dragged myself kicking and screaming into the world of rock and roll and pop music.

I listened to the car radio every day, driving from our apartment in Forest Hills to Manhattan, where I would go to try to make my connections in the field of commercial music, and hoping to find work. I made mental notes to learn what went into those records that I heard and the arrangements in particular, but I was embarrassed enough to be seen listening to that music that when I stopped for a traffic light, I turned my radio off or just rolled the window up so that the unknown driver next to me would not be able to hear the music coming from my car. What a lot of angst for nothing.

Eddie Newmark recommended me to a producer who took a chance and hired me to arrange my first rock and roll record, the name of which I've long forgotten. I approached the arrangements with the same enthusiasm as anyone would who wanted to make an individual imprint with his work, and I thought that I had found a more unique sound for this particular rock and roll song.

The producer walked into the studio as I was getting started with the band. He looked around at the musicians getting ready to play, and not seeing a set of drums, he asked me with a look of incredulity on his face, "Where is the drummer?"

I told him that my concept was to have violins play the back beats pizzicato, along with the electric guitar hitting the same beats with a stopped chord, which I thought would be a more subtle effect than the drummer doing the same thing. Every other pop record had the drums playing the back beats; it was an integral part of what was rock and roll. I thought that the same effect could be achieved in a fresher way and with more subtlety, with the violins plucking the strings, along with the guitar, and still continue stylistically with the "feel" of the records of the day.

"You don't have drums on a rock and roll record?" the producer asked, his voice now rising in anger, accompanying his already contorted, angry-looking face. "How can you have a rock and roll record without drums?" He was, of course, right, I came to realize. There were ways to be inventive; that was just not one of them.

Another time that my attempts to be creative as I was finding my way in the commercial music world were cut down was when I was doing an arrangement of a commercial as an audition piece, hoping to get a job for a company that created music for advertising, known as "the Music Makers." It was owned by Mitch Leigh, a composer who was best known for his score for Broadway's *Man of La Mancha*, and it was one of the leading music production companies for advertising in New York. Mitch Leigh had also studied with Nadia Boulanger, and he kindly responded to me when I was introduced to him as someone who could possibly work as a staff arranger for his company. Mitch himself wrote the tunes for the jingles, a "head" arranger wrote the lead brass and woodwind parts and established a concept rhythmically, and the "staff" arranger filled in the missing parts, the second and third trumpets, the second and third woodwinds, and so on—a kind of a musical connect the dots.

I was introduced to the head arranger, and he gave me a chance to show that I was qualified by arranging a tune that featured a horn as a theme over animation of a young boy seen tooting a horn on the screen. This jingle had already been completed and was already on the air. Again, I tried to find a more unique and creative approach to this assignment, by adding two additional horn parts doing contrapuntal melodic lines, which I believed would make it less literal, and more magical. After all, I reasoned, it was just animation of a boy with a little horn in the first place; why not take some risks?

"How could you use three horns?" he exclaimed—that head arranger, and chief opportunity squasher—when I brought my finished score to him. "There's only one horn on the screen, why would you score it for three horns?" He was right of course. There might be room for magic in a jingle, but that was not the way to do it. Nor did I get the job, and I needed it badly.

Transitions are fraught with obstacles as every stepping stone one takes in a particular direction is a slippery one and easy to fall from. Surely one can make changes from accepted conventions that are commonly used, but only after one understands what made those conventions work in the first place. I wasn't there yet.

⸎

After living in Forest Hills for two years, Joan and I moved, for the same amount of rent, to a larger apartment in Far Rockaway so that I'd have my own room to work in, as our son, Robbie, was now starting to walk, and it was more difficult for me to keep working in the living room, as I had been doing. We were now living much farther from the city, about an hour from

New York, and getting into the city on a daily basis was difficult as there was sometimes not enough money for gas, or even the train. At that point, I had a faithful standby. I had a Bell and Howell 8 millimeter camera that Joan's parents had given us that I brought to a local pawn shop where it would bring three dollars, just enough for me to get into the city for the day, to try to make my connections to get work. I retrieved that camera when I had enough money, but I pawned it again so often that I just kept it wrapped in the pawnbroker's brown wrapping paper for the next time that it was going back to him. I couldn't afford to park my car in a parking lot in the city, so I became familiar with parking spaces many blocks away where there was slim chance that I would get ticketed. I did get ticketed of course, many times, but the parking violations just went unpaid. I had no choice. There were times that my brother Manny and I would meet for lunch in the city, and we'd share an egg salad sandwich, which was usually the least expensive sandwich on a menu. I never got depressed from this or lost any conviction of what I needed to do, but it was difficult, nonetheless. There was one time that I was desperate enough to call every person either I had worked for or who had left me with the feeling that he would be calling me with work at a future time. I tried the honest tact of saying that if there was ever a time he planned to use me for a project, this would be the time that would make the difference in my life. The people I spoke to were all very empathetic and promised that they would call, but not one of them did. I learned quickly that there are boundaries with people who employ you, and it is futile, if not harmful to one's career, to try to step over those boundaries. I never did that again.

Mademoiselle would never allow me to feel badly that I wasn't able to pay for my lessons. She was my teacher and I was eager to learn. It was simply that. It was never an issue with her. She said to me that one day, if I was able to, I could do something in return for someone else. That's a legacy that I'm proud to continue. She always expressed her concern to me, however, that I had enough to eat. I always assured her that I did even when it was not always true.

At a critical point financially, someone gave my name and telephone number to a producer doing a rescore and reedit and mix of a Japanese sci-fi picture. The producer, who was also the American distributor of the film, Joe Balucci, called, and I went to his studio to meet with him hoping that I might have a film to work on.

He had a very large studio, filled with antiquated moviolas and ancient equipment. It was very surreal looking with strips of film hanging from every corner of the room and more film stretched from one side of the room to the other. He was alone and recutting the picture himself and obviously had his own technique for doing it.

This was one of those really bad Japanese sci-fi pictures from the sixties, where there were mostly Japanese actors whose voices were dubbed over into English, so their lips moved but obviously not to the words spoken. Billy Crystal does a wonderful imitation of this. Every now and then Robert Horton or some of the Americans in the cast would return the dialogue with their lines that were not dubbed in, so it looked like they were appearing in two different pictures cut together.

Joe asked me to help to rescore the film. He had no money to compose and record a new score, but he wanted to hire me to find prerecorded library music and help him cut it into the picture. This is not at all uncommon, even today, as there are "canned" music houses that supply music already recorded that you can buy and track into a film.

He offered me five hundred dollars, and I agreed to do it. However, driving home from the city, I started to feel very badly about having to spend the next few weeks in selecting and cutting together canned music cues for this awful picture, even though the money was significant to me. When I got home, I called Joe back and said that I just couldn't do this job even though I had agreed to it. He wouldn't let me off the hook and said that I was going back on my word, that he was counting on me to do the job, and that I'd see that it wasn't so bad, that I would find the music easily and it wouldn't take me much time at all.

So I relented . . . on the condition that he not put my name on the screen, and he agreed to that. Even then, with no screen credits to my name at all, I knew that this would not be a good credit for me to live with.

For a composer, going to the "canned music house" where Joe sent me, to choose cues from a library of prerecorded music, was tantamount to going to a butcher shop, albeit a musical butcher shop, because you pay for the use of the music by the number of cues and lengths of each cue.

"I need some tension music for this scene."

(Audition various pieces of prerecorded music.)

"That's good, cut me off about 1/4 pound."

"Now I need some rhythmic, dramatic music."

"About 1/3 of a pound."

"Now chase music . . ." and so on.

It was awful. And I hated every minute, having to piece together completely different cues to try to make them work for each scene that needed scoring. Joe cut the music to the picture at my designation, and I must say he was very appreciative of what I was doing for the film.

In several of the scenes, I even put music in that I had written and recorded for other projects. A song here, a demo there. It was a real hodge-podge, but finally it was completed, and I was done with it, and I earned my money.

That movie did find its way to theaters with the title *The Green Slime*. Unfortunately, Joe did not live up to his end of our agreement and put my name on the screen so that the full screen credit read, "Music by Charles Fox and Toshiaki Tsushima." Tsushima was the original composer whose music was dropped, but I did retain a few of his original cues for the film. I don't really know why Joe put my name on the screen, as it had no consequence to anyone but me.

Wouldn't you know that this picture has come back to haunt me from time to time to this day, as it continues to get shown on TV. Many times over the years I've taken a ribbing when I would show up at a recording session or a dubbing theater and someone would say, "I saw your movie, last night, *The Green Slime*. . . . Nice picture."

I even get e-mails and letters occasionally from people who want to know if I wrote this theme or that for the film. And when people would ask me why I would do a movie called *The Green Slime*, all the while trying to conceal a chuckle with that question, I would always answer, "For five hundred dollars. Now why would you want to watch a movie called *The Green Slime*?" That usually put an end to it.

The Green Slime incidentally is a green liquid murky substance that finds its way under doors and devours and destroys everything it touches, including humans.

Fortunately, it didn't destroy my career.

⤷∞⤶

I was introduced to a country songwriter from Arkansas, O. C. Francis, who stood six feet nine inches and weighed about three hundred pounds. He wanted to get into the record business in New York, and he offered me a hundred dollars a week to write songs with him that we would publish, and for me to run the publishing company office. I knew nothing about country music, or the publishing business for that matter, but a weekly paycheck of a hundred dollars quickly convinced me that I could learn.

O. C. rented an office in 1697 Broadway on the corner of 54th Street. This was the "other" music publishing building after the famed Brill building a few blocks away, which was known as the heart of Tin Pan Alley. Our building was connected to and built over the Ed Sullivan Theater, where the *Sullivan* show was broadcast from in the early days of television. Today that same theater is where the *David Letterman Show* is taped for broadcast later that same day.

O. C. Francis was a gentle guy for such a big man, and spoke with a thick southern accent. When we'd start to write a song together, I would sit at the upright piano in the office, and he would bend way down from his six foot nine inch height and lean on the top of the piano on one arm, and he'd say, "Chord for me, son," as though a piano was just another form of a guitar, and I was there to be his accompanist while he came up with lyrics. And so I chorded for him, and somehow we did write songs together that were recorded by several artists. Roberta Sherwood recorded two songs for a single record release, a group of R & B sisters another, and Neil Sedaka even recorded one of our songs, and although it was never released, we did watch him record it during his recording session. To help promote a record we released with the sisters, on the label that we started, named Olen Records after O. C.'s first name, O. C. was convinced that payola was alive and well in radio and he was prepared to find out personally. He asked me to come with him to a local R & B radio station in Long Island City, just across the 59th Street Bridge, to talk to the program director. I was not comfortable at all with that prospect, and actually, I was frightened that this was against the law. Nothing in my makeup or my background prepared me for this misadventure.

Indeed, payola existed at that time, but it was obviously done under the table by people who knew each other. For a six foot nine, Southern-accented guy from Arkansas and a twenty-two-year-old innocent-looking white kid to walk into an all-black radio station in 1963, proposing that money be passed under the table to get radio play, which could land everybody in jail, was if nothing else stupid or laughable . . . take your pick. The program director greeted us cordially, and O. C. did all the talking. I did all the worrying. I really can't remember how he phrased the proposal, but the program director reacted with indignation, proclaiming his being offended that anyone would even suggest that payola was a possibility at his station, and O. C. was quickly cut off from believing that there was any chance of his offer being accepted. I believe that there was even some mention that the police should be alerted to this proposal, but the program director did not do that and in fact, as I recall, he even said that he would listen to the record to see if it had any merit in being played on his station at all. We left the radio station, and I was so happy to be out of there, alive.

Fortunately for me, as it turned out, my job was short-lived, as O. C. decided that the record business was not for him. The paycheck aside, I was very happy not to have to go to an office every day and masquerade as a publisher and record man, so I had no regret about the job ending.

❦

Then a wonderful opportunity presented itself, or so it seemed.

I was introduced to Dizzy Gillespie by his attorney, Bernard Stallman, with the hopeful thought that I would compose and arrange some material for his band. I was thrilled to know him and be invited to his house and have this opportunity. Dizzy gave me a collection of his records to listen to, and I spent hours with him at his house in Jamaica, Queens. I even began to fantasize about the possibility of one day becoming his pianist.

Dizzy was wonderful to me, not condescending at all to a young, aspiring musician, but very warm and friendly. I went to his house many times to hear his band rehearsing in the basement, and we even played chess together during that period. I don't recall ever winning a chess match against him. All the while, I was writing instrumental pieces for him. Eventually, I played what I wrote for him, and he liked them and chose four among those that I wrote and asked me to arrange them for his quintet. It's easy to imagine the thrill that it was for me when he brought his band in to rehearse my pieces for the first time. James Moody was the saxophonist, and he and the other band members all complimented me and said they liked what I had written. It was a great and memorable day for me.

Shortly after that, Dizzy went on the road and performed my music wherever he played on his tour. I was thrilled that he was playing my pieces and was hoping that he would then record them as well. When Dizzy returned from his tour, he confronted me with a dilemma that to this day resonates within me as being so unbelievable that I still have a hard time coming to grips with it. He told me that when he was getting started, he wrote songs that other people put their names on and that he expected that from me as well.

"You mean . . . Dizzy . . . you want to put . . . ? But Dizzy, surely you don't want to put your name on my music?" I stammered.

He repeated his intent without any hesitation or apology, but that was the way it had to be. I thought to myself, Dizzy Gillespie improvises brilliant new melodies all night long. It made no sense to me. But I was devastated. I worked for so long and so hard to please him. My sense of right and wrong and fairness was thrown off balance. Why would the great Dizzy Gillespie, composer of "Manteca" and "A Night in Tunisia" want to put his name on my work?

I still replay this scene in my memory bank, thinking that I must have heard badly. But I know I didn't. I still want to excuse him and give him an out in my mind, but I have no explanation that makes any sense. During this same meeting, and before he brought up the issue of the composer credit, he asked me to give him a bill for the arrangements that I did, and for the copying charges that I advanced the copyist. He told me my bill was too high, that he only paid twenty-five dollars for a small band, and fifty dollars for a big band arrangement. I don't recall how much my bill could have been, but for five musicians, and charging the exact page rate for five musicians set by the Musician's Union, it couldn't have been very high. And I would gladly have written arrangements of my tunes for nothing, just knowing that he was playing my music. Then he changed the subject to the ownership of the copyright. When I wouldn't agree to his soft-spoken but none the less resolute demand, he refused even to pay me the money that I had already advanced to the copyist.

I was shocked and saddened after all this time to be at this point with Dizzy Gillespie. Rather than accept what had happened quietly, I told this story to someone at the Musician's Union, and the trial board decided to bring charges against Dizzy. It was with great ambivalence that I went to the trial board for a hearing, but I felt very justified, albeit heartbroken.

During the hearing in front of the Musician's Union trial board, Dizzy stated that he performed my music in a number of cities about twelve times, and then decided that he didn't like my work, and that he never actually hired me to arrange my pieces, even after he put his "Dizzy Gillespie for President" stamp on all the music, which had an imprint of him playing his trumpet. The trial board members were obviously excited and happy to have the great Dizzy Gillespie in their presence, and he was charming and at ease with them and joked with them, and they responded enthusiastically. Ultimately, it came down to a common courtroom dilemma, who are you going to believe? He admitted that he liked my music, that it was "highly unique," and that he performed the pieces in many cities before deciding he didn't want them. The Union believed everything he said. I didn't stand a chance. However, the trial board did rule that he must reimburse me one hundred dollars for the copyist's charges. For me, it wasn't so much the loss of income for all my work, although that was very meaningful to me at that point in time, or even the loss of not having my music recorded by Dizzy Gillespie, which certainly would have meant a great deal to me in many ways, but more so for the loss of a hero. I would have paid him for the privilege of the experience that I had.

I still look back at my relationship with Dizzy and remember playing chess with him and hearing James Moody and the others in his band playing my music, and wonder how it could have turned out as it did. Did I perhaps misunderstand him? Misinterpret his words? Hurt and confused, but undaunted, I formed a jazz quintet of my own, and recorded those four songs. While they were never released commercially, they remain a remembrance of that period of time in my life.

❧

I began to get occasional work as an arranger for commercials from a very nice fellow who took a liking to me. He played the bass and was connected with a few advertising agencies. Mac Shopnick must have been an army man at one time, because when he counted off the tempo for the orchestra to begin playing, he would count off with the military marching call by saying, "Hup! Hup! Hup two-three-four!" in the tempo of the piece. If the members of the orchestra had not been seated in front of their microphones, I'm sure they would have gotten up and started to march.

I started to do all of Mac's arranging work. Mostly, it was to arrange songs that were written by in-house staff people at the agencies, and my work was based on a concept driven by the visual approach to a particular spot. I worked on all of the Parker Brothers games commercials such as Monopoly and Clue. I also worked on all the Robert Hall commercials using their main theme song as well as their Christmas jingle. The melodies and the lyrics for those jingles still reside, unfortunately, too close to the front of my mind.

> When the values go up, up, up,
> And the prices go down, down, down,
> Robert Hall in season
> Will show you the reason
> Low overhead, low overhead.

And . . .

> Sleigh bells ring, and children sing,
> It's back to Robert Hall again.

I wrote arrangements for many singers for those songs, emulating the sounds and styles of the latest hit records on the radio. For me it was a great training ground to learn to write in all musical styles. I worked on too many commercials to mention here, but it helped to prepare me for my work in film as the music had to be synchronized to the film if it was a TV spot, or with the dialogue if it was for the radio—fifty-eight seconds for a one-minute TV spot, or twenty-eight seconds for a thirty-second version. Not a fraction of a second more or less.

Occasionally I would land a job on my own, to compose the music for a commercial. That was clearly a step up in my career and income. The first time I was hired to compose original music for a commercial, it was for White Owl cigars. The requirement was to compose the theme that would be played by an electric guitar solo, and for budgetary considerations, the same guitarist would then overdub a second accompanying guitar part, and then a third line, which would substitute for the bass.

We hired one musician, Vinnie Bell, the great studio guitarist. I wrote several guitar parts, which he was to record separately and overlay the individual lines to form the whole piece. The producer of the commercial must have realized that this was a first for me and proceeded to eliminate me from any discussion of my music. If he had a thought or comment or suggestion for a musical change, he directed those comments directly to Vinnie Bell, as though I wasn't there and as though it wasn't my music. Vinnie, a great musician, and a sensitive man and a nice man, recognized my dilemma as I was standing right next to him while he was working to satisfy the producer with the suggestions that the producer made to him. Dear Vinnie turned to me with each suggestion, and asked me if that would be all right with me. I was feeling quite helpless and lonely in that studio as I was trying to keep my dignity intact, and his including me in the discussion was something that I never forgot and always appreciated. I'm sure that he would not even remember that particular recording session, but many times, people respond to other people with kindness and help that come very easily from that person and yet have such importance to the recipient of that kindness. We went on to do many recording sessions together over the years, and Vinny Bell remained my friend and first-choice guitarist for most of my recordings in New York until I left for Los Angeles.

Little by little I started getting more and more work in the pop arranging field. I made records with artists with the unlikely-sounding names of the Lollipops, Lorna Dune, and the Peels, with songs with the equally unlikely titles of "Juanita Banana" and "Rosita Tomato." My credits were starting to look like a shopping list.

One day, it was suggested to me that I call Robert Russell Bennett, who was Richard Rodgers's great orchestrator and a fine composer. He had orchestrated all of Rodgers's great Broadway musicals and his powerful *Victory at Sea* series as well. He had studied with Nadia Boulanger many years before me, and the hope was that perhaps he was willing to meet with me and offer some suggestions with my career or help in some way. He was very gracious when I called him and agreed to meet with me. I met with him at his office, and he seemed genuinely interested in my background and wondered how he could help me. Was I familiar with pop music and theater music? Perhaps I could show him something that I wrote in those fields, and he could then recommend me for work. I really had nothing that fit into that category, so I said that I would write a composition for theater orchestra and would bring that back to show him.

I wrote a dance suite in the style of Leonard Bernstein's *West Side Story*, which was as close to that world as I was familiar with. I orchestrated the piece for a large theater orchestra, and a week later, I brought the completed score to Mr. Bennett's office. He seemed impressed and offered to help me. He said he would make some inquiries on my behalf and get back to me.

After a short period of time he called with the following thoughts. He spoke to a school in Vermont, Bennington University, I believe, about my getting a job as a composer in residence and becoming an assistant teacher. He said, alternately, that he had spoken to Skitch Henderson about me, and he was willing to meet with me with the prospect of his using me. I told him how grateful I was to him for both opportunities, but at this point in my life, I couldn't see myself as a teacher. However, I was thrilled to have the opportunity to meet and possibly work for Skitch Henderson, who was a major figure in popular and symphonic music in New York, so he set up an appointment for me to meet with Skitch.

Charles with Skitch Henderson. *Courtesy of the author.*

Skitch was very friendly to me from the beginning. He lived with his wife in a house on 57th Street just above the recording studio that he owned, called Studio 3. It was not a very large studio, but comfortable for a small orchestra. It was always impressive to me that he could simply come down the stairs from his apartment to his studio, still in his slippers, to record. The engineer was a man named David Sarser, and we became friendly. The first assignment for Skitch was to help him with an industrial film that he was doing the music for. I gave him a short composition that I had already written for a small orchestra, and he found use for that piece in the film, and recorded it with a large orchestra in Germany along with the other music he had for the film. That was the first time I heard any music of mine with a large orchestra, and it sounded rich and full and was quite thrilling. Skitch got the job as the musical director for *The Tonight Show* starring Johnny Carson shortly thereafter. From time to time he would ask me to arrange a song that would feature him at the piano with the *Tonight Show* orchestra. Doc Severinsen was the lead trumpet player in the band, and it was a great band to write for. Several years later I would do an album with Doc that I arranged and that included a couple of my songs. Every now and then, Skitch would ask me to write an original theme that the band could play when they went on and off the air during a commercial break. He would sometimes call on me as well to play the piano or harpsichord in his Studio 3 if he was conducting and needed an extra keyboard player.

One day, after I had written a number of themes for the show, the librarian for the *Tonight Show* band, Shelley Cohen, asked me if I was with BMI (Broadcast Music, Inc.), or ASCAP (the American Society of Composers, Authors and Publishers).

"What's that?" I asked.

"They are the performing rights societies that pay you money as your music is performed on the air on radio or television."

"Really?" I said.

I didn't have any awareness of the performing rights societies or their function, and was very happily surprised. The first on the list happened to be BMI, which I called to arrange for an appointment. They confirmed that indeed they would pay me for my music being performed on *The Tonight Show* and anywhere else on radio or television where my music was performed, in this country and in every other country. I was thrilled with the prospect of income from my themes on the air, and signed with them immediately. I never even inquired at ASCAP to see what the difference might be between the societies. I've been a member of BMI ever since that time in 1962. It's been the only constant business relationship that I've had in my whole career, and has always been a happy one. At BMI I've had many friends and fans over the years, and people who believed in me at every step along the way. It would be hard to say that about many relationships.

It was an exciting time for me, getting started writing music for TV and records. I made several of my own albums during that period. Among those records was an instrumental Latin record for the MGM label, *Anatomy of Dancing*, and *All*, a pop instrumental album featuring two alto saxophones, with Mike Gold, my high school friend, overdubbing both parts, and the jazz quintet group that I started, with the music that I wrote for Dizzy Gillespie that he didn't record.

My career seemed to be moving along in the right direction.

I was with Ed Ames the afternoon that he performed on *The Tonight Show*, and whose infamous tomahawk throw will forever be remembered as one of the most memorable clips from that show. I wrote the arrangements

Courtesy of the author.

for his performance that day. After we finished rehearsing with the band, Johnnie Carson handed Ed a tomahawk and asked him to throw it at an outlined caricature of a cowboy drawn on a wooden wall about fifteen feet away. Ed was costarring at that time on *The Daniel Boone Show*, playing the role of an Indian and Boone's sidekick, but he had never actually thrown a tomahawk on the show. So time after time the tomahawk he threw would not stick into the wooden board, leaving the drawing of the cowboy unmarked. Finally, a stage hand came up to Ed and suggested that he turn the tomahawk around so that the blade side faced up, toward him. One throw, it stuck, and the stagehand marked the spot where he stood so that he could duplicate it for the show.

Sure enough, when Ed threw the tomahawk that afternoon during the taping of the show, with one throw it stuck, right in the middle of the cowboy's crotch with the handle pointing straight up. Ed was so amazed and embarrassed that even with his laughter and everyone else's hysteria, he started moving toward the wooden backboard to remove the tomahawk. But Johnnie Carson, fully aware of milking the moment, grabbed Ed's arm and wouldn't let him retrieve the tomahawk, and the image of that circumcised cowboy is an indelible part of TV history.

A little-known part of that history is that the song that Ed sang that night, which I arranged, which probably only he and I remember, was "Try to Remember," the song that he made popular from the show *The Fantasticks*.

⌘

In 1964, the World's Fair opened in New York on the site of the 1938 World's Fair in Queens, which formerly held the Aquacade. New York was ablaze with construction in preparation for the event. The already overburdened highways were being widened to accommodate the influx of tourists expected during the next two years of the fair. I didn't know at this point that I would spend the better part of 1964 working at the World's Fair with Ray Barretto's charanga band. Ray was one of the great conga players, who made his name initially playing with Tito Puente and doing the top studio work until he formed his own band and became one of the venerable stars of Latin music.

Our band was very often matched up and alternated playing with some of the great Latin bands of the day. Some were big bands with trumpets, trombones, and saxes, like those of Tito Puente or Tito Rodriguez, and some were conjuntos consisting of just trumpets and rhythm like the great Cuban band Sonora Matancera or La Playa Sextet. Our charanga band consisted of two violins, flute, and a rhythm section with singers, of course. Even though a charanga band usually has no brass, we still made some of the most intense, swinging, and driving rhythm imaginable, and when we played places like the famous Palladium, on 54th Street and Broadway, you could feel the whole dance floor shake in tempo with hundreds of dancers in sync with the music. It was a great sensation to be part of that.

For one of his albums, Ray and I wrote a few songs together, which I arranged and we recorded with the band. Ray's big hit number was called "Watusi," and it was one of the few Latin crossover records that ever went on to be a hit on the American pop charts. It consisted of a simple vamp that went on forever, with an occasional flute solo, that accompanied the lead singer and Ray, who were speaking in Spanish, carrying on in an argumentative way that the people thought was fun. I guess I must have known generally what it was about, but I never knew what they actually said as I didn't speak Spanish. But the audiences did, and they loved it. Ray's orchestra was very popular at that time.

The band was hired to play at the World's Fair, in the Caribbean Pavilion. The Pavilion was open on three sides so that the music would attract the crowds of people passing by at the fair. We played mambos and cha-chas late into the night, but the pachanga was all the rage at that time. We played five days in a row, and were off for the next five days, as we switched off with another band, so we actually worked five out of ten days. But it was steady employment, and paid well, and was an improvement in my earnings.

Our uniforms for that job were white rumba shirts, with blue ruffled sleeves, and a red bandana around our necks. Picture the Desi Arnaz orchestra on the *I Love Lucy* show. I'm sorry now that I don't have a picture of our band in that uniform. There was no dancing in the club, we played strictly in concert, on a stage, past a huge bar where there were many tables where people sat and listened.

Every night I'd show up with my rumba shirt, which Joan cleaned every day, but with it still looking like it had just come out of a washing machine . . . which it had. I noticed that most of the other musicians in the band, who were Latino, came much more nicely dressed, because their rumba shirts all looked pressed and starched, so that the ruffles on the sleeves stood out freshly ironed. Mine was clean, but didn't look like the other players' uniforms. I asked my friends in the band how they got their shirts to look as well as they did, and the answer was that their wives cleaned and pressed and starched their shirts every day. I didn't know how my wife Joan would take to that, but it was inevitable that I'd ask her. One day, I told her that all the other musicians' wives pressed and starched their shirts every day when they came out of the washing machine. I held up my clean but wrinkled shirt to her, and asked her if she would starch and press it for me. She looked at me with a look of incredulity and simply said, "Jewish girls don't iron rumba shirts." I considered this for a moment, as I looked from the wrinkled shirt, to Joan, and back to the shirt. . . . I knew that my days in Latin music were coming to an end.

⋘⋙

Prior to the World's Fair opening, I got my first opportunity to compose the music for a film, a short documentary film that would be shown many times a day at the Kodak Pavilion at the World's Fair. In preparation, I had very little to draw from in approaching synchronizing the music to film. I don't believe that a film composition class was anywhere on the horizon at any level at that time, so I learned by doing. I called Skitch Henderson to ask him how I should go about doing it. He said to me to come over to his house, and he would lend me his stopwatch, which had film footage in addition to seconds and minutes on the sweep hand. He also gave me something called a "Ready Eddy," which was a circular plastic chart that translated film footage into seconds. Armed with both of those devices, I began my work in film. To this day, after more than one hundred films, I still use the same kind of stopwatch that Skitch lent to me, to guide me in synchronizing my music to the screen. The "Ready Eddy" was necessary only when the moviolas didn't have second counters as well as footage counters and became entirely unnecessary when I began working with music editors, but that wasn't until years later, in Hollywood.

Working to film came easily for me, and I was very happy to be composing a score after doing so much arranging. The producer of the film, Jim Manila, came to my house, and I played every cue for him at the piano, describing what was going on at that moment in the film as I was playing it. That is something that I have continued to do on all my films subsequently, although since the seventies, I have video playback to show the film instead of talking about it. Now, of course, it's all through the computer.

Jim loved the music that I had composed, especially for the ending of the film, which had, as I recall, a joyous, exalted-sounding culmination of the themes that I wrote for the film. As the story of the film developed, so did the music accompanying it. "Why not," he said, "use that joyous section more often and throughout, especially at the beginning of the film." Now I was totally perplexed. My classical background and formal training, in learning to develop the musical material in an organized manner, was now coming into direct conflict with a producer, the person who hired me, asking me to extract only the sections that he liked for the film, and relocate those sections to parts of the film that I didn't intend for that music. I was overjoyed at how much he loved the ending music, but could not conceive of it being used any sooner. After all, the reason I believed that it worked so well at the end was that I developed those themes so that little by little they took on a larger meaning and came together with a conclusive burst of joyous energy that brought it to the high point musically, which he liked so much. If I started with that, with no introduction or development of the themes, it would not have the same effect at all, and would not take on that larger meaning.

"Try it," he said, and so I reluctantly complied.

"Great, I love it," Jim said after hearing the change in relation to the beginning of the film.

And so there I was, left with a high point in my music with absolutely no idea of how I got there musically. In fact, musically, it made no sense to me at all, but Jim Manila loved it and called me for future work for other short and documentary films, which he did so well. But in moving forward in my career, I had to learn to deconstruct my sense of musical form from time to time. However, the more experience that I had, the more I learned to work within the confines of a given situation on the screen and became very comfortable with developing my musical material without going against my musical instincts.

Around that time, I wrote the following letter to my teacher in Paris. It was always a consoling act to write to her. I felt that she understood me so well that I could be completely open with her. This was a part of my letter to her, and her response to me.

> *My Dear Mlle Boulanger,*
>
> *When I think that nearly a year has passed since my last letter, I cannot find the words to express my apologies. I pray that you are well and hope that you will not be too angry with me. There is so much that I want to tell you though I feel so close to you that I think you must already know.*
>
> *My son is nearly two years old now and is so bright. He sits for long periods of time at the piano—never banging but picking out single notes and always singing at the same time. I am really so proud of my wife and child. We are struggling and yet there is so much to be thankful for.*
>
> *I am forced by my own choosing to earn a living writing commercial music. It is very difficult for me to work with people who are more interested in a marketable product than in music. But I know and love only music, and I must bring to any kind of music the same care and concern for the truth that I would*

*if it were my most important work. In this way, I can keep my
mind alive to fight for time to do my own composing. . . .*

My Dear Charles,

*Let me, alas hurriedly (tell you) how happy your letter
made me, which was sad. This—well, never look on what can't
be changed.*

*Here you are, with a cherished wife, a little boy, facing the
growing of your life—Help it in exercising it as always (until)
that movement becomes part of oneself.—Well, this needs some
comments and would lead to nothing.*

*Feel simply assured that my affection remained always
the same to say enlightened by your moving letter which
reaches me where your heart is to be heard.*

*So many wishes, and hopes for your work, for meeting
your wife and child, and for one day, maybe, another meeting.*

Most Faithfully,
Nadia Boulanger
9 Mars 1964

For some parts of that same film for the Kodak Pavilion, Jim wanted the
modern sound of an electronic score in addition to what I was writing. For
the electronic music, he hired a man who was otherwise a professional photographer, and was a musician of sorts as well, who owned a new electronic
instrument called the Ondioline. It was a keyboard instrument that had a
two-octave range that was very harsh and brassy sounding. The volume was
controlled by a lever that one pushed sideways with his knee to increase or
decrease the level. It was actually a horrible-sounding instrument, but recording the sounds made on that Ondioline, and altering them by tape manipulation, produced an otherworldly sound for that period, however unmusical
that sound was. I was, however, impressed enough by the possibilities of new
electronic sounds that a noncomposer could make that I decided to enroll in
the electronic music laboratory known as the Columbia/Princeton Lab on
the campus of Columbia University. The teacher, Vladimir Ussachevsky, was
the composer who, along with his collaborator, Otto Luening, was one of
the originators of electronic music by tape manipulation. Oddly enough, for
someone who didn't like electronic music and never had any interest in attending a university in the first place, in order to take that class, I had to first
be officially accepted to and enrolled in Columbia University as I could not

just audit the class. Fortunately for me, the school, to their credit, understood my background and interests, and gave me a special test in order to accept me to the academic program, from which I could then enroll in the electronic music class. I was accepted to the school, and after I was officially enrolled, I was able take any other classes that I wanted, so I decided to take an advanced French language class, in order not to lose the language that I had worked so hard to learn when I was in Paris. After a month or two, that class conflicted so often with my professional work that I finally dropped out even though I was enjoying being a student again. But I did continue in Ussachevsky's class for the whole year, which fascinated me with all the possibilities of constructing music with this new facility of musical language.

In this day of synthesizers, samplers, and computers all being processed digitally, the Columbia/Princeton Lab would now seem like an archaic studio that you'd be more likely to find in the Smithsonian Museum. But in 1965, it was one of only five in the world that had that capability at all, and the others were in France, Germany, and Israel, so composers came from all over the world to work in this studio, and as a result, it was in operation twenty-four hours a day, and I was excited to be part of this experience.

In the studio, there were banks of generators that produced all manner of electronically initiated sounds such as saw tooth waves, square waves, and sine waves. One could produce and record individual notes that then had to be spliced together. The length of each splice depended on the rhythmic value of each note according to the metronomic tempo and the speed of the tape machine. When one put together a musical phrase by splicing all these individual notes in a rhythmic order, one would then make a loop of this melody and send the result into any number of sound-altering devices such as ring modulators and tape delay equipment or simply through echo chambers. All this was to produce one track of music that would be recorded on a monaural tape machine. Working track by track contrapuntally, you would eventually have four separate tracks of music that when started simultaneously, all four mono tape machines would produce the finished musical work. It was a very long process, but there were some very sophisticated and well-wrought compositions that were achieved in this manner. For me, it opened my ears to electronic music, which I had detested while I was a student in Paris, where it was a regular part of avant-garde concerts.

At the Theatre Odeon, there was the occasional concert of only avant-garde musical works by composers such as Ligetti, Stockhausen, Berio, Nono, and Henri Pousseur, who were always in attendance, as well as, of course, Pierre Boulez, who was the musical director and who conducted most of the works in his extraordinary manner. The concert series was known as "Domaine Musicale."

It was always a thrilling event, and it brought out all the music students in Paris in addition to the musical cognoscenti. The audience would cheer, whistle, and shout their bravos at the top of their voices, or boo loudly. There were no holds barred. People responded enthusiastically whether it was negatively or superlatively.

I wrote again to my teacher:

My Dear Mlle Boulanger,
I have been fortunate enough to have been permitted to work (composing) at the Columbia University electronic music laboratory. I must admit that I first went there with a wary eye, full of grievances against it and a great feeling of indifference towards it as music. That was eight months ago. And now I find myself enchanted with the possibilities. It is such a new world of sounds with endless varieties.
Of course there is a great amount of technique to learn, so I have been doing only short pieces. But I am planning now to begin work on a ballet in September. Unfortunately the studio will be closed for the summer, so I cannot begin sooner. . . .

Within two years, I would purchase my first synthesizer shortly after it was invented, directly from its inventor, Robert Moog. The Moog synthesizer, as it was commonly known, was so new when I received it, that Moog had not yet gotten around to writing an instruction manual, and I had to experiment with the instrument and its myriad possibilities of sound in order to learn how to use it. But, for me, it was a progression that I was prepared for because of the class with Ussachevsky at Columbia. I spent weeks in my basement studio in our first house in Cedarhurst, Long Island, experimenting with the possibilities that the instrument offered, but friends who would visit me in my studio, as I sat in front of this huge array of knobs and dials, thought that I looked more like a mad scientist than a composer.

The Moog synthesizer—which I bought with money advanced to me from BMI—was very groundbreaking and quite impressive to look at. It was a very large instrument consisting of modular parts with banks of oscillators, sound generators, and sound-altering modulators and ring modulators and played on a keyboard that acted as a voltage controller. It offered a whole new world of musical and nonmusical electronically produced sounds that could be altered in many ways, and it was all controlled by a keyboard, so for the first time, one could play notes generated by electronic sources. The instrument for all its impressiveness, however, produced only a single musical tone. No polyphony or harmony was yet possible; however, in a few years, there was an additional keyboard controller available that allowed me to play two musical lines at the same time. I also bought a four-track tape recorder to be able to record up to four tracks of musical information, one track at a time, and more than four tracks if I bounced tracks back and forth, combining them. So composing music was a process of first creating the sounds and then working line by line and instrument by instrument to build a composition.

The first film that I composed the music for, using my new synthesizer, was a short film entitled *The SS Manhattan*. The SS *Manhattan* was an oil tanker that was especially constructed as an icebreaker as well, which was capable of crushing through the Arctic ice in order to bring back oil from that part of the world. The music I wrote also contained elements of sounds effects that I constructed electronically so that the sound of howling winds, and of the huge boat crushing against the ice, were all part of the musical score. It was fascinating and exciting to me to be able to compose the music and create the musical sounds at the same time. From that point on, I very

Charles at home in Cedarhurst, Long Island, with first Moog synthesizer. *Courtesy of the author.*

often incorporated all the electronics that were available into my orchestral scores when appropriate.

I started scoring documentary films and short films for the U.S. Information Agency using smaller orchestras and sometimes in conjunction with the new electronic sounds. The films for the U.S. Information Agency were allowed to be shown only outside the United States, as they were films specifically designed to spread the work of American technological progress and innovation to the rest of the world. One of those films, entitled *Destination Moon*, was about preparing pilots for space flight and was made about five years before we landed a man on the moon. I also scored one small, independent feature film called *Below the Hill*, with a small chamber orchestra alternating with a jazz combo. It was never distributed to theaters or television that I was aware of, but it still gave me the opportunity to learn the craft of film scoring, and it was actually a touching little film about the demise of a small mill town in Massachusetts as a result of the closure of a large textile mill.

⟨⟨⟩⟩

During that same time frame, I became friendly with a record producer, Elliot Mazer, who also worked as a publisher for EB Marks Music. He hired me to do arrangements on several occasions. One album that I was particularly proud of was by an artist name Jake Holmes, entitled *A Letter to Katherine November*. It was an autobiographical album of songs that Jake Holmes wrote that recalled his life and marriage and subsequent breakup with his wife. I was supposed to do an album with Elliot for Janis Joplin with her group, Big Brother and the Holding Company, but it never happened, as she went off on her own.

Elliot did, however, hire me to do two arrangements for a record featuring a television star, and that would ultimately have a great and far-reaching effect on my career.

Barbara Feldon was the costar of the popular TV series *Get Smart*, along with Don Adams. She played Agent 99, and that was, not coincidentally, the title of one of the two songs we recorded. At the session, the producers of the *Get Smart* series were there, David Susskind and Daniel Melnick, along with Bob Israel, who handled the music for their company through his own company, Score Productions. They must have been impressed with my work, as I remember Danny Melnick putting his arm around me congenially and saying to me that he thought that I would be great to do films. He must have been reading my mind.

As a result of my work on that record, Bob Israel hired me to score my first TV movie—which was shot on video—a remake of the film *Johnny*

Belinda, starring Mia Farrow and for the same producers, Susskind and Melnick. They all liked my score, and I felt that I was definitely making progress toward my career as a composer for film. After the music scoring sessions were completed and the music was edited into the film, the next stage was the dubbing mix, which incorporated all the elements of dialogue, music, and sound effects into the proper balance. At the dubbing session, David Susskind offhandedly mentioned that he wanted to sell his Jaguar XKE. I said that that was my dream car. He looked at me and said, "Why don't you take it for spin during the lunch break?" Irving Robbins, a very knowledgeable musician, was the musical supervisor for the film. Irving, or "Binny" as he was known, said he would go with me as he knew a lot about cars. I really was not in the market for a car, and couldn't afford one, especially a Jaguar, used or otherwise, but I didn't know how to extricate myself from that dilemma gracefully, so I said that I would take the car for a spin. Over the lunch break Binny and I drove David's car up and down the East Side highway. He concluded that the car was in bad shape and that I shouldn't consider buying it. Now I was in a tough spot, working with my first important producer, who was a well-known celebrity in his own right, having his own television show. When he mentioned wanting to sell his car, I really didn't mean that I was ready to buy a Jaguar in the first place, but simply said that it was my dream car.

"What do I say to David?" I asked Binny.

"Tell him that it's just too much car for you; he'll understand."

After lunch we were back on the dubbing stage, and the first thing that David asked me was, "How'd you like the car?" I repeated the words Binny suggested and embellished it a bit, hoping to make it a little more palatable to David's ears.

"It's a beautiful car, but too much car for me," I said.

"Too much car for you?" he responded loudly and incredulously.

If he said anything more to me that day, or ever, I don't recall, but that was a quick end to my relationship with David Susskind, even though he liked my score very much.

However, Bob Israel continued to hire me.

The first project he asked me to compose for TV is still on the air, I believe, forty years later, the theme for *Wide World of Sports*. There had never been a sports anthology show on television before, but this turned out to be the first of several TV series that I did that could be considered the first of a new genre and therefore very uncertain of its potential success. *Wide World of Sports* was, however, a great success and even though the first of its kind, it is still on the air recapping the week's highlights in sports, and still using my theme. The cue sheets do not list my name as composer, as I was paid five hundred dollars to write it as a buyout. I was twenty-five years old and happy to have the opportunity to write for TV, and to earn five hundred dollars, and the long-term implications of performance royalties weren't even on the radar screen yet in my life, as I was still trying to earn the monthly rent. And Bob Israel liked my work very much and used it as an audition piece for him to get me other work.

We recorded the theme for that show at Plaza Sound Studios in New York, with an orchestra that included strings. After they heard it, the consensus of opinion between the network and the producers was that it should be stronger and brassier to match the power of the sports that it was meant to evoke. I traveled to London with Binny and Bob Israel to record a new orchestral version of the theme with a large brass section, woodwinds, and percussion, and this time without strings, at CTS Studios in Wembley. The engineer was Eric Tomlinson, who would one day come to Budapest to work with me on the film *Love at Stake*. The assistant engineer was John Richards, who many years later would move to Los Angeles, at my request, to become the head engineer and mixer for the studio that I was a co-owner of, Evergreen Studios in Burbank.

Recording *Wide World of Sports* at CTS Studios in Wembley, London. *Courtesy of the author.*

The printed version, however, of the *Wide World of Sports* theme credits me and Irving Robbins as jointly being the composers, which I never understood because Irving (Binny) had nothing to do with the composition at all. And although I was promised 50 percent of all ancillary rights beyond the use in the TV series by Bob Israel, five hundred dollars was the only amount I ever earned from that theme, as presumably he has received all the income from it. However, it led to other work, which I needed in order to earn a living as a composer, and was very happy to have, and for a few years, Bob Israel kept me pretty busy doing.

⨂

He asked me to write a new theme and library of music for Goodson and Todman, the game show kings, for a remake of their hit game show *What's My Line?* I had the same understanding with Bob Israel that this would be a buyout of my music, but this time he paid me one thousand dollars. Again we went to London to record, this time with Mark Goodson present. I did the same for the other Goodson-Todman shows, *To Tell the Truth* and *Matchgame.*

For each show that I composed the music, I had a similar scenario in presenting the music to the producers. Goodson-Todman's offices were the entire thirtieth floor of the Seagrams Building, a landmark on Park Avenue. At the appointed hour I would be shown into the large conference room filled with many of the Goodson-Todman employees: producers, directors, and office staff. At the far end of this huge room was a sixty-six note piano. I never found out why they skimped on the size of the piano—the room was surely large enough for a full-sized eighty-eight note piano.

Bill Todman would usually come into the room to greet me and then leave before hearing the theme. It was always Mark Goodson who was the person I had to please. He would normally stand at the end of the piano alongside of the high notes. While I played, he would lean on the top of this small upright, on his right elbow, with his head cupped in his right hand, not looking at me, but rather, staring at the ceiling away from the piano, and in his left hand he held a huge cigar, which he puffed steadily while listening.

As I was about to perform the theme on the piano; in my head I heard it fully orchestrated with brass and woodwinds and percussion, but all I had to demonstrate my music was this three-quarter-sized piano. I began to play the theme, nervously at first, and tried to put all the sparkle and energy into the music that I could muster.

After finishing playing the theme, I was usually greeted with a deafening. . . .

Silence.

No reaction at all.

Just people staring at me.

Then Mark would interrupt the silence, look at his staff around the conference table and ask them one by one what they thought of the theme. But not knowing what Mark's reaction would be, they were evasive in committing themselves to a position either way.

"Nice beat."

"Sounds good."

"Not sure, need to hear it again," were the usual comments.

Finally, Mark would say, "Let's hear it again," and I would start the theme again from the beginning, a little more confidently this time, while Mark took his usual place alongside the piano, still leaning, still puffing. This time however, as I played, at some point I would look down at the floor and I would usually notice that his foot would start to tap along with the beat of the music. When I saw his foot tapping, I knew I had him. I knew he liked it.

One time that I recall, however, Mark didn't like the theme I had written, and I was asked to wait outside the conference room while he and Bob Israel presumably considered the options. While I was waiting, and believing that I knew what it was about that theme that he didn't like, I opened my briefcase, took out some score paper, and wrote a new theme in the interim. When Mark and Bob came out of the conference room, I told them that I had a new theme to play. They both seemed very surprised and impressed and asked me to let them hear it, and we went back into the conference room together. After hearing me play it at the piano, Mark dismissed it summarily and suggested that I go home and come back yet again with another theme. I learned quickly from that botched attempt to write a new piece on the spot that a producer would rather know that you worked very hard and long in satisfying an assignment rather than to think that it came off the top of your head. It is often very true that one has to work long and hard to come up with even the simplest-sounding music, but it's equally true that sometimes it's the initial burst of music that turns out to have just the right statement. I've learned to trust my instincts and know intuitively where the difference lies.

Mark always came to London to be present at the recording of the theme and library cues that I wrote for his shows. He made his occasional comments, and each session that I did for him and Bob Israel was fun and successful for me as well as a learning experience. I loved working in London. The musicians were always wonderful to work with, and London was close enough to Paris that I would always fly over there to see Mlle Boulanger or at least to buy flowers to send upstairs to her, from the little flower shop downstairs from her house.

Mademoiselle once asked me as an aside, which she would often do in the middle of a lesson, if I knew Quincy Jones.

I said I did.

"He's such a lovely man. He sends me beautiful flowers when he's traveling and can't come here for his lessons. He sends me postcards from all around Europe. He plays in a jaaaazzzzzz band." And with the word "jazz," her face would make a quizzical expression that implied that she didn't understand that kind of music.

However, Quincy's sending her flowers when he was away must have made an impression on me, because in the years to come, whenever I was in Paris, I would always send her flowers from that little flower shop in front of her apartment house.

She made that same face on another day when she asked me if I knew Michel Legrand. He was already well known, and of course I knew of him and his music. He had studied with her as well.

"It's too bad about him," she said. "He's such a talented man, but he writes music for the mooovies." With the word "movies," that same quizzical look would appear on her face. She simply didn't understand music that wasn't classical in nature and composition.

Joan always came with me to London on these trips, and we always saw it as a great opportunity to travel a bit and spend some time alone together, knowing that the children were being wonderfully taken care of by her mother at home.

⬥

For one of the Goodson-Todman shows, I wanted to add the electronic sound of the Ondioline to the theme. There was no Ondioline available in London, so the company flew Monsieur Ondioline, the inventor of the instrument, and his wife over from Paris, and they brought their instrument with them. (Years later I used that same sound on the instrumental section of the *Happy Days* theme. It was a really not a very pretty sound; it was a harsh, unmusical sound, but the few times I used that instrument, it was effective for its unusual color.)

My understanding with Bob Israel before writing the music for those shows was that I would not be receiving anything beyond my initial fee, regardless of the longevity or success of the shows and my music being performed on the air. I never resented these buyouts of my music as I saw it as a stepping stone in my career, and Bob truly believed in me and my work, and he was the only one offering me this kind of work. I didn't, however, expect to see another person's name appear as composer of the music. But I knew that hopefully one day I would be in a position that I could afford to accept work only when I would be fully credited for it.

That happened in less than two years in 1967, when Bob asked me to write the theme for a new series, a weekly football game in prime time, *Monday Night Football*. No network had ever programmed a regular sporting event in the evening in prime time. Would women object to this seeming exclusion from prime-time TV? No one knew. I was offered the same business arrangement as before; however, this time I simply said no, I wouldn't take any more work that didn't credit me as the composer when I was the composer. Bob said that if I insisted in holding to that, he'd have to hire someone else. I had made my decision, and there was no turning back. I felt that I had paid my dues, and if I didn't break with the past at this moment, I might never. Fortunately for me, the people at ABC network insisted that they have the same creative team that did *Wide World of Sports*, and as a result I received the same fee that I was offered, and still retained all my rights as composer of the theme. *Monday Night Football* is still on the air, but my theme was replaced after seven years by someone named . . . Bob Israel.

By that time I had already been in Hollywood for several years and could only laugh at the irony of it. I always liked Bob Israel and thought of him as a friend, and considered that he gave me opportunities that no one else was offering me, so I appreciated that and was able to put the rest of it in perspective. He also got me my first film, *The Incident*, which led to my wonderful friendship with the director, Larry Peerce, with whom I did seven films over the years including the film that brought me to Hollywood, *Goodbye, Columbus*.

Larry Peerce was the director of my first motion picture and remains a very dear friend of mine more than forty years later, and I treasure every memory of our working together over the course of seven major films.

By 1967 I had done a number of short films and documentary films, a television remake of *Johnny Belinda* for David Susskind and Daniel Melnick, and one of the TV plays from the end of the "taped live" TV dramatic era called *ABC Stage 67*.

Bob Israel introduced me to Larry Peerce, who was working on his second film, *The Incident*, after his powerful film debut with *One Potato, Two Potato*. I don't recall Bob's connection with this film, but I was hired to "score" the film, working with Terry Knight, whose credit would be "composed by." I'm not sure of that distinction of titles because to me, they are one and the same. But Terry was a rock and roll songwriter and record producer who would several years later produce the albums for the Grand Funk Railroad. His father, I learned, owned a string of movie theaters in the Midwest, and had put money into this film, and it was understood that Terry would do the music for it.

As Terry presumably had no experience with film, I was brought in to work with him in scoring it. I had no problem in accepting this role and, in fact, was delighted to have the job and the opportunity regardless of the ambiguity of credits. As it turned out, Terry's only contribution to the film was an end title song called "Is It Over Now." That left me with the rest of the film to fill in the notes.

The Incident was filmed in black and white, and it was an extraordinarily real and frightening film set in New York and shot mostly on a set that was a complete mock-up of a New York subway car. The interiors were shot in this car, built on the soundstage of the old Biograph Studios, where Charlie Chaplin made several of his films. The film centered around two New York tough hoods who terrorized everyone in the subway one night. In New York, at that time, there was always some fear of riding in certain parts of New York on a subway at night. This film played to those fears. It starred Tony Musante and Martin Sheen as the hoods, and Beau Bridges as the young soldier who finally challenges them. I believe it was all of their first film assignments, as well as mine.

I scored the film with a very rhythmic, percussive, hard-edged-sounding orchestra, and took every advantage of the new electronic sounds that were starting to emerge. Larry was wonderful to work with, encouraging me at every turn and appreciating my approach to the film. We agreed on the tone and placement of all the musical cues. And it was great fun hanging out with him. It was serious filmmaking and easy friendship with lots of laughs. I played all the cues at the piano for Larry in advance, describing what the orchestra was underscoring at that moment, which gave him a chance to comment, and for me to make changes if necessary before I orchestrated the music.

I was already loving my entrée into the world of filmmaking. Larry and I would repeat the experience of working together in films as diverse as *Goodbye Columbus*, *The Other Side of the Mountain*, *Two-Minute Warning*, and one of my personal favorites, *A Separate Peace*. Too many times, composers get typecast in a certain genre of film in their careers. The best is when there is trust between a director and a composer that transcends a particular style. That's what I enjoyed so much with Larry—the trust he placed in me, and my desire to make the film as good as it could be. And the friendship we've had.

The Incident, a 20th Century Fox picture, opened in New York with a much ballyhooed premiere on Broadway, complete with klieg lights, and it was very exciting to be part of that. The film, however, was so dramatic and real in its portrayal of New York, with its worst fears, that at its most intense moments, it brought out such anger in some moviegoers in certain theaters where it was shown that some audience members actually vandalized the theater, and the film had to be withdrawn from those theaters. In the film, near the conclusion, the soldier played by Beau Bridges could no longer take the terror spread on the subway riders and finally stood up to challenge them. A bloody fight ensued. At the end, the two bad guys were lying, bloody, on the floor of the subway as it pulled into the station. The train stopped and that familiar ticking of a subway car standing still was heard. The riders continued sitting for a long moment as if waking up from a nightmare, and one by one, finally got up and passed by the two men lying motionless on the floor. At that moment, Terry Knight's song came in, quietly and plaintively sung by Terry, with just a few piano chords as accompaniment.

> Is it over now?
> Is there no more to say?

Larry heard that song begin over the shell-shocked subway riders stepping carefully around the two bodies and started to scream, "That's terrible. You can't sing that . . . 'Is it over now?' It's laughable! Of course there's *no more to say*, they're dead, the picture's over."

The producer, Monroe Sachson, said, "We have to keep it in, Lar'. We have no choice."

Larry looked at me. "What do we do?"

I was low man on the totem pole. I had no say in getting that song out of the picture. I was happy to have the job. And it remained in.

To this day, when I'm with Larry, if the situation warrants, at a key moment I might sing, quietly, "Is it over now?" And it still elicits a scream from him—forty years later.

Years later, when we were dubbing the film *Two-Minute Warning* at Universal, which dealt with a lone shooter who terrorizes everyone in the Coliseum during a Super Bowl game, when it came to the end of the picture, as a gag, I had the music editor build the song from *The Incident*, "Is It Over Now?" over the end of the film. I waited with anticipation until the song came in, and sure enough, Larry roared when he heard it.

I'm so fortunate for the career and films and friendship and fun that I experienced with Larry Peerce over the years.

❧

Bob Crewe is one of the most successful producers and songwriters in the history of pop music and cowrote and produced all the Four Seasons hit records and had a successful record company and publishing company as well. A dear person and friend, Harriet Wasser, who did publicity for me at that time by getting my name into the trade papers when I had finished a project, was a good friend of Bob's as well. She arranged for me to meet Bob, hoping that it would spark a collaboration.

I met Bob Crewe at his office, and he was, and he is to this day, one of the most energetic and artistically talented people I've ever known. Today, and for the last ten years or so, he has turned his talents back to art, for which he was originally trained. I have several works of his in my house that I see and love and appreciate every day as I pass them. At that time, he was one of the leading record producers, and we talked about doing a project together. He knew of my background in classical, Latin, and jazz and said that he had long wanted to do a project that contained all those elements. He had a pianist that he wanted to work with and suggested that I meet with him and begin to develop an album concept that was based on the classics, but one that would combine all the elements of jazz, Latin, and pop music.

I spent some time with the pianist that he had in mind, and I told Bob that I really didn't think that he was up to the challenge that this album would demand, so Bob left it up to me to find the right artist. My friend Jack Michaels knew of a young pianist, who he said was great and that he could play in every musical style. I met with Ben Lanzarone, and we hit it off right away. He had a fine classical technique and was a great jazz player, and really, he could play anything, and coincidentally, Ben also graduated from the High School of Music & Art two years before me.

Bob Crewe was heavily into astrology at that time, and he was accustomed to speaking to his astrologer before he began a new business relationship or a major project. Ben and I each had to ask our mothers for the exact time of our birth, which Bob then reported back to his astrologer. The astrologer gave the collaboration the thumbs-up sign, and we three Scorpios began to work on the album.

My concept for the record was to take various themes that I chose from the classical literature and use them as a springboard to write new compositions based on the individual style of a particular composer, or perhaps, to develop or do variations of the actual classical theme, incorporating all the elements available to me in contemporary music. Ben and I worked to develop a pianistic style for him as soloist that would become an indelible part of this concept. It was a very good collaboration, and Bob and Ben and I became good friends, and remain so to this day.

I wrote ten new compositions and scored them for a symphonic orchestra with a rhythm section and, of course, featuring Ben at the piano. Once we got into the studio, Bob Crewe's experience and talent as a producer came into play, and it proved to be a great three-way collaboration. We were all very proud and excited with the album we made, and for me, it came at the perfect time.

Bob Crewe's label, Dynovoice, was distributed by Dot Records, which was owned by Paramount Pictures' parent company, Gulf and Western. Paramount had just finished a film called *Barbarella* starring Jane Fonda, which was a science fiction spoof very much in a campy, psychedelic, sixties style. There had been a score already written for the film, which Paramount dropped. They then asked Bob to get involved in the new score, which clearly needed to have a fun and futuristic approach to it, with a sixties musical sensibility. We had just finished the Ben Lanzarone album together, which led to great acclaim, if not great record sales, and soon after that, an album for the Bob Crewe Generation, and Bob knew that I had already scored a major film, *The Incident*. As a result, fortunately for me, I was presumably the natural person at that moment for him to bring in to work with on *Barbarella*. He and I would write the original songs, and I would score the film. Bob rented a house in Southampton for that summer, and as Joan and I were now living in Far Rockaway, I started a daily commute of two hours each way in order to work together with him on the songs. After a week or so of all that traveling and at Bob's invitation, Joan and I along with our two boys, Robbie and David, moved out to Southampton to stay in a guest house on the property, while Bob and I continued working on the songs. We wrote the main title song, "Barbarella," and four other songs that we would use in a scoring sense, over the action, as commentary on the film. After we finished work on the songs, Joan and I returned to Far Rockaway, and I began my work composing the score.

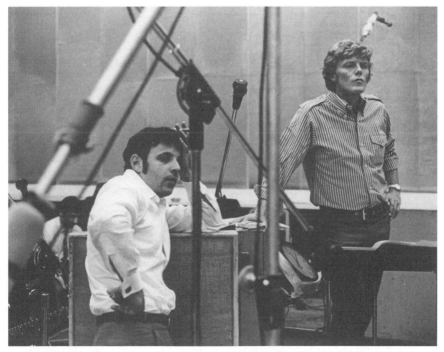

With Bob Crewe, recording the score of *Barbarella*. *Courtesy of the author.*

It was a dream project for me, and was an important enough picture for Paramount Pictures to send the head of the music department, Bill Stinson, to oversee the recording of the music. The producer, Dino De Laurentiis, and director Roger Vadim were there for the scoring of the film, which took about a week. No one at Paramount knew of the young composer that Bob Crewe had brought in to the project, so they sent Paul Haggar—who would grow into legendary status in postproduction at Paramount—to New York to work with me as my music editor. I had done many short films and even one feature up to this point, so I was comfortable with my role, but I had never worked with a music editor before, and I had no idea how he could help me.

Paul and I became fast friends. He explained to me that we could "spot" the film together with the director, Vadim, to determine all the places where the music would go, and then he would break down the film for me so that I would have all the action and dialogue on the screen notated down to a tenth of a second. That was the way it was always done in Hollywood and still is. I sheepishly responded that I'd already done all that. Composers in Hollywood just did not do their own spotting notes and breakdowns, but in New York there were no music editors that I knew of who did that for composers, so I learned to do it by myself, working with a moviola.

"What about click tracks and streamers?" he asked.

"What's that?" I replied.

I think he started to get worried now. He told me about the book by Carol Knudson, who had organized a table of beats that would synchronize music with film based on a specific tempo or click track. I had heard about this "fabled" book in Hollywood, but I never knew that it actually existed. However, I thought that I'd give it a try, and use a click track on the main title. At the recording session, I was truly amazed that it worked so well that, while I followed the click track tempo in my headset as I conducted, all the hit points in the film landed exactly as I intended. However, as I learned to write music that would synchronize to film without any aids, but rather by knowing the film so well and learning intuitively how to make the music breathe as the film moved, I have mostly worked without clicks all these years. That leaves me free as a conductor to move a tempo faster or slow it down as I watch the film in front of me, while I'm conducting. I generally put timings on my score every measure or two and indications of what's on the screen at that moment, and that way I always know exactly where I am in relation to the film. Now, with *Barbarella*, I learned about click tracks, and though I have used them a lot over the years as well, for the most part, I still like to work directly to the film without being locked into clicks.

Vadim and De Laurentiis loved the score that Bob and I wrote and thought it captured the sci-fi camp aspect and still brought the dramatic action to life for the big screen. For me in particular it was the right film at the right time, because I had been up for director Larry Peerce's next film after *The Incident*, entitled *Goodbye, Columbus*, and that was a Paramount picture as well, and the head of the music department was in New York to attend the recording sessions.

After the score and dubbing were finished, I had the not unpleasant task of going to Paris to meet with Vadim and his wife and star of the film, Jane Fonda, to teach her the song "Barbarella." She had to learn the song so that she could hum along with it, on a voice-over, as the opening credits were run over the footage of her shedding her space clothes and getting ready to sleep for a long intergalactic voyage. Jane and Vadim lived in a lovely farmhouse outside of Paris, and they sent a car to bring me out to their house. Jane was pregnant with her daughter Vanessa and was very welcoming to me to their home. Bob Crewe and I were supposed to come back that summer to St. Tropez to work with Jane on writing and producing an album for her, but ultimately she decided not to make a record.

Vadim and I drove to a neighboring farm where there was a piano. He had a red Ferrari and drove like the wind. That short and fast ride through the French countryside probably planted the seeds for my getting a red Ferrari many years later.

Not long after my return to New York, I was in the city one day and called Joan from a public phone booth on the street. "Call Stanley Jaffe right away," she said. Stanley was the producer of *Goodbye, Columbus*. So with my heart beating very quickly I called Stanley immediately. "How'd you like to come to Hollywood to score *Goodbye, Columbus*?" he asked. I was standing in a phone booth on the street in New York City, and for the first time, I saw my life coming together as a composer. I can still hear those words and Stanley's voice in my ear many years later. "Wow, of course I would!" I echoed back immediately, and my life changed again with that phone call.

Hollywood, 1968–Present

$\mathscr{P}$aramount sent a limo to meet us in Los Angeles when I arrived with Joan and our two sons, Robbie and David (our daughter, Lisa, wasn't born until two years later). I was expecting to be in Los Angeles for two months working on the film, so we flew out together as a family and settled into a very lovely apartment on a high floor, on La Cienega Boulevard just off Sunset, over-looking the city. What a way to be greeted in Los Angeles. Our first ride in a limousine, passing palm trees and swimming pools in the middle of winter, and this is where they made films. It was exciting and exhilarating being in Hollywood and working on my third major film at the age of twenty-eight. I sometimes think that when one is struggling in his life, if someone would come along to say that all will be fine in a matter of time, you could relax a bit and not be so fearful of the future. But since no one has those powers or could know that in advance, what episode in a career will lead to another, it causes you to work harder, prepare more, and therefore possibly help to guide the course of future events more in your favor. I always felt that people whose gifts came more easily than mine could have more predictability and more balance in their everyday lives. I always believed that my main resource was that I was willing to work longer and harder than might be necessary. Staying up through the night, sometimes several nights in a row, became part of my regular work hours.

Sometimes I would make a month's worth of corrections on a simple harmony exercise by taping layers of corrections one on top of the other, so that I could refer back to earlier attempts by just lifting up each newer version. I remember one time when it was already evening and dark outside. There was no more than a single light near the piano pointing to the music that at that moment highlighted the center of my universe. Mademoiselle looked at the newest correction to this simple harmony exercise and paused as if lost in thought for a moment, and finally looked up and said to me, "People might think it foolish to spend all this time on the smallest detail, which goes by in a second, but we alone know how important and meaningful that detail is to our work."

One day, while I was working at the piano in my basement studio, in our first house in Cedarhurst, Long Island, a workman came downstairs to check on the water heater, and he saw me at the piano. When he was finished with his work, he went back upstairs and asked Joan, "Is that what your husband does for a living?"

She answered that it was.

"He's a lucky guy to be able to earn a living at the piano," he said.

She answered matter-of-factly, "You might not think so if you knew that he's been there for two days and hasn't slept yet."

I don't recall if I ever said I wasn't able to do a project even with an impossible deadline, and similarly, I don't recall not finding a way to be available if someone wanted to meet with me, regardless of the hour or inconvenience. I was always willing to make it work, somehow. "No" was simply not part of my vocabulary. But now, suddenly, the years of struggle didn't seem so long, and I felt that from here on I could really begin to fulfill the dream of a composing career.

The next day, in a car that the studio rented for me, I drove down Melrose Avenue for the first time. When I got to the corner of Gower and the Paramount Pictures lot, I was greeted with a huge billboard of *Barbarella* that had my name on it. I was directed by the guard at the main gate to the music building, where there would be a parking space for me with my name printed on it. As I pulled up in front of the music building, I stopped and noticed that my space was between those of Neal Hefti on one side and Henry Mancini on the other. I couldn't believe that I was parking next to Henry Mancini. There were the only three parking spaces with composers' names printed on them, and one of them was mine.

I was greeted by my friends from Paramount who had come to New York to work with me on *Barbarella*, Bill Stinson and Paul Haggar, who was going to be my music editor on this film as well. I was then introduced to John Hamell, who would supervise the recording, and Phil Kagen, the orchestra contractor, who was an older man, and who had contracted for Stravinsky and Stokowski and many others at the Hollywood Bowl. After a brief chat, I sat down with John Hamell and Phil Kagen to discuss the orchestra that I'd need for the score. As I didn't know any of the Los Angeles musicians, Phil started to recommend specific musicians after I described what kind of players I wanted for each chair.

"How about Shelly Manne on drums?" he suggested.

"Shelly Manne, could I really get Shelly Manne to play for me?"

"Of course," he said. "How about Conte Condoli on lead trumpet, Bud Shank on woodwinds, Pete Jolly on piano."

I was in musical heaven. I had practically worn out a record that I had of Pete Jolly with his jazz quintet, and to think of Shelly Manne and Bud Shank playing for me was beyond belief.

"How many trumpets? How many woodwinds?" Phil asked.

"Perhaps two trumpets and two woodwinds." I didn't need a large orchestra, as I knew the score would have a contemporary "pop" edge to it, to accompany this romantic comedy of a mismatched duo based on the novella by Philip Roth. The movie, like the book, was set in Westchester, NY, and the Catskill Mountains, and the world of a nouveau riche Jewish family and a young, cynical Jewish boy, totally alienated from that world. This was a world I felt I knew and understood, and I felt very confident about what the film needed musically, other than the songs that the very popular singing group the Association were writing and going to record.

Phil continued. "How many violins?"

"Perhaps ten or twelve," I answered.

"Violas?"

"Two or three."

"Celli?"

"Two."

When it was all said and done, there was a thirty-five-piece orchestra, which is what I had told Stanley Jaffe that I'd need when we were in New York. At one point during our discussion of the orchestra, John Hamell got up and walked over to a window and looked out onto the street in front of the music building. When he was out of earshot, Phil leaned in close to me and said quietly, "Charlie, you have a little, stinky orchestra here."

"Really?" I said.

"Yes, this is Hollywood. You're not going to make a good impression."

"Really?" I repeated.

"Yes. This is Hollywood," he repeated in a kind but affirmative voice. "You could have twenty violins, ten violas, and ten celli. Why do you want a stinky little orchestra?"

A moment later, John Hamell came back to where we were sitting and joined us again. I made a quick decision to take Phil's advice. I hadn't come all this way to be laughed out of Hollywood. "John, I've been thinking about the number of strings, and I think that I could use some more."

"No problem," John echoed back.

"How about . . ." long pause ". . . twenty violins?"

Short pause. . . . "That's fine."

"And . . ." long pause. "Ten violas and ten celli?"

Short pause. . . . "That's fine," he said.

I was feeling very excited to have such a large orchestra to work with, and I was relieved not to be looking foolish on my first Hollywood film. After finishing with the orchestra call, John suggested that we all go for lunch to the commissary across the street from the music building, where there was a specific table at which composers who were working on the lot sat together.

A few minutes later we were sitting at a table in the commissary, and shortly afterward, in walked Henry Mancini. John waved him over to join us at the table and introduced me to him. Henry Mancini, one of the greatest (and nicest) composers to ever work in film, sitting next to me as a colleague. I remembered back to one night in Forest Hills when Joan and I were relaxing in bed and reading a story in *Life* magazine about Henry Mancini and his great success. We both wondered if it was even possible to dream that high, and here I was having lunch with him on my first day in Hollywood. During lunch, Henry asked me at some point if I was in the Motion Picture Academy. I said that I was not.

"We could use some new blood in the academy. How many films have you done?" he asked.

"This will be my third film."

"Perfect, he said, "you have to have three major films to be considered for membership. You can't apply. You have to be invited and have two members sign a card to request your being invited in, and then it has to be approved by the executive committee of the Music Branch. I'll sign for you. Do you know anyone else in the Academy who will sign?"

I didn't know anyone in the Motion Picture Academy. "Nobody," I answered.

"Okay. I'll ask Elmer to sign for you as well."

I thought to myself, "Elmer Bernstein and Henry Mancini inviting me to join the Motion Picture Academy! This is a day I'll never forget." And as you can see, I never have.

Months later, after I finished my work on *Goodbye, Columbus* and was back in New York, I got a very nice note from Henry saying that my application had been turned down by the board, but only because *Goodbye, Columbus* had not yet been released, and by the next board meeting, I would certainly be approved. After that next meeting, I received a formal letter from the Motion Picture Academy that the board had voted to invite me to membership.

(Within a few years, I would be invited to be a member of that executive committee of the music branch, and since that time I have served on that committee almost continuously for more than thirty years, the last three as a governor of the Academy.)

Later that same day, the first and most memorable on the Paramount lot, I was back in my apartment and told Joan of all that had happened. "I can't believe I have a sixty-piece orchestra to score the film." I'd never had that large an orchestra, and I wasn't sure that I even wanted that big a string section for this intimate film with a pop style score, but I was excited nonetheless.

The next morning, at 9:00 AM I received an angry phone call from Stanley Jaffe. "Charlie, did you go fucking crazy here in Hollywood? You better come in to my office to see me right away."

I got dressed and rushed in to the studio and sat in front of Stanley's desk. "In New York you said you needed a thirty- to thirty-five-piece orchestra. I counted the number of musicians you put out a call for. You have a sixty-piece orchestra. That's twice my budget. Do you really need twenty violins?"

Short pause. . . . "No, not really. Ten to twelve will do."

"And how about ten violas and ten cellos? Is that necessary?"

Very short pause. . . . "No. Two violas and two cellos will do fine."

In an instant, I was back to a thirty-five-piece orchestra, which was all I really needed in the first place. That was the one and only time I let myself be intimidated about the number of musicians that I felt I needed to do a film properly.

The following day, I was asked to attend a meeting with Stanley Jaffe and Larry Peerce in Bob Evans's office. Bob was the head of Paramount Pictures. For this meeting, I dressed with a suit and tie, which I certainly would have worn to an important meeting in New York, and I assumed that it would be appropriate when meeting the head of the studio in Los Angeles as well. As I entered his office, Bob was leaning way back in his chair with his hands clasped behind him supporting the back of his head, and with his feet up on his desk. When I saw him, I realized that Hollywood was a little more casual than New York, and I quickly got the message, as he was wearing short pants and thongs on his bare feet. That was the one and only time that I ever put on suit and tie for a meeting in Hollywood.

Because of Mademoiselle's formality, her male students had to wear a jacket and tie when coming to her house for a lesson. A man without a tie was naked as far as she was concerned. Leonard Bernstein once came to her house, she told me, without a jacket and tie, and put his arm around her shoulder saying, "Chère Nadia." She was offended by that greeting, but still, he was Leonard Bernstein, so she accepted his casualness.

I always wore a suit and tie in Paris because I never knew if I would see her unexpectedly even on a day that I didn't have a lesson scheduled.

I had a great time working on the film and recording the music at the fabled Goldwyn Studios in Hollywood. Everything went as well as I could have hoped for. Shelly Manne, Bud Shank, and Pete Jolly were wonderful to work with, and they all became friends of mine and played for me many times over the years, as did many of the other musicians. Stanley Jaffe gave me full screen credit when my contract called for only half a screen, as appreciation for my contribution to the film, and gave me a gift of our first color television as well.

Goodbye, Columbus was a big hit film and established the acting careers of Ali MacGraw and Richard Benjamin. Larry Peerce, after this, his third film, became one of the top directors in Hollywood, and Stanley Jaffe soon afterward was appointed the president of Paramount Pictures. As for me, I always remember it sweetly as the film that brought me to Hollywood, and of course, it didn't hurt my career either.

Aside from the horrendous amount of rain that pummeled Los Angeles continually for those two months in 1968, my introduction to California was a joyous one. Bill Stinson congratulated me for my work on the film and said that before I went back to New York, Paramount had a pilot for a new TV series that he thought I'd be perfect for, and he wanted me to meet the producers of the show and Doug Cramer, the president of Paramount TV, and Tom Miller, the VP, who would be directly in charge of the production. *Love, American Style* was going to be a new concept for prime-time TV. A comedy anthology series that would have three separate stories, each independent of the other, and with separate casts. In addition, there would be comedy blackouts in between the stories. The only connecting link between the stories physically was a bed, an ornate-looking brass bed (which was actually made of iron, because it took a lot of abuse, sometimes being pushed down a street on wheels, sometimes floating in water) that was designed for the show. That bed would come to be known and sold commercially in stores as the *Love, American Style* bed. The original producers who created the show, Arnold Margolin and Jim Parker, stayed with the show for the first three years, and then the producers changed from year to year, as the directors and actors and screen writers changed from week to week. The only other connective link for the entire run that the show had on prime-time television was me. For five years, I scored all the episodes that were scored for the show, usually eleven out of the twenty-two that were filmed each year. For the shows that I didn't score, my music editor, Bob Kreuger, tracked those shows with music that I had already composed and recorded for other episodes. That's a common practice on TV series.

I wrote several songs for the pilot episode, including the theme song, with one of the producers and creators of the show, Arnold Margolin, who wrote all the lyrics. For the pilot, I gave the show a musical identity that had a contemporary record sound and style in the approach to scoring that was somewhat different from the more traditional scoring style that was predominant on television at the time, and I received a lot of encouragement from the producers and Paramount that I was on the right track.

I finished my work on the show and was back in New York with my family when I learned that the pilot had sold, and that the producers and Paramount wanted me to come back in the summer to begin work on the series. The producer of the show, Bill D'Angelo, was quoted in the *New York Daily News* at that time, saying, "The concept of the hour is designed for a youth-oriented audience. Our young people are interested in style and flair. With Charles Fox's music, the show will have a hip, contemporary sound."

We offered the main title song to a very popular young group at that time, the Cowsills, who were riding high on the charts with their record *Hair*. They were going to record "Love, American Style" as the theme song for the show, and it was going to be their next single record as well. I flew from California to Saratoga Springs, New York, where they were performing in concert, one blizzard-filled night, to meet with them and go over the recording and the show's needs. They came to California for the actual recording sessions. For the next entire year, I was commuting back and forth between NY and LA, doing an episode or two and flying back home to be with my family while the next episodes were being shot and edited. My second son, David, was three years old and didn't understand why I wasn't home all the time. He was confused about what California was as he knew only that it took his daddy away from him. He would hang onto my leg when the time came for me to leave again. It was always difficult saying good-bye each time that I had to return to LA to work, and I was so happy getting on the plane, when I had finished my work, to come home. We had just bought our first house in Cedarhurst, Long Island, one year earlier, and Joan and I felt so lucky to have such a big, beautiful house after all we had been through. But it was clear that it was more important to keep us all together. After that first year with the show, my agent, Marc Newman, informed me that Paramount didn't have any other composers that they flew back and forth to New York every few weeks and had to pay a per diem as well. I would have to decide to move to California if I wanted to continue with the show for the next year. It wasn't a hard decision to make at all. I was already committed to working on a musical film at Universal called *Pufnstuf*, a children's film based on the successful Saturday afternoon series produced by Sid and Marty Krofft, which I would write all the songs for, and I would score the film as well when it was finished. And of course I wanted to continue with *Love, American Style*. That was my show.

As well as everything was going to that point, I did have some difficulties with the man who was head of television music for Paramount at that time, Leith Stevens. That was part of my learning experiences in Hollywood.

In all my recording experience, I was used to getting off the podium and going over to the instrumentalists individually to confer with them about their parts on a one-to-one basis. One would not normally think of a conductor as being shy about talking to a whole orchestra at once, but I guess that I might have been at that point in my life. There was a microphone on the podium where I could press a button and be heard loud and clear by all the musicians, but I was accustomed, especially with the musicians in the rhythm section, to have a more personal contact with them. Leith Stevens used to set a stop watch every time that I left the podium to have a brief discussion with a musician regarding his part.

That recording stage on the Paramount lot, where I recorded most of the television work, was on the Desilu side of the lot, which was originally owned by Lucille Ball and Desi Arnaz. Indeed, I'd walk past Lucille Ball often as she would get out of her chauffeur-driven car and go into her office, as her office was just down the street from the *Love, American Style* bungalow where I had an office as well.

At the end of each recording session, Leith would give me a tally of how many minutes I spent (ergo, wasted) during the session. Leith was a fine composer who had done many films in Hollywood, and he always seemed friendly toward me, but for a while it seemed to me that he was out to "break me," or at least, make my days more difficult. I don't remember Leith complimenting me on my music as much as I remember him, at the end of each session, giving me the break-downs of all the time that he felt that I wasted because of all the time that I spent off the podium.

One day, my agent, Marc Newman, told me that he had spoken with Leith, who said that he was very fond of me and thought of me in a fatherly way, and that he felt that I could have a good career in Hollywood, but that he was pushing me very hard to learn the system so that I didn't fall on my face and get into budgetary problems with recording, which would hurt my career. I was very glad to get this feedback, as it now made sense to me why Leith seemed to be always on my back. But still, I did not look forward to those recording experiences with him.

Recording new music was always an exciting time for me, as everything that I had heard in my head was now being played by wonderful musicians, and I could see it working with the film as I had conceived. I had a very difficult time initially in getting used to the recording schedules that were necessary to get everything accomplished and recorded during the scheduled hours of recording. It was usually budgeted to record five minutes of music an hour. According to the Musician Union rules, you had the right to keep a musician only one hour beyond his initial call, and after that he was free to leave if he had another session, or if he was able to continue, the overtime became extremely costly. Either way, there was always tremendous pressure to record all the music that was necessary for the film.

Composing a certain amount of music each week also presented a similar problem, in that everything that the film needed or demanded had to be accomplished on a weekly basis. On paper it seemed reasonable enough. If you had thirty minutes of music to compose, and five or six days to accomplish that, you had only to do the math and figure out that you had to compose five or six minutes each day. Each musical cue could be just a few seconds long, or several minutes long, depending on its role in the film. Each musical start, no matter how short, had to be conceptualized as to its purpose and importance in the film. No matter how well I planned my work schedule, and no matter how many hours a day I worked, it always came down to having no sleep at all the night before a recording session. There were times that it was already 3:00 AM, and even though I was practically falling asleep at the piano, I had yet to write several minutes of music that would be recorded that day. I've always loved my work, but there were times that I was just fighting to stay awake. Indeed, there were times that I'd wake up with my face literally on the piano. After that brief nap, I was awake again and could again enjoy the discovery in composing. Later that morning, with my writing finished and in the copyists hands, I would begin recording with the orchestra, and was ultimately energized by the recording process. But there were even times every so often when I would have a night without sleep, a full day of recording, and then have another night without sleep in front of me. That was a killer. I don't know how I got through those days.

And yet there were other times that I would finish my work for the day, and then turn my attention to songwriting. As soon as I started to work on a song, I was refreshed again, and hours passed unnoticed. This schedule went on for weeks and months at a time.

❧

When the Emmy nominations were announced that year, I was totally unaware of that aspect of the business, and it never occurred to me that it was even a possibility for me to receive a nomination, so I didn't even bother checking the newspapers when the announcements were made. It wasn't until I received telegrams of congratulations from Paramount, the TV Academy, and ABC Television that I learned that I was nominated for *Love, American Style*. One day, years later, I was having lunch with Martin Starger, who had been the president of ABC TV at that time, and who was the one who sent me a letter of congratulations. He, of course, didn't remember that particular letter as he had sent many like that each year, but I could finally thank him personally for something that was so significant for me at that time.

In 1970, the Emmy Awards were not yet broadcast on television but were presented simultaneously at ballroom dinners in Hollywood and in New York. I was back in New York for the show, and I invited several of our good friends to join Joan and me at a table that I took for the event. My friends and Joan and I had a great time that night, and as I had no thought of winning, I wasn't nervous in the least. It was just a great and fun party, and I felt very exhilarated and honored simply to be there. When the nominations for best theme song were read, our friends and I were all so busy talking and laughing that no one paid any attention to the fact that this was my category. When the presenter announced my name and Arnold Margolin's—who was in Los Angeles—as the winners, it took a few moments for it to sink in. Somebody at my table finally said, "Wait a minute, didn't they just announce your name?"

I thought I might have heard my name slowly registering in my ear. "Really?" I said. Again, from the stage, it was announced, and this time I heard it. I had won the Emmy Award in the first year of my first series. Our table was way in the back of the ballroom, and by the time I made my way up to the stage, even though I was hurrying, the presenters assumed that the winners were in Los Angeles, and they were moving on to the next category. At that point, I appeared at the side of the stage, and the presenter of the award noticed me standing in the wings, looking, I suppose, very awkward. "Are you Charles Fox?" she asked. I nodded yes, and walked up to receive my statuette.

"On behalf of Arnold Margolin, who is in Hollywood, and myself," I thanked the academy and left the stage. It was the kind of acceptance speech that producers like. "Thank you" and off. I was in a daze, suddenly being rushed into a publicity photo area with flashbulbs popping in my face. I was nominated each year for the next four years in the category of Best Score, and in the fifth, and final year of the show, I was fortunate enough to receive the Emmy for that as well.

Sometime during the first year that I was working on *Love, American Style* and commuting back and forth between LA and New York, I was hired to compose the music for a short film starring Marcel Marceau. It was a film about thirty minutes in length in which Marcel played all the characters on board a ship, including the captain, the steward, all the musicians and crew, and featuring his familiar character Bip, who wanders aboard a ship one night that is docked in the New York harbor in pursuit of a beautiful, haunting woman who is a figment of his imagination and who turns out to be only a dream. It was a very challenging assignment to create the score completely electronically with my new Moog synthesizer, including emulating the music that Marcel's various characters were miming with their imaginary instruments, as they were portraying the ship's orchestra.

I began work in New York shortly before moving to California and completed it at the house that we were renting in Beverly Hills on Cove Way when we first arrived. Marcel came to Los Angeles to work with me and lend his support if not his input. I met him at the airport and brought him back to our house. Before dinner that evening, Joan had a fleeting thought of miming serving dinner, but good sense and hunger prevailed over a laugh. Marcel was a charming man, as nice as he was brilliant in his work, and the film, *First Class*, had a brief but successful run in film festivals, winning several honors.

A little-known fact in films is that at the time we did *Barbarella*, Marcel was a character in that film, and he uttered the only words—actually, word—that he ever spoke in a film, to my knowledge. His one spoken word on the screen was "No!" A second tidbit in film history is that the rock group Duran Duran took their name from a character in *Barbarella*.

Working on that "first class" film established, for me, that the use of synthesizers in a musical way in film was indeed possible. To that point in time, it was used mainly for musical effects or sound effects in sci-fi pictures. Throughout the years that I've worked in film and television and records, and in my several electronic studios that I've had in my house, each one more elaborate than the previous one, sounds produced electronically became part of the orchestral colors that I used in my music, especially in film.

❧

During my first year in Los Angeles, while I was working on *Love, American Style*, my agent, Marc Newman, wanted me to meet his brother Lionel Newman, who was head of the music department at 20th Century Fox and a member of the Newman dynasty in Hollywood. Their brother was the great composer Alfred Newman, whom I met just once several years later in the commissary at Universal while he was working on *Airport* and I was working on *The Other Side of the Mountain*, shortly before he died. Marc thought that the best way to meet his brother was by doing a project at Fox and asked me if I would do a single episode of the Fox series *Nanny and the Professor*. I scored one episode of that series, and Lionel became a friend and champion of mine at that studio, and over the years I did a number of films for Fox. Over the course of my whole career in Hollywood, that was the only time I ever did an episode of a series that I did not write the theme for and start from the show's inception. However, Marc was right, doing it was a good introduction to Lionel and 20th Century Fox.

One of the first films I did at Fox was *The Laughing Policeman* starring Walter Matthau as a detective investigating a multiple homicide. It was directed by Stuart Rosenberg. Walter Matthau was mostly known for his brilliant comedic roles, but he was superb in the stark, dramatic film.

When Stuart was doing preparation for the film, which was shot in San Francisco, he spent days riding in a squad car in which the detective that he rode along with had his car radio set to a station that only played forties-era big band music. So when it came to score our film, that was a stylistic point of reference that he wanted to continue for the Matthau's character.

Audiences watching a film would not be expected to know how the choice of what to play as background music coming from a radio or stereo, or TV or elevator speaker, known as "source music" in films, affects the audience's perception of the characters on the screen. Much thought and discussion between the director and composer goes into those choices, as source music that's used also has an effect on the overall film but in a more subliminal way.

I am very aware of the music that comes from various sources as I go about my normal day, or when I'm traveling. It sometimes amuses me that when I'm in an airport lounge or elevator, I sometimes hear music coming from a "source" that I recognize as being wrong for the scene. But since this is not a scene in a film, but real life, it's hard to argue with that. Still, my instincts dictate to me what kind of music I should be hearing.

❦

After completing my first year of *Love, American Style*, I began to work immediately on the musical film *Pufnstuf*, based on the successful TV series of that name, and produced by the brothers Sid and Marty Krofft. I was set to write the musical score after the film was shot and edited, and in addition, I was hired to write all the songs, which would be recorded first, and then filmed with the actors lip-syncing as is normally done in musicals. As the speaking lines for many of the actors on screen, including the Pufnstuf character, as well as the other sweet but strange-looking characters whose costumes were inhabited mostly by little people, were dubbed in after shooting ended, I used studio singers to represent each character's singing voice in the film and for the chorus work. An original, live-action musical was a dream assignment. Harry Garfield, the head of music at Universal, welcomed me warmly to the Universal lot and told me that he'd have as much work for me there as I wanted, and to consider Universal my home. I already felt that way about Paramount, so Hollywood was already turning out to be a dream come true.

I didn't have a lyricist set to work with, and the choice was mine to make. When I was in New York during this period, I was visiting my friend, the head of BMI in New York, Ron Anton, at his office. I told him about this project that I was about to do and asked him if there was someone that he would recommend to work with me and write the lyrics. "Do you know Norman Gimbel's work?" he asked. Of course I knew his work. Lyricist to some of the most beautiful songs from the bossa nova era. Jobim's "Girl from Ipanema," "Summer Samba," and "How Insensitive," as well as "I Will Wait for You" and "Watch What Happens," with music by Michel Legrand from the film *The Umbrellas of Cherbourg*. And he had done two Broadway shows as well. Ron said, "Let me get him on the phone. I think you guys might hit it off and be great together."

So it started, my long-term collaboration with Norman Gimbel. We spoke on the phone that day from Ron's office and made a plan to get together when I was back in Los Angeles.

Norman and I had a good collaboration right off the bat. He was a New Yorker who had moved to California a few years earlier than I, also to work in film. He had a beautiful wife and two children around the same ages as my two older children, and it was a start of a long friendship and successful writing collaboration. We would discuss the character and dramatic content of each song in the film, and what we needed to get across. He would normally call me with a lyric or a start of a lyric, perhaps one verse and chorus, or we would meet and to go over a lyric he had written, then I would get to work on setting the lyric with the proper musical tone for the characters in the film. After that, we'd get together around a piano and go over our joint work and make the adjustments we needed to the lyric or melody. It was a procedure that both of us were comfortable with. It has remained my preferred way of writing songs, writing the music after the lyricist and I discuss the motivation and context for the song, and then I work to an already, at least partially, written lyric, which gives me everything I need to know about the character to begin to craft a proper musical setting and compose the melody. I had a very nice office with a good piano on the lot at Universal, and when we were ready to present a song to the producers, we'd all meet in my office while I played and sang the song. Sid and Marty Krofft seemed to love everything that we wrote, and the whole project was going as smoothly as possible.

The songs came easily for Norman and me, and *Pufnstuf*, the musical, started to develop. We wrote songs for Jack Wild, the young star who was probably fourteen or fifteen years old, who played one of the only roles not in a fluffy, magical, animal costume. The other costumed roles required the acting voices to be looped, after the film was shot and edited. The other "live" performances were those of Martha Raye and Cass Elliot, both of whom played witches. We wrote solo numbers for each of them. Then there were a few production numbers with the whole ensemble of cast members. I met Cass Elliot for the first time only the day that she came onto the recording stage on the Universal lot to sing the song we had written for her called "Different," which laments being a witch and not being like everyone else: "Different is hard, different is lonely." I had listened to Cass's records to study her voice, and then we wrote a song for her in a comfortable key and range, and recorded the track with an orchestra even before hearing her sing the song. When she heard the prerecorded track, which she already had a copy of in order to learn the song before coming into the studio, she remarked to me that the song "fit her like a Hong Kong suit." And she sounded wonderful singing it. Many years later, in 2005, when a compilation of Cass Elliot's recordings was being released on a special CD, I was asked by her daughter and friends to lend my help to try to secure the rights for that song to be included on her CD. I was told that even though it was never released as a single record, Cass's fans have made that song an underground favorite all these years, and there was great interest in that record being available to buy. I enlisted Marty Krofft's help, and that song, "Different," is now on her greatest hits CD.

After completing *Pufnstuf*, I continued working with the Kroffts by scoring their next series, *The Bugaloos*, for which Norman and I also wrote the theme song. The show featured a rock and roll band dressed like bugs that flew. There was no end to the imagination that flowed from the Krofft brothers. They also had a factory that made all their costumes and sets that they designed. It was quite an operation, and Sid and Marty became good friends of mine and were always great to work with. It was an extremely busy time for me as I was scoring that show on a weekly basis, and *Love, American Style* as well. At the same time, Norman and I continued writing songs together for the pop record market, and a true collaboration was emerging. Even while I was busy scoring films and television series, we continued writing songs together and continued growing as a songwriting team. We decided that we would try to find a singer that we could write for specifically, as Bacharach and David had done so successfully in their brilliant collaboration with Dionne Warwick. We felt that if we found an artist with a voice that inspired us to write songs specifically for it, we could work with that artist and develop a sound and style by producing the artist's records. That would give us the outlet for our material and the control to make the kind of records that we wanted.

We went to clubs regularly to listen to new singers, and we met many times in my house with singers who were recommended to us or that we discovered at a club or concert. We had a certain vision of the kind of records that we wanted to make that would have an honest and folk-like quality yet would appeal to a large audience, and we had not yet found that voice. We loved the intricacies of Joni Mitchell's music and lyrics, and the earthy quality of James Taylor and other troubadour-like guitar playing, "honest" sounding artists. It took a long while, many months, before we found the singer whose voice inspired us to create a style and world of music around her sound.

Lori Lieberman was only eighteen years old and had lived in Switzerland most of her life although she was American and born in Los Angeles. She was recommended to us, and when she came to my house and we recorded her singing, Norman and I looked at each other, and we both knew instantly that we had found our voice with Lori. She had a very beautiful, rich alto voice that was perfect and inspiring for the kind of songs we wanted to write. Everything she sang sounded haunting, and considering her young age, she had a knowing quality to her interpretations, and we all felt that we were on the same track as far as style of records that we wanted to make. Lori was also a sweet and lovely person, and the collaboration of singer and songwriters came very naturally and easily, and we all became good friends. We worked with her for several months at my house in Encino, writing songs and developing a style that she could be comfortable singing, all the while making demos with the professional equipment that I had in my studio at home. My friend Dan Davis, who worked at Capitol Records, set up a meeting for us to meet with Maury Lathower, who was head of A & R at that label. He loved Lori's voice, as did everyone at Capitol, and we signed a deal with them to record a number of albums over a period of four years.

We spent the next several months writing and recording, using a basic rhythm section with some of my musician friends, who were among the top players in Los Angeles: John Guerin on drums, Max Bennett on bass, and Dennis Budimer on guitar. I played the piano, and we overdubbed strings, instrumental solos, and chorus parts after Lori's vocals were complete. We were very excited by the records we were making, and we felt that we were accomplishing what we set out to do. Lori sounded so wonderful and rich, and the songs were introspective and probing and unpredictable in form. I did all the arrangements, and that too became part of the overall sound. When we had nine songs finished for the album, and still needed one more

Norman, Lori, and Charles. *Courtesy of the author.*

to complete it, we received a phone call from Capitol that they were anxious to release the record, and could we finish it as soon as possible? We needed a tenth song quickly. Norman had a sketch book consisting of possible song titles and ideas for songs that he had collected. I was sitting at the piano and Norman was looking through his sketch book for ideas for the last song for the album.

"What about a title, 'Killing Me Softly with His Blues'?"

We all liked the "Killing Me Softly" part, but not the "with His Blues" reference. We felt that "blues" sounded like an old-fashioned image, even then, in the early seventies. Norman thought for a moment and said, "What about 'Killing Me Softly with His Song'?" That had a very interesting connotation right off the bat, and we agreed that that would be a good starting point.

That very night, Norman called me with a newly completed lyric, and by the next morning I called him back to sing it to him over the phone. We met again that next day with Lori, who loved it immediately, and that day we made a demo in my house. Lori sounded so beautiful, and the song had such an interesting idea and rich sound, that we thought we had our first single. Everyone at Capitol agreed when they heard it as well.

For some unexplainable reason, when we went to United Western Studios on Sunset Blvd. to record with our band the next day, we just could not capture that same sound of Lori's that we thought was so magical in my house. So we decided to have the studio send their equipment to my house and record her vocal there. My house did not have a vocal booth to ensure having a clean vocal track, and was not soundproofed for a professional "live" recording, although I did a lot of electronic recordings with my Moog synthesizer, so we set up the vocal mike for Lori to sing in the hallway, just outside my room. That way, all the mechanical noise of the tape machines would not be picked up on Lori's vocal microphone. Lori sang so comfortably and beautifully in my house that actually, on that song, the final vocal that we used for the record was indeed that performance she recorded in my house that day.

As it turned out, unfortunately, the day we recorded Lori singing "Killing Me Softly" was Mother's Day, and I had to ask Joan if she would take our kids out for the day so we wouldn't have any extra noise to interfere with the recording. The music business sometimes makes many unfair demands on a family and relationships. That day was certainly one of them. But Joan knew what we were up against, having to finish the record for a particular release date. I couldn't say she was happy about it, but she was certainly understanding. We did finish our album that day, and "Killing Me Softly" was the record that we all agreed, Capitol included, would be our first single.

As much as Capitol loved the album and as much as we pushed them to promote it fully, it received only a moderate amount of promotion because Lori was a new artist, and as a result, it never achieved the success we all believed it had merited. However, Lori's career had begun, and she instantly developed a fan base in the United States and in a number of countries in Europe. We eventually made four albums with Lori, including a greatest hits album even though we had no bona fide hits. Lori performed in the top clubs around the country and in many countries in Europe, notably in Belgium, Holland, and France, and appeared on many TV shows here and abroad as well. She had a loyal fan base wherever she performed. I sometimes played the piano for her or conducted the orchestra behind her. I still have a very special place for her in my heart.

But it was left to Roberta Flack, who heard Lori's album on an airplane, to discover our songs and record her version of "Killing Me Softly," which became a number one hit in just about every country in the world, while establishing a style on her record that has been copied by many hundreds of artists in every country, and in every language since that time.

Roberta was flying on American Airlines one fateful day for us. Among the promotional aspects that Capitol Records had accomplished was to get Lori's record to be the featured album on American Airlines' "Theater in the Sky" during the month that Roberta heard it in the air, while she was flying. In the days before Walkmans and iPods, people wanting to hear music while flying actually listened to the preprogrammed material that the airlines provided. At thirty-five thousand feet, Roberta was a prisoner of our music, and fortunately, she heard Lori's album that day. When she landed, she tried to get in touch with me and was able to get my phone number from Quincy Jones. She reached me at Paramount Pictures, and as I was walking through the music library one particular day, someone handed me a telephone and said, "Here, this is for you." I reached for the phone and on the other end of the line the voice said, "Hi, this is Roberta Flack, and we haven't met, but I'm going to sing your songs."

Roberta had just won the Grammy Award the previous year for her beautiful record of "First Time Ever I Saw Your Face." It was remarkable just to get a phone call from her. That phone call rates in my memory bank as equal to the one I received from Stanley Jaffe to invite me to Hollywood to score *Goodbye, Columbus*. There are certain conversations that took place many years ago that I can replay in my mind and hear as though they're recorded on a CD. It's easy to understand why. That song established me as a songwriter separate and apart from being a composer of motion pictures.

Norman and I met with Roberta Flack in Quincy Jones's office at A&M Records. We talked about writing songs for her in addition to the songs on Lori's album that she wanted to record, including "And the Feeling's Good." We would eventually have a number of cover records of that song as well, including those of José Feliciano and Sarah Vaughan, whose recording session I attended. Roberta did release her beautiful version of it as well on a future album.

After that initial meeting, we did not hear from her for a long time, but one day I picked up the *LA Times* and read a review of Roberta in concert at the Dorothy Chandler Pavilion in LA. The last line of the review mentioned this great new song that she had performed. . . . Ours! Joan and I and Norman went the following night to her concert. She sang the song beautifully, but hadn't quite found her way with the arrangement and production. She also featured the great New York studio guitarist Eric Gale on the song. I knew him from my New York days as he had played on some of my sessions. Roberta would eventually record the song with the version that became a hit, without the guitar solo, but before that, months went by, and I hadn't heard anything from her or about her potentially recording it.

I first learned that "Killing Me Softly" was on its way to becoming a giant hit when I received a phone call from someone at Columbia Pictures Publications in Florida. They wanted to know if the print rights were available to the song. I had never been asked that question before about any song, so I asked him why he was inquiring. He told me that the song was already top forty on the charts, didn't I know that? I didn't. I didn't read the trade papers, *Billboard*, *Cash Box*, or *Record World*, at that time. I had no idea that our song was even released as a single, no less that it was already a hit. I ran down to the nearest magazine stand and bought all the music trade papers. Sure enough, there it was, on practically every page there was something about Roberta Flack and "Killing Me Softly." One paper predicted that "'Killing Me Softly' will be bigger than swimming pools in California." That was an image I never forgot.

Many years later, thirty-two years later, to be exact, on the day that I was to be inducted into the Songwriters Hall of Fame, and at which Roberta Flack was going to make the presentation to me, after she finished rehearsing "Killing Me Softly," which she would sing that night for the show, we were sitting together and chatting in the nearly empty ballroom of the Marriott Marquis Hotel in New York. I said to Roberta how lucky for us that she found the song, and Roberta, who is a beautiful and spiritual person said, "No, the song found me."

⟨∂⟩

When a songwriter gets very lucky and has a major international "hit," interesting and wonderful things happen in your life. For one, suddenly, singers and record producers are interested in finding your "next" hit, and you get calls from them asking if you have a song that might be right for that artist for their next record. You get calls to license the song for commercials to help sell other people's products, and other artists cover the song with their own versions, in languages of countries you've never been to. Elevators and department stores and airline lounges welcome you with your music. People pass you in the aisle of a supermarket whistling or humming your song. Sometimes you even want to let them know who is in the aisle next to them, and you think about approaching them and saying, "That's my song you're humming," but you refrain from doing so and continue with your own shopping, harboring a secret glee. The very title "Killing Me Softly" has been used so many times metaphorically in newspaper headlines, such as "Killing them softly with a tax increase." The title has also spawned a number of New Yorker type cartoons.

From New York, Cairo, Budapest, and Tokyo, people somehow find a way to contact you, and you get letters from strangers in cities and countries you've never been to. Some letters tear your heart out with the personal meaning your song has for them. The best is to hear that two people fell in love while listening to your song. Then it becomes "their" song and will stay with them forever. I heard from people in prison and in the army overseas, and tragic stories, as well as stories of faith. It's so interesting to learn firsthand how people are moved by songs. It's such a fragile moment, such a fleeting moment, to catch someone's attention, with a brief, poetic thought set to music that latches on to someone's life. Such a brief art form, usually sandwiched in among many others as they're played on the radio or TV, and all aspiring to move you and catch your attention so that you'll want to own the record or sheet music and have it when you want to listen to it or play it at the piano. And so little time to do that when people are preoccupied with their own lives. When it happens with a particular song, it's like nothing else. Certainly rewarding for the income it produces from all the sources, but in a real way, even more rewarding for the lives, people have told you, that have been affected. And although "Killing Me Softly" has been recorded in many different languages, it is basically the English language records, and more specifically, Roberta Flack's record, and many years later, the Fugees, who also had an international hit recording with that song, that the world hears. It's amazing to think of the sphere of influence and popularity that American music has on the world. The whole world seems to be listening to American music, and for that matter, watching American films and television as well.

The icing on the cake with "Killing Me Softly" was our winning the Grammy Award for best song that year, 1973.

Of course, after you have a big hit song, you then think you know which other songs of yours will be certain to be hits as well, and then you're disappointed if they're not. Norman and I wrote a song for the film *The Last Married Couple in America* that Maureen McGovern, who is one of the all-time great singers, recorded for a single as well. To this day, I can't understand how that record did not become a hit, especially since it followed another hit that we had with her, "Different Worlds," the theme from the TV series *Angie*. But that's the mystery of the record business.

In 1973, when "Killing Me Softly" was all over the radio and hugely popular, you couldn't turn on a music station and not hear it within a few minutes. Indeed, I had all the buttons on my car stereo set to the leading radio stations in LA, and there were times that I would press button after

Norman, Charles, Lily Tomlin, Roberta Flack, and Isaac Hayes, Grammy Awards, 1973. *Courtesy of the author.*

button and all the stations were playing my song at the same moment. One day I received a call at home from a new director making his first feature film, *The Sugarland Express*, starring Goldie Hawn. His name was Steven Spielberg. He told me about his film and said that he heard "Killing Me Softly" every day as he was driving to work and that it was his favorite song. He said he'd like to come over to my house one day during his lunch break and talk to me about my composing the music for his film. I said that I'd love to talk to him about his picture, and we scheduled a meeting at my house. I hadn't heard his name before, but when I was at Paramount Studios later that day, I saw my friend Tom Miller, and told him about my phone call from Steven. "Oh, he's great," Tom said, "He made a TV film called *Duel* that was outstanding. You watch him, he's going to be one of the top directors." Tom, along with his producing partners, Eddie Milkis and Garry Marshall, discovered Henry Winkler, Tom Hanks, and Robin Williams for their TV series *Happy Days*, *Bosom Buddies*, and *Mork & Mindy* respectively, and had a great insight to talent.

Steven came to my house during his lunch break, so Joan prepared lunch for us to eat as we talked—tuna fish salad, she remembers. She has an uncanny memory for things like that. He was really an impressive young guy, serious but with great warmth and very likeable. The film, as he described it, sounded wonderful and had a really upbeat ending. He left me with a script and asked me if I would read it and call him to talk about my doing the film with him.

We next met at his office at Universal and discussed the film, and the possibilities for the score. I knew that I was going to enjoy working with him. During our meeting, he had a call from England, from the great English director John Schlesinger, of *Sunday, Bloody Sunday* among many others, who was planning to come to America to shoot a film and was calling the young Steven Spielberg to ask him his opinion about actors and technical matters. I came home from that meeting and told Joan how brilliant and knowledgeable he was. I didn't hear Schlesinger's questions to Spielberg, but his answers made those very clear. He spoke with such precision about aspects of filmmaking, and camera use for different actors, and lighting, and gels for certain actors, that I was completely impressed with his knowledge. I expected to do that film when it was ready for music, and I was looking forward to it.

Unfortunately for me it was not to be. Steven called me one day filled with apologies. He said he wanted me to score his film, but Zanuck and Brown, his producers, had worked with John Williams on their previous picture and were very insistent that John do the music for *The Sugarland Express*. Steven said that this was his first film, and he couldn't force the issue with his producers, and hoped I understood. I did, completely, as those things happen in one's career. He was so nice about it, and I recognized his position, and I was busy with other work, and that was that.

And then he turned out to be STEVEN SPIELBERG!

And as the world knows so well, John Williams and Steven Spielberg forged one of the great collaborations in film and musical history and helped to create a new appreciation and reverence for the art form that we all benefit from, composer, filmmaker and audience alike. However, when I replay that scene in my mind, and think back to my first meeting with Steven at my house, and our having lunch together while we were discussing his film, I harbor a thought that perhaps it was the tuna fish that I asked Joan to serve that day. What if instead she had prepared a Caesar salad with chicken, or even a turkey sandwich, would things have turned out differently? I'll never know.

Years later, Matthew Robbins, who wrote the screenplay for The Sugarland Express, would write the libretto and become my collaborator along with choreographer Michael Smuin for the ballet *Zorro!* that we created for Michael's company, Smuin Ballet.

❦

That same year, 1973, Norman and I had another big record, but this time the memory of its success was forever marred by a tragic occurrence.

I met with the director Lamont Johnson at 20th Century Fox to discuss his new film that I was hired to score. This would be, as it turned out, the beginning of a long friendship and collaboration in which we would do nine or ten films together over the years. Lamont has always been such a pleasure to work with, because although he's very strong in his vision of the film he's working on, and how to bring about the best results for that vision, I can always turn to him if I have an idea, musically, that seems radical or out of the ordinary for that film, and he's always responded with intuitiveness and trust.

The Last American Hero was based on a short story by Tom Wolfe and starred Jeff Bridges in his first film. It was a story of a loner, living with his family in the backwoods of Georgia. His father made moonshine in his illegal still, and Jeff's character would deliver the moonshine to the recipients, all the while racing his car, filled with the booze, to avoid the local police, who would chase after him. When his father was arrested and sent to jail, after the police destroyed the still, Jeff went off to the stock car racing circuit, for which he was so well trained by virtue of his run-ins with the police. The film is his story.

As part of the score, I suggested to Lamont that it might be a good idea to write a song that would give us insight into Jeff's character, in as much as there was a lot to read into his expressions and mannerisms as he was a loner who kept a great deal inside of himself. Lamont was wary of a song being interpolated into this dramatic, earthy film. He didn't want the picture to get "slick" with the addition of a commercial song even though he knew it could benefit the commercial potential of the film. He also hated the idea of a song if it was used at the beginning of the film over the main title and gave away what the picture was about. I couldn't agree more. That was not what I envisioned. I saw the opportunity to get to know Jeff's character and vulnerability a bit so that we could have some understanding of what drives him. I brought Norman Gimbel into the project, and we came up with an idea for a song that would start with an introduction to Jeff's character over the main title, and would continue to unfold with new verses as the film developed, and still have the possibility of it being a hit record down the line. That idea

Lamont liked very much. Norman came up with a lyric that did exactly what we hoped we could accomplish for the film. I've always felt that that lyric was among the very best from Norman's pen.

The first singer that we chose to offer the song had a hit record at the moment, and we all felt that he could be the right voice for the earthiness of Jeff's character. That artist agreed to record our song for the picture and as his next single as well, and his manager made a deal with 20th Century Fox. The record, however, was not forthcoming, and too much time had passed. He was in the process of producing an album and never got to our song. After a while, I started receiving phone calls from Lionel Newman and from the producers of the film, asking me when they'd have the completed recording of the song. It was not forthcoming. I was told that based on the dubbing schedule and the release date for the film, if the song wasn't completed soon, we'd be forced to record the song with a studio singer, which would have no commercial advantage in promoting the film or the record. I sent that message back to the artist, and soon after that I got a call from him and his manager on a three-way phone call. They were very sorry to tell me this, especially after taking so much time, but he would not be recording the song after all. He didn't think the song was a hit song after all. Now, everyone has a different opinion about what could be a hit song, given the record market at any particular time, and even the most successful industry executives and producers are right in their picks only some of the time, so I had no quarrel with his belief in the song or not. But that he agreed to do it, and took so much time, then decided to change his mind and not do it left me in a position to possibly have lost my opportunity with another name artist. In the music business, it's hard to regain momentum once an opportunity is lost.

We decided then to quickly offer the song to two other artists at the same time, which was not normally done, but we were up against a deadline and needed a quick response, and a quickly produced recording for use in the film. We decided to offer the song to John Denver and a new artist whose first record, "Operator," was moving up the charts. Both artists heard the song only over the phone and both agreed that they would sing it. It was now a difficult decision for us to make. John Denver was a major recording artist and had a wonderful free spirit to his sound and style. Jim Croce had a very earthy quality to his voice, and although he had not yet had a hit record, we were sure that he would go very far with "Operator." We decided that Jim's voice more closely resembled the attitude and rugged quality of the character played by Jeff Bridges. The song was "I Got a Name."

I discussed the key and the range of the song with Jim and his producers in New York, Tommy West and Terry Cashman. I arranged and produced the tracks that he would sing to for the film at the 20th Century Fox recording stage in Los Angeles, and brought these tracks with me to New York.

Jim opened the door for me as I arrived at his producer's office. After our brief hellos, he asked me if I would play the song again for him, as he heard it only over the phone. I sat at the piano and sang the song for him. He told me that he knew that he wanted to sing the song because it would make him feel closer to his father, who died when Jim was young and left many dreams unfulfilled. Then he said he'd like to play a new song for me, and accompanying himself with his guitar, he sang "I Have to Say I Love You in a Song." I thought it was beautiful and told him so. It's been one of my favorite songs ever since. I always remember that first encounter with Jim Croce as a special one, with two songwriters trading songs with each other. He was a pleasure to work with on my tracks for the film, and several weeks later I returned to New York to be present at his recording of the record version of the song at the Hit Factory Studios. From the moment I heard him first sing the song for me, to adding the strings for his record, I knew we had something special.

Jim's untimely death in a plane crash while flying in a little plane on his way to a concert was a great loss for the music world. I remember him showing me a schedule of small plane hops that he kept in his back pocket because he used it so often. "I Got a Name" was an instant hit when it was released as his next single after "Bad, Bad Leroy Brown." He was touring, featuring our song as his new record, when his plane went down. Suddenly the world focused on his music and records in a way that's reserved for the true icons of the entertainment world. Three of his albums were on the charts at the same time. "Time in a Bottle," another one of Jim's beautiful songs, couldn't be held back until ours had reached the top of the charts and played itself out. The disc jockeys themselves played both songs, and as a result, he had two hit singles at the same time. To this day, I think that there is a special reverence for Jim Croce and his music, and I was always grateful to have been a small part of that.

Jim's wife, Ingrid, once asked me if I would look through the unfinished songs that he left, and if I would help to finish some of them. I told her that I was honored that she would ask me, and she said, "Who else? You were the only other songwriter whose song he sang." Unfortunately it was not to be. Her house was damaged by a fire, and the unfinished songs were gone. Their son, AJ, is a fine musician and pianist and performer in his own right, and now carries on the Croce musical legacy.

❧

Many artists have recorded "I Got a Name," and from several of them, I've heard personally the meaning that the song had for them, but none more touching than from Lena Horne. In 1981 she had a one-woman show, *Lena Horne, A Lady and Her Music*. It had a limited run in New York and was a sell-out hit. Lena is one of the great performers and actresses, and this was a tour de force performance for her first Broadway solo outing. I knew that she was performing "I Got a Name" in her show, and I was thrilled about it. She had, several years earlier, recorded a version of that song with Michel Legrand arranging and conducting. As much as I loved her and admired Michel Legrand, I never thought that that record version captured her special quality. One day, the songwriter Alan Bergman asked me if I'd seen Lena's show in New York. I said I hadn't. He said I should run to New York to see it, that I'd never hear a performance like that again, and that it was worth going in to New York for. I wasn't able to do that at that time, but I did attend one of the first performances of her show when she opened at the Schubert Theater in Los Angeles.

The show opened with a brief version of her classic signature song, "Stormy Weather," and the audience responded as expected with great warmth and enthusiasm. Then she immediately began to sing my song. She started easily at first, with a simple almost rubato approach, but with a lolling rhythm underneath. As the song progressed, she and the orchestra grew more and more intense and rhythmic and dynamic, and she made the song her own, departing from it for a moment here and there to include a sentiment about her father, to whom she addressed the song, still in tempo with the music, as she was singing. The intensity of her performance was so moving and dynamic and kept on building that the audience finally responded, as if on cue, rising to their feet in the middle of the second number of a show, as though the energy level in the theater was just too great to keep sitting. The total effect was incredible, and Alan Bergman was right—for a songwriter, it would have been worth a trip across the country.

I hadn't met Lena Horne (and I still haven't), and I never expected to be moved as much as I was by her performance, so I didn't arrange for a backstage pass in advance to pay her a call after the show. But the next day, I did send a bouquet of flowers to her dressing room, with a note saying, "Thank you from a grateful composer."

The following day I received this letter from her:

Dear Charles,

I'm so happy that I finally have word from the composer of my favorite song. You can't understand what a deep meaning it has for me. I think of my father each time that I sing it, and I realize any sort of statement I am making is to say thank you to him.

Thank you for writing such good music. Please don't stop.
                                            Gratefully,
                                            Lena Horne

Talk about how songs move people. For a songwriter it doesn't get any better than that.

One day, during my first year in Paris, I passed a record store that had an album featured in the window by a very popular Latin American band known as La Plata Sextette. I had written two songs for them before I left for Paris, but I didn't know if they recorded them or even liked them. When I saw that their new album was released, I ran into the store excitedly and reached for it in the window to see if they recorded my songs. Sure enough, there they were, "Holiday Cha Cha" and "Hollywood Cha Cha."

I was so excited to see my name on a record that it didn't even bother me that they left my last name off. The composing credit said, "Composed by Charlie." Good enough for me. That was my name and those were my instrumental pieces, and I had two songs on the album. I ran to the front of the store holding the album and held it up to the proprietor, and pointing to my name I said, "C'est moi! C'est moi! Charlie! (pronounced, Sharlee) "C'est moi!" my voice filled with emotion.

I don't remember her reaction or even that she had one, but no matter, I'm sure that she was as excited as I was. I couldn't afford to buy the record at that moment, and I didn't even know anyone who owned a record player in Paris, so I didn't buy it, but the proprietor let me listen to it in the store before I put it back, and I floated on air all the way back to my room, with the thought that I had my first record release. I was eighteen years old and on my own in Paris, and this gave me a tremendous boost.

Some of the truly wonderful experiences for me as a composer have to do with hearing my music being performed. Even though I hear the music and the orchestra playing it as I write, it doesn't compare to the experience of standing in front of the orchestra and conducting, or sitting in a concert hall and hearing an orchestra on the stage. For a film composer who also does work on television, you're in the studio so often that it's a regular part of the work schedule. Weekly series demand that the music also be scored on a weekly basis. Movies made for television usually budget two to four weeks for the composer to write the music, or even as little as one week is not unheard of if an "on the air" deadline demands it. For a theatrical feature, depending on how many minutes of music must be written, orchestrated, and copied, anywhere from three weeks to several months to complete a score if it's a score that's practically nonstop in a film over two hours in length. And there are times that the composer is faced with even a week or two to complete a major motion picture, if it's a replacement score for example, and there is a release schedule to contend with. After a composer finishes recording the musical score, it then has to be cut into the film for the music tracks to be synchronized to the scenes they were scored for in the film, then dubbed in with the sound effects and dialogue, so that all the sounds are heard at the proper level in relation to each other. Then the film goes through the technical processes of timing, color correction, cutting a negative, and striking prints. All these steps can take weeks, so they usually work backward to see when the music and sound effects must be finished in order to make these schedules for a certain release date. The composer usually starts to work even before the picture is completely edited in its final form, but invariably, changes are made to the film, and often to scenes that will affect the timing of the music sequences, even while the composer is working on the score. As a result, one can't really lock into the music in its final form until the film has had a final cut. So the one thing a composer must be, aside from good, is flexible. We are very often caught in a vise between the picture being ready for us and having to be finished recording in order to make the "dub" by a certain date. You sometimes have to fight for an extra day or weekend just to get the work done. And of course, you have to be as good and artful as you can be, and give the film all it needs and deserves within that schedule. But through it all, it is a wonderfully satisfying challenge, and ultimately, such an important part of how a film is perceived.

Now, and since the original *Star Wars* film, the sound in theaters has come alive with the Dolby surround sound process in theatres. We are now used to a full spectrum of sound and music and effects coming from the sides and rear of the theater, as well as from the screen, so that there are more options to balancing the dialogue with the sound effects and the musical score. It's not nearly the battle it used to be in films, not so long ago.

When I began working in film, in the late 1960s, the sound in the theaters was guided by a horrible cut-off of the top end over 5000 cycles on the actual soundtrack on the film. It was known as the "Academy Roll-Off." Television, before stereo, had a top-end axe as well. I never really understood why the sound in theaters couldn't keep up with everyone's home stereo and allow a full spectrum of sound. Music never really sounded as full and rich as it did when it was being recorded on a recording stage once it came under the axe of the Academy Roll-Off. Dubbing mixers did add back frequencies over 5000 cycles to give the appearance of a brighter top end, but it was basically to give the sound an aura of having a fuller spectrum. And because the films mostly had monaural soundtracks at that time, all the effects and music had to be carefully balanced with the dialogue, not to overshadow it, and at the same time, not to get lost under it, or for the music to get drowned out by the sound effects, particularly in a loud action scene. That is still as true even with surround sound, but it's easier to balance because there's much more space in the audio spectrum. However, that said, the films today generally have many more sound effects tracks to balance because improvements in technical capabilities through digitization have allowed directors more latitude, so probably it is just as daunting if not more so. But at least today we can make minute changes and updates in a dub, going back and forth, whereas it used to be necessary to dub a film reel by reel, ten minutes at a time, with no ability to stop and go backward to improve a balance. It was a constant battle to fight for the maximum effect of the music helping the film. If it got lost, it didn't help the scene it was intended to work with. As a result, on most of my films, I usually sat through the whole dubbing process, realizing that it was my last opportunity to see that the music was mixed properly into the film along with the rest of the sound. After working sometimes day and night to complete the score, and following that, being on the dubbing stage day after day at 9:00 AM, it was difficult sometimes just to stay awake. And sometimes I lost that battle. But I always considered that to be part of my job to help with the final aspect of the filmmaking process. I know that many of my composer colleagues wouldn't dream of being anywhere near the dubbing stage after completing the score, leaving the final balance entirely to the director. I can fully appreciate that, as sometimes it's long and painful to watch the film dubbing process, as the same ten minutes of film can be worked on for hours at a time, and very often a composer has another picture ready to begin work on. And it is up to the director, after all, to finish the film as he or she sees it and hears it, but I always found the directors I worked with to be appreciative of my involvement to the end of the dubbing process, and in fact would usually ask me if I could be there at least for part of the dub, and they would usually rely on my input to help dub the music into the film at just the right level.

For a composer who loves to work in film, there is nothing like sitting in a theater and watching a film you've scored, when the music is playing full screen, making the film come alive as only music can do. Whether it's a delicate scene of discovery or relationships or fear or joy or exhilaration, when the music breathes along with the film, and moves to connect all the sequences of events and arrives just at the perfect moment on the screen, and is heard at just the right level, perhaps even from just a corner of the screen, it is the most satisfying aspect of filmmaking from this composer's point of view. The music may sound exceptionally rich and full and wonderful and exciting or even beautifully delicate and warm and transparent as it's being recorded on a sound stage, but it's when that music is heard alongside the film at the right level that it truly fulfills its purpose and comes alive on the screen.

At the same time, when the composition as it's written for the film is complete unto itself, and filled with thematic development, and subtextural counterpoint, and a satisfactory conclusion tying together all the elements, it can be like any other composition listened to in a concert hall and can stand up next to music that was not written to accompany a film. That is the challenge. To conceive the musical score written for a film to be completely effective on the screen and to be completely satisfying in a concert hall or on records as well.

I never found it limiting to work within the confined space of preexisting timings to synchronize with the action on the screen, nor did I find it limiting to have to use certain orchestral colors to support the scenes in a film. It's all part of the process, and I see it as a painter would, who approaches his canvas with a certain palette of colors. It's not limiting to have just grays and browns and whites, if that is the concept. Sometimes it even dictates a form or shape to the music and opens up a perspective about what's possible that you might not have thought about. I always found the process of making a film fascinating and fulfilling, and through all the deadlines and difficulties in the process, it's a superb way to spend your time and earn a living as a composer.

To me, writing music for television films is exactly the same as it is for theatrical motion pictures, just for a smaller screen, with smaller budgets, and less time to compose the score. But the musical needs of TV films are identical to the big screen, with certain exceptions of course:

Theme songs, music bridges, playons, playoffs, bumpers, acts in, acts out, and "goesintas" as my friend Artie Butler says, as one scene "goes into" another. But that's the world of sitcoms, and that is another world of music.

TV sitcoms are more the world of make-believe situations than real drama of the human condition. However, they seem to echo real-life situations, often, in a very skewed way, and therefore, the humor. As such, there are certain stylistic conventions that have developed over the years that are pretty much standard in the industry.

The laugh track:

It's happy, it's joyous, it tells you when to laugh at a situation, and just how much to laugh. A snicker, a titter, a nervous laugh, a giggle, a howl, a belly laugh, hysteria, it's all there. It's all in fun, of course, and used only because TV producers want to make sure that you "get it."

Four-camera "live" sitcoms are normally shot in front of an audience, so that for the most part, the reactions are real, but they're still "punched up" on the dubbing stage with an artificial laugh track when the taping is completed. Filmed shows have no live audience, so the laugh track is completely artificial.

When *TV Guide* reviewed the new show *Laverne and Shirley*, the reviewer wrote about our song, "The show was shot in front of a live audience, and so should the composers of the theme song be."

Norman Gimbel was furious and wanted to sue. I thought it was rather harsh, myself, for a reviewer to be calling for our death. After all, it was only a television theme song—how much could it have offended him? However, I took it in the self-serving spirit that the reviewer intended.

But don't get me wrong. I loved working on sitcoms and TV series in general, and some of my most enduring and popular work so far has been connected with some of those shows.

∞

Love, American Style had as one of its episodes within the hour format a story about the 1950s. ABC considered it as a pilot for a new series at the same time, but decided not to give it a go as a series, presumably believing that a show about the 1950s wasn't ready for primetime. After George Lucas's film *American Graffiti* was released and became a major hit, with Ron Howard starring, ABC decided it might be the right time for our series, and decided to give *Happy Days* a regular time slot.

Tom Miller and Eddie Milkis were the producers, and this was their first series as producing partners—the first of a long line of shows that have left a lasting legacy in the history of television—along with Garry Marshall, the creator of most of their shows and executive producer. I was fortunate enough to be with them on much of their ride. They asked me and Norman to write a theme song to sound like it could have been a hit in the fifties. We approached the song with the hope that it could be a genuine hit in the seventies as well. I scored the first few episodes of the show and eventually wrote a library of cues, some theme based, that the music editors would cut into the show as though it was scored that way. That is a very common practice in TV series. Everyone at Paramount, including our producers, Tom and Eddie and Garry Marshall, loved our song. However, because *American Graffiti* used the 1950s classic Bill Haley's "Rock around the Clock" as a major theme in the film, ABC decided to use that same song as the main title of *Happy Days* as well, and licensed the use of that song for the first season. Our song "Happy Days" was used at the end as an end title. The first year of *Happy Days* was shot on film, without a live audience, and Ron Howard had the starring role. The show succeeded well enough to earn a second year on the air in prime time, but barely. However, at the beginning of the second year on the air, the show was starting to catch on, and Paramount started getting tons of fan mail for "the Fonz," Henry Winkler, the 1950s loveable tough guy character with an infectious smile, who singlehandedly recoined the fifties expression "aaaaaayyyyyy." Sometime during that second year, it was decided to do the show on tape with four cameras in front of a live audience, and feature the Fonz in the starring role. Garry Marshall would warm up the audience with his glib and wonderful sense of humor, and the audience responded with cheers and love when the cast was introduced. To be in the audience when the cast was introduced was to sense the importance that this show had to the television viewers and to the history of the medium. They were ecstatic to be there. The producers decided that with all this change, they might as well give our song a chance as well and use it as the main title theme song, as it was originally intended. With this new format, the show went to number one in the ratings, Henry Winkler became a major star and ultimately one of the most beloved characters in TV history—his leather jacket permanently enshrined and on view in the Smithsonian Museum of American History in Washington—and our song, "Happy Days," with a record by a group called Pratt and McClain, became a worldwide hit. That was in 1975, shortly after the show itself became a worldwide television hit. It's awfully nice to know that you have a show that's being seen and enjoyed around the world that carries your music as an indelible part of it.

Doing as much work in TV with lighthearted fare, in both series and television films, as I had been doing, I was concerned about being typecast as a composer of comedy shows only. Tom Miller was the VP of Paramount Television when I first met him, and Eddie Milkis was head of postproduction. Tom was probably the person most responsible for me being offered the *Love, American Style* pilot when I first came out to California. Tom and Eddie were both wonderful guys, and they became good friends of mine and were always the best to work with. And fortunately for me, they liked my music. Their first project together as producers was a dramatic TV film about women in prison starring Ida Lupino in one of her last roles. I knew that they were making this dramatic film, and I felt that we were good enough friends, and that they were appreciative enough of my music, to tell them straight forwardly that I would love to do the music for that film, called *Women in Chains*. They both echoed how much they loved my lighthearted, romantic music, then asked if I felt that I could score a dramatic film as well. I said that I had already scored dramatic films, as my very first film for director Larry Peerce was *The Incident*, which was as dramatic a film as one could imagine, and I felt strongly that I could do their film justice and I really hoped that they would give me that opportunity. They respected me enough to make a quick decision and offer me the film. For me, I knew instantly that *Women in Chains* would break the syndrome of being cast only for comedic and romantic films, although I loved working in that style as well, and those films oftentimes offered a chance to write a song that could make a significant contribution to the film. Immediately after concluding that discussion, they said that they had a pilot for a new comedy series starring Ted Bessell and a chimpanzee, called *The Chimp and I*. Would I do that as well? I laughed at the irony of that and said, "Of course I will." So my long and happy career began with these two wonderful guys as well as the extraordinary Garry Marshall who would make television history with their shows and continue with some of the great and enduring theatrical films as well.

As a small footnote to this story, when *The Chimp and I* went on the air as a series, it was retitled *Me and the Chimp*, because Ted Bessell didn't want to take second billing to a chimpanzee.

Happy Days continued as one of the most popular shows on television, and very often it was the number one show. During one of the episodes, Laverne DeFazio and Shirley Feeney were two new characters introduced as potential love interests for Richie Cunningham and the Fonz. The two girls, Penny Marshall, sister of the show's creator, Garry Marshall, and Cindy Williams, made such an impression with their brief roles on the show that ABC asked Garry, Tom, and Eddie to put together a twenty-minute presentation of excerpts from the girls' appearances on *Happy Days* and add some new footage to see if there was a series potential there. Tom, Eddie, and Garry believed that a complete looking-and-sounding main title always helped to sell a series. They asked me and Norman to do a main title song to the newly shot footage of the girls romping on the streets of Milwaukee—set in that city because that's where Tom grew up—and having fun in a lot of situations, including the beer factory where they worked.

Normally, in order to compose a song that really suits the characters and situations on a show, we'd have to know more about the people and the lives they portray on the screen, including situations that haven't been written yet, so that the song wouldn't get outdated by the show it introduces. I always go into a series hoping and expecting that it will have a long TV life and aware that the theme music has to remain fresh as well as sounding familiar, like an old friend.

There was no complete story or script to work from, but Tom and Eddie described Laverne and Shirley as two girls who were blue collar workers, working in a beer factory, but hoping and dreaming about bettering their lives. Norman and I wrote a song that personified the two girls as hoping and wishing their dreams would come true. Garry, Tom, and Eddie heard that song, which had a lyrical message and tune, and felt that the song did not represent our characters. Our characters were tough and street-wise, and they were not going to let life pass them by, but they were going to make things happen. That, of course is a very different song in tone and character. It was only after they heard our first attempt to characterize the show in a song that they realized who those girls would become. So Norman and I wrote a second song, this time called "Making Our Dreams Come True." There's not much difference on paper between "Hoping our Dreams Come True" and "Making our Dreams Come True," but the latter implies very strong personas, and that was our girls. The lines the girls speak in tempo, while playing hopscotch just before the song begins, "Schlemeel, Schlemazel, Hasenfeffer Incorporated," came about spontaneously as the girls were filmed just fooling around for the main title footage. It was suggested by Tom Miller because that was a camp song of his and he thought it would be fun. I incorporated the tempo of that phrase into the introduction to our song, and had a burst of trumpets coming at the end of their phrase to lead into our song. Over the years, so many people have asked me what those opening lines of the show meant.

The producers loved the new song and I set out to find the right singer to record it for the show. I was at Magic Mountain one day with my children, and happened to pass a pop group performing, which featured a girl singer who had a strong but lyrical voice and sang with wonderful intonation. Sometimes, strong, powerfully voiced singers tend to sing somewhat out of tune, but not this girl, Cyndi Grecco. I introduced myself to her, and said that I thought that she might be perfect to sing our song for this new show, and I asked her right there if she would do it.

ABC liked the presentation and thought that this series could follow *Happy Days* in the next time slot and carry the same audience, and they scheduled it as a midseason replacement. Right from the first episode, the show became a hit following *Happy Days*.

At the same time that the "Happy Days" record was moving up the charts, it seemed a natural that a record of the *Laverne and Shirley* theme could do the same. There seemed to be a little bit of a trend on the record market with television theme songs that started with John Sebastian's recording of his song "Welcome Back, Kotter," based on that series. I called a friend of mine, Larry Utall, who owned a boutique, but important, record company, Private Stock Records. Larry was a really good record man who knew the business very well and who had a solid streak of hits on his label. He was familiar with the show when I called him and thought our song could be a hit as well. He gave me the go-ahead to make a record that he would release on his label. I recorded Cyndi at a studio in Orange County that was owned by José Feliciano and his wife, Janna, who was also Cyndi's manager. I added a tenor saxophone solo section to the record that we didn't have time for on the series, and that opened the record up and gave it an infectious, happy, party sound.

Larry Utall loved the record and had a terrific promotional idea to launch the single. He said to me that if I could get the stars of the show, Penny Marshall and Cindy Williams, to spend a couple of hours with a promotion man and me, visiting two or three radio stations, taking some publicity photos and perhaps doing a short interview on the air, and do the same with photos at the three music trade magazines, *Record World*, *Cash Bill*, and *Billboard*, he felt we could break into top forty radio immediately, and the record would be an instant hit.

Tom and Eddie agreed that it would be a wonderful thing for the show if the theme song became a hit and that it would certainly help to propel the series even more. They worked it out for me to go with Penny and Cindy during their lunch break one particular day. Private Stock Records had a limo and a promotion man pick the girls and me up at Paramount Studios to do a quick but extremely effective mini-tour of LA at the top stations and trade magazines in town. Penny and Cindy were wonderful. They were so much fun, and so nice, just as they appeared on the show. When we brought them back to Paramount, I told them how grateful I was for all they did in helping to launch the record. They said they had a lot of fun doing it and hoped it would work and become a hit record and bring a greater audience to the show. Somehow all that came to pass. I love when the record business works hand in hand with the film and television world. It's very satisfying, and one certainly helps the other.

As Larry Utall promised, the record "broke open" in LA, which helped to carry it into top forty radio around the country. "Making Our Dreams Come True" was an instant hit, and Norman and I had two songs climbing up the hot one hundred charts at the same time.

I sent Penny and Cindy each a large bouquet of flowers as a small token of my thanks for lending their support. I called the flower shop that I dealt with, and along with the flowers that I had the florist deliver to their dressing rooms at Paramount, I asked them to enclose a note saying,

Dear Penny (or Dear Cindy),
Thanks for "making my dreams come true."

Love, Charles

It seems a little corny to me now, but at the time it felt like the right thing to say.

That same week, I had a series of recording sessions booked for a film that I was working on. There were last-minute editorial changes on the film, and we had to delay the recording sessions. That didn't happen very often, but on occasion it did if a film was being tested with an audience, and the studio and producers and director decided to make some changes that would affect the music. I called the orchestra contractor at Paramount, Carl Fortina, and told him of my phone call from the studio, that we had to delay our orchestra call. He said that'd be fine, but it was too bad for one of the string players, a woman who had returned home early from a vacation to play in my orchestra. Even though she was my first-call player on that string chair, I would never have expected anyone to cut a vacation short to play for me. There would be many other times that she would be in town to take the call.

Feeling badly for her canceling her vacation, I called that same florist to send this woman flowers with a note saying,

I'm sorry it didn't work out. See you next time.

Love, Charles

I didn't know until the end of the month, when I received my bill from the florist, that they mixed up the orders and sent the wrong flowers and the wrong note to the wrong person. I don't know if Penny Marshall or Cindy Williams received the note from me saying, "I'm sorry that it didn't work out, see you next time," but I do know that the musician received her flowers from me thanking her for "making my dreams come true." I didn't call anyone to explain after I found out. I just assumed it was past the point and left it alone. However, shortly after that, I heard that this woman and her husband had separated. I was sure that this was entirely coincidental to her receiving my flowers and wrong note . . . at least I always hoped so.

Norman Gimbel and I were fortunate enough to repeat that success on the charts a few years later with Maureen McGovern singing our song "Different Worlds" for another Garry Marshall, Miller, and Milkis series, *Angie*, starring Donna Pescow. However, with the theme from *Wonder Woman*, and a record that I produced of that song, and *The Paper Chase* featuring a song with Seals and Crofts, and even *The Love Boat* featuring Jack Jones singing the song that Paul Williams and I wrote, magic did not strike again in the record market, even though all three of the shows were hit series as well. Jack Jones did tell me, however, that when he performed *The Love Boat* theme in person, the reaction from the audience was as though it was his biggest hit.

Vol. CCXLIX, No. 16   Hollywood, California, Thursday, December 1, 1977   Price 35 Cents

Hollywood Reporter, December 1977. Courtesy of the author.

I never felt that the record business was a predictable one or even that I understood it well, even when I was fully into writing songs and producing records and had records released continually. Trends come and go, and I always felt very lucky to have a song take hold and become familiar to people to any extent. I've always seen it as a very ephemeral world, and sometimes as a songwriter, you can get very lucky. I never considered songwriting the main thrust of my work, even though I had more successful songs than I could ever have dreamed. I always saw it as an adjunct to my composing career in film and television. It was too hard to get records as more and more singers were writing their own songs, too unpredictable and too unrewarding if nothing happened with a song. I've always loved to get up in the morning and work on my current film project. I love being involved with the characters on the screen or on the page with a book musical, and with the storytelling process. I love a film where I have to flesh out just the right orchestral colors and just the right thematic and compositional touch to embrace a scene musically, and bring out all the nuances that that film demands. I truly love the process of discovery in enhancing a moment on the screen and tying it with all the others, to give it a sense of form and cohesiveness. At the end of each day (or night as it so often happened), when I was doing a film, and when I was too tired to continue working, I would close that notebook in my mind, perhaps have a cup of coffee, and turn all my attention then to a lyric that I wanted to musicalize. Fully refreshed with this new musical experience, I could go on for hours at the piano. That was, generally speaking, my daily routine with composition. Even when I worked on theater projects having as many as ten to fifteen songs to write for a show, and with collaborating with book writers and lyricists, I always seemed to start my day by composing, and preferably in longer forms. There was more for me to get into. Of course, that was partially due to the fact that films had deadlines, and at the end of a period of time, I had an orchestra hired to perform and record the music for the film. And that was my one recurring nightmare, standing on the podium with an orchestra in front of me, and having no music to play. I didn't need a therapist, however, to help me figure that one out.

❧

In 1975, I scored what was one of the most beautiful and touching films that I have ever worked on, *The Other Side of the Mountain*. It was another of the films that I did with Larry Peerce. The producer was Ed Feldman, whom I also count among my good friends and with whom I've done a number of films as well. It was the true story of a young Olympic skiing hopeful who had a tragic accident during a downhill race in Alta,

Utah, and ended up as a quadriplegic. The young Jill Kinmont was played by Marilyn Hassett, who had a bright, fresh-as-the-morning, exuberant smile about her. She trained at Mammoth Mountain in the high Sierras. Her coach was the man who owned and built the ski resort and ski area, Dave McCoy. Mammoth Mountain is also where Joan and I owned a condo right next to the mountain for many years, and where we skied often during the winter along with our children, who learned to ski there. Obviously, the territory of the film was close to my own heart.

The film opened up on the fifteen-year-old Jill Kinmont cruising down the beautiful, wide-open bowls in Mammoth and shouting, "I'm Jill Kinmont and I ski," as a sort of pronouncement of her ebullient character. The main title music that I wrote for that opening featured a trumpet solo floating above a piano weaving fast moving notes, establishing the momentum of movement and all accompanied by a string orchestra playing a long lyrical line, with supporting low strings. It was meant to capture the freedom and exhilaration of skiing fast and downhill on a magnificent snow-carved mountain. The story progressed as Jill was making her qualifying runs to secure her place on the Olympic skiing team. Everything changed after her accident, and from there to the end of the film, it was about survival. Could she have any kind of a life after that, living in a wheelchair, and paralyzed from the neck down? To make it even worse, near the end of the film, her fiancé, played by Beau Bridges, who loved her and stayed with her through it all, is killed in a small plane crash somewhere over the mountain range near Bishop, which is about an hour's drive from Mammoth. It is the true test of whether she can go on in life, after that. Of course, the music had to change along with the picture, and after her accident, it became a reflection of her anguish and emotional and physical struggle.

As I was recording the orchestra on the sound stage at Universal, the real Jill Kinmont sat in her wheelchair next to the podium while I was conducting, watching the screen and listening to the orchestra playing. She was sitting close to me, but behind me, and as I was busy with the orchestra, I couldn't see how moved she was at hearing the music underscore her struggle and emotions as she watched herself trying with all her strength to bring a single potato chip up to her mouth. Many of the musicians could see her, however, and they were all obviously aware that this was the woman being portrayed on the screen, so those orchestra members were very moved in turn by this experience. Jill's mother, who was there at the recording session, told me afterward that she had never before seen her daughter that emotional, even as she was going through the same experience in real life. Between watching the actress portraying her on the screen, and the way she internalized the musical expression accompanying that scene, it brought out emotions in her that had been long suppressed. I think that that is one thing that music can do so well, to dig down deep into someone's inner being, and reach for a part of it in a way that no other art form can.

I got to know Jill a little, personally, as we spent an afternoon together while a photographer took pictures of us for the back of the album cover and for publicity for the film. Part of the time, while they were taking photos, I was at the piano playing, and she was listening, and in others we were sitting together and chatting on the countrified grounds of the Hawthorne School in Beverly Hills, where she taught. She later moved back to Bishop, California, which is on the way to Mammoth, from LA. She continued teaching in a small school that had many Native American children enrolled as there was a large Native American population living in that area. Every time Joan and I would pass Bishop on the way to Mammoth, we'd always say that next time we should allow the time to visit with Jill. But we always had the children, and after four hours of driving with still one hour left to go on the trip, we were anxious to be home already, in the mountains, and always decided to continue directly to Mammoth, so I haven't seen her since that day in Beverly Hills.

As I was getting close to finishing my work, composing the score for the film, I had an idea about adding a song at the end of the film that would serve as a sort of postlude to the story, leaving the audience with an uplifting feeling about Jill's life after the close of the film. The last scene is with Jill in her electric wheelchair, which she could control, and her mostly Native American students walking on a country road next to Jill, in a beautiful, autumnal scene that looked like there was not a care in the world to be had. The children are laughing and interacting with Jill, and she seems very at peace with the world and has regained that beautiful smile. There was a central musical theme that I used throughout the film that was Jill's theme. I never had any intention of using it as the basis for a song, but after the music for the film was completed, it seemed that with a lyric added to the theme, we would have a song that could project her life and attitude into the future. Both Larry Peerce and Ed Feldman liked that idea, and I asked Norman Gimbel to write a lyric to my existing theme. Norman captured just the right expression, lyrically, and it brought the end of the film through the end credits to a deeper dimension for the audience to take with them.

The song was called "Richard's Window," titled after Dick Buick, who was Jill's fiancé and who was killed in the plane crash. Norman's lyric used Richard as a more poetic sounding name, and the song is about Jill inheriting his vision and attitude in life, by using the metaphor of "Seeing life through Richard's window to the sky." When it was released in England, the film itself was retitled *Window to the Sky*, after the song. We thought that Olivia

Newton John had just the right quality to her voice for the song that needed to be sung in a quiet, personal style, as a very private moment. This was not going to be produced to sound like a hit record, but you always hope it can find its way to an audience in every case.

We offered the song to Olivia, and she agreed to do it. I arranged and produced the song for the film, and she was lovely to work with. (She was as well when I worked with her on *Grease*, but that's another story.)

The song, and Olivia's recording of it, helped to bring a positive feeling and message to the end of this very moving film that had so much anguish portrayed in it. It was never released as a single record but was part of the soundtrack album. However, Norman and I were fortunate in that our colleagues in the Motion Picture Academy nominated the song for an Oscar, and both the song and my score were nominated for Golden Globe Awards. Although we didn't win any awards the nights of both of those shows, they were still wonderful experiences, and it was extremely rewarding to be recognized for the work that went into the film. And, as I never had any expectations of winning, there was no disappointment at all. It was thrilling to be at the Academy Awards, and have a song nominated and sung as part of the show. And at the banquet and celebration after the show, Joan and I shared a table with Elizabeth Taylor and George Cukor, so we certainly enjoyed the ultimate Hollywood experience.

⪥⪥

In June 1976, an Air France plane flying from Athens to Paris with 250 people on board was hijacked en route by members of the Popular Front for the Liberation of Palestine and two members of Germany's Baader-Meinhof gang and taken to Entebbe, Uganda, where it landed at the Entebbe airport. The 103 Israeli civilians on board the aircraft were held captive by the PFLP with the help and guidance of the Ugandan dictator, Idi Amin. The non-Israelis were released. (This incident occurred three years before the Iranian hijacking of an American plane whose passengers were held captive for almost a year, until a successful release was negotiated by President Reagan, and only after a rescue effort failed.) The world seemed to stand on edge as the Jewish and Israeli hostages were constantly threatened with death, if fifty-three militants being held in jail in Israel and four other countries were not released.

On the eighth day of captivity, after the hijacking, the Israeli army staged a daring and successful raid on the Entebbe airport by landing three Hercules transport planes in the middle of the night and executing a commando raid to capture the airport and overtake the Ugandan soldiers and PFLP members and rescue the Israeli hostages and bring them back to Israel.

The plan worked miraculously, and all the hostages but one survived the attack, and only one soldier lost his life during the daring raid. His name was Lieutenant Colonel Yonatan Netanyahu, and he was the brother of Benjamin Netanyahu, the prime minister of Israel. The world was stunned by the audacity and success of the raid, and it gave a great emotional lift to the free world and especially to Jews the world over. It was the kind of story that inspires movies to be made about it, and indeed, soon after the raid and release of the hostages, several movies were rushed into production.

Twentieth Century Fox announced that it would begin production on a film called *Raid on Entebbe* for TV. Golan-Globus, an Israeli-owned production company, began a theatrical film, *Entebbe: Operation Thunderbolt*, and Warner Brothers TV in association with David L. Wolper Productions rushed a quickly written script into production for a film called *Victory at Entebbe*. I received a call from Larry Marks, who was head of music for Warner Bros., to ask my availability for the later project. Luckily for me, I was available to begin work almost immediately. Normally when a composer is asked to score a film that has not yet begun shooting, the work to do the scoring would not take place for many months and could even be a year away. Even a TV film on a rushed time schedule would still take weeks of shooting and editing before a composer would begin his work. In this case, with *Victory at Entebbe* being one of three films hoping to be the first to be completed and shown to the world, I was literally asked to begin my work immediately even though filming had not yet begun. To this day, that remains the most unusual timetable and schedule that I've ever had in my career. This was to be a film shot on video and transferred to film for expediency in shooting and editing. As of this writing, it is not at all unusual for a film to be shot on high-definition digital tape and then transferred to film, but in 1976 it was hardly the norm as the finished film would still have a videotaped or quasi-live look to it. The film featured an all-star cast including Burt Lancaster, Elizabeth Taylor, Anthony Hopkins, Richard Dreyfuss, Kirk Douglas, and Helen Hayes.

I received the two hundred-page script by messenger the same day as the phone call asking me to do the film. It was 50 percent longer than most scripts and was planned to be a three-hour movie. When I received the script, I sat down immediately to read it, which I did in one sitting, both mesmerized and extremely moved by yet another story of horror and cruelty perpetrated on innocent Jewish people, but in this case one that ended with such a dazzling act of heroism by the Israeli Army, and ultimate victory. It fired my reaction to the events, and I immediately went to the piano in my studio and proceeded to write the whole ending of the film, which was such so powerful and uplifting. I don't recall ever being so moved by a story, especially in script form, that the music just poured out of me, effortlessly. Of course there was no film shot yet, so I expected that I'd have to modify what I'd written to make it work for the film, but at least I had the basic theme and developmental ideas to use as I needed.

The first day of shooting came almost immediately, and after only one or two days, a tragedy interrupted it. The actor and comedian Godfrey Cambridge, who was playing the Ugandan dictator, Idi Amin, died suddenly of a heart attack on the filming stage. He was replaced by Julius Harris, and those scenes already shot that included the Idi Amin role had to be reshot. After each day or two of shooting, a video was sent to my house of the quickly edited version of the dailies, and in some cases, the unedited dailies themselves, so I could begin my work. Normally, I wouldn't begin to compose the music for a film until it had a "locked" or "final" cut, or pretty close to it, but there was not going to be an edited film to work with in this case. For each two or three days of shooting, I'd discuss the spotting of the music with Larry Marks and begin my work. Every third or fourth day after filming began, I'd be on the scoring stage at Warner Bros. recording the music for those scenes, shot only a few days before. I met the director, Marvin Chomsky, for the first time, only after the first few days of filming, on the day of the first music scoring session. He came down to the scoring stage to introduce himself and wish me luck and tell me how happy he was that I was doing the film. He stayed only until I had recorded the first cue, and then had to get back to his work on the shooting stage. I never saw him again until the film was completed. In every other film I've ever done, I've spent a great deal of time working with the director, discussing the film and the music as we both saw it, and then we would "spot" the film together, to determine where music would go and how it would play with the film. When I record the music, conducting the orchestra as I watch the film in front of me, the director as well as the producer and editor would always be right there to offer comments and support to me. So, to meet the director only once, and briefly at that, and not to work in collaboration with him was highly unusual and mandated by the schedule we were all under. In spite of the time constraints and pressure, and urgency in producing the work on schedule, it was an entirely satisfying experience for me as I believe it was for the others working on the film, having to rise to the demands put on all of us.

I didn't sleep very much during this period. I'd go to bed at 3:00 or 4:00 in the morning, after a long day's work at the piano and my desk, and set my clock for four hours' sleep to begin working again the following day. There were days when the orchestra was already assembled on the scoring stage at Warner Bros., and I was still at home putting finishing touches on that day's music to be recorded, knowing that that music still had to be copied, and parts distributed to the individual musicians. This schedule went on every three or four days for weeks on end. Sometime during this period, I came down with serious flu-like symptoms, but couldn't give in to my physical weakness that came as a result. I was taking antibiotics for my illness and pain pills for my aching bones. Another time, I would simply have taken to bed until I was well enough to work again. This time, I didn't have the luxury of time to give in to my body. I had to continue my work, regardless. One day I was on the podium conducting the orchestra, and as a result of being loaded up on all the medication, and still not sleeping more than a few hours a night, I was actually having to fight sleep and the urge to close my eyes, even while my arms were moving as I was conducting. I never heard of anyone falling asleep while standing in front of an orchestra conducting, but it was a real threat at that moment. I called Joan after the next "take" we recorded, and asked her to rush down to Warner Bros. to bring me medicine to stay awake. In all my years of impossible schedules and deadlines, I always carried Benzedrine with me in my pencil case, just for such emergencies, although this was like none other. Over the years, I used it very seldom, and never after just one night without sleep, but only if I had to go a second sleepless night and then needed to be awake and refreshed for the following day to record the music I'd been writing. A half of a Benzedrine tablet could get me over the hurdle. I never saw it as a drug, but as a lifesaver in emergencies. This day was an emergency.

After I finished recording each day, the scenes that had music were dubbed that same night in the dubbing theater, so that the music was mixed together with the dialogue and sound effects at the proper level. After those reels were dubbed each day, they were sent for processing immediately, and the day after I finished my final recording session, the film was shown on ABC TV, and a day after that, the theatrical release opened in theaters in Israel.

After the film was completed, I went back into the studio with an orchestra, this time to do a record version of the *Victory at Entebbe* theme, which would be distributed worldwide by Warner Bros. Records. The following day after finishing the record, Joan and I were on a plane to Acapulco to take a much needed break and rest.

Years later, I was asked by Nate Lam, my good friend and the cantor of Stephen S. Wise Temple in Los Angeles, and who is responsible for bringing much new music into the services at the temple and for special musical events, if I would turn my music for *Victory at Entebbe* into a concert piece for orchestra that would be performed with a symphony orchestra at an upcoming concert. I happily agreed to do it. In my reworking of the music, I used basic themes and moments from the score and composed a new suite that made a complete musical work with its own internal form, so that it could stand alone in a concert setting. It was not just a putting together of musical cues from the film as they were heard in the film. This is something I've done a number of times with my film scores, in order for me to give the music I'd written added life in a concert hall setting as a stand-alone work. Along the way, I spoke with my friend, composer and conductor Michael Isaacson, who was going to conduct the premier at the concert. I told him how the piece was progressing and mentioned that it was turning out to feature the piano to the extent that it was practically a piano concerto. "We'll have to get a piano soloist to learn the part," I said.

"Why don't you play the piano solo yourself?"

"What is the date of the concert?"

"October 30th."

"October 30th, that's my birthday," I said. "My fiftieth birthday. I really don't want to make a big deal over my fiftieth birthday, so perhaps I will play the piano. That's something I'd look forward to doing on that day, playing with the orchestra."

So I committed to the performance.

The day of the concert came, the rehearsals had gone well, the orchestra played beautifully under Michael Isaacson's direction, and the packed house at Stephen S. Wise was fully engaged with the music. I did enjoy the experience of performing with the orchestra very much, and the audience's reaction was the icing on the birthday cake. After the performance, Nate Lam called me back to the stage and told the audience that it was my fiftieth birthday that day. With that, a huge birthday cake was wheeled out with a grand piano pictured on it and too many candles to count, while the symphony orchestra played "Happy Birthday" and five hundred people sang along. And I had said I didn't want to make a big deal over my birthday!

After the concert a man came up to me to express his feelings of how moved he was to hear my work. He told me that he was one of the Israeli commandos involved with the actual raid, and that the music brought him right back to that moment, to the tremendous tension involved with the experience of being part of it, and to feeling the ultimate victory and success of the mission. That was, for me, the most moving comment I could imagine hearing, and I told him how much I appreciated his telling me this, and for his part in the raid itself.

Victory at Entebbe Suite has been performed many times since that premiere performance, with many orchestras. I conducted several performances myself with the Columbus Symphony and performed the piano solo with the Los Angeles Jewish Symphony Orchestra several times with Noreen Green conducting. I didn't have the pleasure of hearing the piece performed when Noreen conducted it with the Jerusalem Symphony in Israel. However, I did conduct the piece myself in a concert in Ariel, Israel, with a wonderful Russian émigré orchestra. For me, it's the ultimate satisfaction to write a film score that becomes an indelible part of the film and then goes on to have an afterlife on records and in the concert hall. All the sleepless nights to complete the score are long since gone, but the music, inspired by that most dramatic event, will hopefully go on reaching out to people recalling that moment in history.

The *Victory at Entebbe Suite* was recorded by the Israel Philharmonic with Michael Isaacson conducting, for the Milken Archive series of recordings. I performed the piano solo part on a session in Los Angeles. During that recording session, which took place at Evergreen Studios, the studio that I was a co-owner of, history intervened.

Events in history have a way of winding themselves through our lives as we live them. Those are the sometime occurrences about which we always remember exactly where we were and what we were doing at that moment in time. I was in the middle of performing the piano part for *Victory at Entebbe* when Michael Isaacson, who was in the control booth producing the session, interrupted my playing on the intercom to say, "Come into the booth, we're at war with Iraq." The first Gulf War had begun. The bombing of Baghdad had started, and it was all over the world's airwaves. I went in to the control booth, and we watched the events as they were happening. For the first time in history, people could watch a war happening in real time, broadcast by CNN. Bombs shattered the nighttime silence, at that very moment in time.

That's another aspect of television, being able to broadcast the events of the world, on a moment-by-moment basis. The same television set that brought the film of an earlier event in history, for which I was now recording the music, was bringing us the news of another life-changing event that would be the basis for future films made about that subject one day. How ironic the world we live in today can be. The first Gulf War was a short-lived war. The U.S.-led coalition forces were quickly victorious in routing the Iraqis from Kuwait and liberating that country and their people with as few casualties on our side as could be imagined. Yet lives of families of those casualties are changed forever. The U.S. decision to end the war, short of going into Baghdad and bringing Saddam Hussein to justice, left over the seeds that grew into the later Gulf War, which is having a far greater consequence on the world, and as of this writing, its outcome, and how that impacts all our lives, is yet to be determined. I can't help thinking of the irony of the medium of television, which brings us the world news, local news, and epic events happening live, and on another channel at the same time, an innocent sitcom like *Happy Days*, for which I worked to create just the right musical signature. I often think of the phrase that Will and Ariel Durant wrote at the beginning of their epic tome, *The Story of Civilization*:

Civilization is a stream with banks. The stream is sometimes filled with blood from people killing, stealing, shouting and doing the things historians usually record, while on the banks, unnoticed, people build homes, make love, raise children, sing songs, write poetry and even whittle statues. The story of civilization is the story of what happened on the banks.

After thirty minutes or so of watching CNN, I went back into the studio to complete the recording of my piano part for *Victory at Entebbe*, but in those few moments, the world had changed.

❦

Lamont Johnson, who directed *The Last American Hero*, asked me to work with him on the film *One on One*, the story of a young high school basketball star played by Robby Benson, who was being drafted to accept a scholarship to play for a major university. His life gets caught between basketball, feelings for a young student, Annette O'Toole, and the pressure put on young athletes to succeed. It was a very good film.

The musical concept for this film, even before I was invited in, was to have a song score developed as part of the overall musical score. That is to say that a number of songs would play over certain scenes, and it would be part of the storytelling process, not necessarily moving the story forward as in a musical, but adding emotional commentary and reflective expressions with the use of contemporary songs, which would give the film an added style and promotability with a younger market. The songs would be used over the action as one uses orchestrated music to underscore moments. The hugely popular group the Eagles were originally going to write the songs, and for whatever reason they didn't, I was fortunate enough to be asked.

Larry Marks, the head of music for Warner Bros., asked me who I wanted to work with to do the lyrics, and I said that I was such a fan of Paul Williams's work and that his lyrics were so inventive and musical, and I'd love to do this with him. Paul loved the film and was happy to collaborate with me, and we've been friends ever since.

This was a dream project, a lovely, uplifting film where you have someone to root for. Paul and I had a good and easy collaboration, and the songs were going very well. For the most part in our working together, I gave Paul a melody or part of a melody to start with, and he added the lyrics. I was more accustomed to starting my work after the lyrics were written or at least partially written, but writing the melody first worked fine for me as well.

Paul was also touring as an artist during much of the period that we worked on this film, so we did a lot of work together over the phone. I

The music team from *One on One* clockwise from left: Paul Williams, Dash Crofts, Jimmy Seals, and Charles with Robby Benson (center). *Courtesy of the author.*

remember one phone conversation that we had very late at night, which fit into my work schedule as well as his. I had given him a melody to accompany a romantic montage between Robby Benson and Annette O'Toole. Paul called to say that he'd been working on this song titled "My Fair Share." "What do you think of this . . . ?" And he spoke the lines, rather quickly, but I heard the beautiful poetry in it:

> Lost, lost as a child's first thought
> I must have arms to hold me
> Lost without loving care
> I must have my fair share.

I said to him, "Paul, read it again more slowly. It's too beautiful not to absorb those words easily."

And he repeated:

> Lost, lost as a child's first thought.

"How beautiful is that?" I thought to myself.

We wrote five songs for the film, and we asked Seals & Crofts to sing them for the film and release a record along with it. They loved what we wrote and joined the project. I produced those songs for the film, and along with Robby Benson, who is a singer and songwriter as well, we all spent a lot of time together in the studio. I did have an orchestral score to write additionally in which I also included some of the song material. It was a great project and a wonderful time for me.

The only difficulty I had in recording the songs was that in order to be in sync with the film, you had to record directly onto 35 millimeter film, which took more time to do punch-ins on vocals, and became frustrating for Seals & Crofts. In a recording studio where one made records, masters were made on multitrack tape, and punching in when recording the vocals to improve a vocal line was done instantly. At that point in time, however, there were no recording studios in Hollywood to facilitate the process by synchronizing tape with film. As a result of this project, I asked an engineer that I was working with, Rick Riccio, why couldn't we record on tape and still run in sync with film?

He said, "It's entirely possible and easy to do right now with the current technology." He assured me of that, and as a result, one evening over dinner I mentioned that to my friend, composer and arranger Artie Butler, and his wife, harpist Gayle Levant, that I thought a new studio could be built that had the best of both worlds for film as well as records. We all had spent a lot of time in recording studios, and they also thought that was a great idea, and the concept and partnership for Evergreen Studios was born that night. Soon after that we bought the Magnolia Movie Theater in Burbank, and with John Edwards's architectural designs, and Rick Riccio's engineering guidance, we converted the building into a large, modern facility to house two recording studios that were innovative, state-of-the-art recording facilities for motion pictures and records, which eventually expanded to include the huge sound stage on the lot at CBS Radford. Everyone from Frank Sinatra and Michael Jackson to Placido Domingo recorded at Evergreen, and many of the motion picture and TV shows through the eighties and nineties recorded their soundtracks there. We ran that studio for twenty years, in between our writing work.

Jimmy Seals and Dash Crofts had that magical sound when they sang in harmony. Indeed, when I sang with them sometimes to illustrate a point, I thought that the three of us sounded so good together that I suggested that we make the group into Seals & Crofts & Fox, but they wouldn't go for it. A single was released of "My Fair Share" and was soon being played all over the radio. The record was a moderate hit stopping just short of top twenty, but we were all very proud of our work, and "My Fair Share" remains for me one of the most beautiful records I've ever been involved with, and is still played often on the radio to this day.

I coproduced the soundtrack album with Louis Shelton with Seals & Crofts singing the five songs at their own studio, Dawnbreaker, in San Fernando. The poor engineer for the record would have to put up with Jimmy Seals, Dash Crofts, and Louie Shelton smoking their pipes all day, and the Cuban cigars that I smoked at that time. I believe there were times when it was hard to see each other through the smoke. I loved working with Jimmy and Dash, and we became good friends. They were avid golfers, and sometimes in the middle of a recording session, one of them would say, let's take a break and go hit some balls, and fifteen minutes later we were on a golf course. It was the first and only experience I ever had when I would bring golf clubs with me to work.

⊗

Lionel Newman called me and asked me if I would do the pilot for a new series, *The Paper Chase*, based on the successful film of the same name. John Houseman was the star of the film, and he was the producer of the show as well, playing a powerful and impressive professor of law at Harvard University. I met with John Houseman at his office on the Fox lot and discussed the show with him. He told me about the main title, which would introduce the various cast members, the students, each of whom was coming from a different part of the country, with excitement and apprehension written on their faces as the camera followed their individual journeys to Harvard. All the while we would be hearing John Houseman's voice narrating over the footage, words pertaining to the difficult work that the students would encounter, and the law school experience at Harvard, and his encouragement as he prepared each student for the challenge he or she was facing in this new phase of life. The main title footage would follow the characters from their home towns as they made their way to Boston. At the end of the main title we would cut back to John standing at his podium in the lecture hall, as he was in the process of lecturing to his class.

John asked me what I thought of music playing in the background under his narration. I told him that I thought that would work very well, and specifically, that a main title really should evoke an impression of the show through its musical style. I then added that I had a further thought: Since we hope and presume that the show will be on the air for many years, surely the same narration week after week will quickly get old, as the audience is already aware of all the information in his narration. "Why not start with the narration, and then gently segue into a song that would describe the fears and anxieties of the new students, that could be a universal statement of approaching something new in your life?" I suggested.

"What about the narration?" he asked.

I said that at the end of the song, "we could segue back into the narration as we cut back to the close-up on you, so that the song gently comes to a conclusion and ends with a brief instrumental section under your narration."

He wasn't sure that he liked that approach since it pretty much eliminated him from the mail title, but he said that he'd think about it. I began to work on the body of the score. Lionel called me one day to say that he heard from John, who was very uncertain about my wanting to replace his narration with a song. Lionel, whom I always found very supportive, said to me that he told John that since he hired me to do his show, and put his trust in me, why not give me a chance to do it the way I envisioned? With that, John agreed to let me write a song for the main title. Norman came up with a lyric that I thought captured all the anxieties and fears of the new students and resolved itself as the students were seen entering John Houseman's class. The song was called "The First Years."

The first years, are hard years, much more than you know.

I asked Seals & Crofts to sing the song for the TV series. I recorded the score and their vocals for "The First Years" at the Fox studios, and we dubbed the song into the main title just as I originally suggested. I thought it worked very well, and so did everyone at Fox, including John Houseman, or so I thought. The show went on the air and was a fine series, filled with insight, dealing with the struggles of the first-year law students under the tutelage of a brilliant and caring professor. The series received lots of praise from the critics but couldn't find a wide enough audience. At the end of the season, the show was nominated for an Emmy for best series, and I received an Emmy nomination as well for best score. However, with all those accolades, CBS didn't believe enough in the show, and it was canceled after the first year.

Over the years I've worked on a number of comedy series that were reviewed badly by the critics, and subsequently went on to become long-running shows and take their place in television history. Ironically, here was a show that all the critics applauded, and it lasted only one year in prime time. *The Paper Chase* did, however, find an afterlife in syndication, and continued on the air, on local stations, with new episodes for several years. I was not asked by John Houseman to stay with the series, and when I turned it on one day to see if they kept my song, I found that John had gone back to his narration for the whole main title and lost my song. Obviously that concept did not work well for him.

❦

Filmmaking, like theater, is truly a collaborative medium. I've never been afraid to express my views of what will make the film better, and certainly from a musical vantage point, I've always found the directors and producers I've worked with eager to hear my thoughts and concepts and happy to implement them if they agreed with them, and very often they have. But finally, as in theater, there has to be one person at the helm to make decisions. In film, it's mostly the director, and in television, almost always, the producer.

I enjoyed my working relationship with John Houseman, and obviously he acceded to my approach to the main title for the first year of the show and changed back to the narration after the first year. I still believe that for the long run of a show, it helps to have a musical identification that the audience recognizes and looks forward to each week, rather than hearing the same introduction to the same characters spoken each week. For that same reason, I never personally liked theme songs that told you what the story was about, as opposed to those that set the tone of the show and perhaps introduced the characters and the underlying thematic context—and of course, writing something so attractive that when people hear the theme, they will leave the refrigerator and happily turn back to their TV sets.

The theme should feel like a good friend, an old friend who comes back each week to entertain you.

Presenting theme songs to producers for a new series was always a challenge, even when I was fully ensconced in Hollywood and I would come prepared with a complete-sounding demo of the theme. It was sometimes difficult to get the producers to hear it properly. I would show up at a producer's office on a studio lot and find that there was no tape machine or cassette machine to play my demo. There were times that I had to ask the producers to come outside and sit in my little two-seater car to listen to the theme on my car stereo. Sometimes there would be four people or more, standing outside my car and waiting for their turn to sit down in the car and listen to my music.

When I was writing the theme song for *Wonder Woman* to Norman's lyric, the producer, Doug Cramer, called me one night while I was at the piano working. He asked me if I would play the theme for him over the phone. That was not at all unusual, as I had many times played themes and songs for singers and producers over the telephone, with the telephone tucked in under my chin. But this night I could hear loud music and noise in the background from Doug's end of the line. I asked him what that music was, and he said that he was at a party but was anxious to hear the theme for his new show, and not to worry, that the loud music on his end wouldn't bother him at all. In fact, it didn't, and he liked the song immediately.

Playing the "Love Boat Theme" was probably the most unusual circumstance that I ever had. Aaron Spelling and Doug Cramer were the producers. It was their show that started as a two-hour movie of the week, which I scored. After two or three more full-length movie versions of *Love Boat*, it went on the air as a one-hour series. Doug Cramer had been the president of Paramount TV when I did *Love, American Style*, and before working on *Love Boat*, he first described it to me as "*Love, American Style* on the water*,*" a comedy anthology—however, this time, with a recurring set of characters who worked on the boat as new stories unfolded each week. When the show was picked up as a series, I suggested to Aaron and Doug that we add a lyric and vocal to the instrumental theme I had written, and they loved the idea. I asked Paul Williams to write the lyric. When I arrived at Aaron Spelling's offices on the lot at 20th Century Fox, he and Doug were excited to hear the new song. Aaron rubbed his two hands together gesturing gleefully, and said, "Let's hear what you've brought us." I looked around the room for a tape recorder to play my demo of the song and saw that there wasn't one in the room.

"No problem," I said. I came prepared with a cassette tape as well. Aaron asked his secretary over the intercom if there was a cassette machine available, and she came back in a few minutes and said there wasn't one in the building. "No matter," I said, "there must be a piano available somewhere on the Fox lot; I'll just sing the song live at piano." A few minutes later, Aaron's secretary announced that there was no piano available at all at that moment anywhere on the lot. Now we were reaching an interesting point. How to let them hear the song without a piano or tape machine of any kind? I looked at Aaron and Doug and shrugged my shoulders and they looked at me and shrugged their shoulders. Finally I said, "All right, here goes. . . .

"Love, exciting and new. Come aboard, we're expecting you. . . ."

I sang a cappella, snapping my fingers to the tempo of the song to give it a sense of rhythm. Aaron and Doug listened with great interest to this unique performance, and both exclaimed how much they liked it at the end. Fortunately for me and Paul Williams they were able to hear the song through this highly unorthodox presentation. We asked Jack Jones to sing the song, and it became his signature song, he told me, even though he never had a hit record per se. The show was a huge hit, and even today, thirty years later, it's still being shown on TV around the world. After it had been on the air in prime time for ten years, Aaron and Doug asked me to update the theme with a different artist, and so we asked Dionne Warwick to record a new version of the song. She sang it beautifully with the new production that I made for her, which was markedly different and updated from the original. The show would last two more years in prime time, and it's been in syndication around the world continuously since that time. Unfortunately, Jack Jones was very hurt by our replacing his version on the air, and I don't think he ever forgave me for doing so, even though I had no choice. I was simply requested by the producers to give the theme some new life with a new version and a different artist. We did that with *Happy Days* as well after the tenth year on the air, when I brought Bobby Arvon in to sing a new version.

I've come to believe that there is an art to presenting new material and new songs to singers and producers and directors. Making complete-sounding demos of a song is usually the best way for TV and film people to hear it, and absolutely necessary in the record field, and everyone today seems to have good equipment to listen to the recording. In musical theater, performing a song at the piano is still de rigueur, the old-fashioned way, or as Sammy Cahn used to say, "of demonstrating the song."

Sammy and I wrote several songs for the film *The Duchess and the Dirtwater Fox.* Most of them were written for Goldie Hawn, who performed the songs on a stage in a saloon, in a town that looked like it was right out of the Old West. *The Duchess and the Dirtwater Fox* was a film written and directed by Mel Frank, who wrote and directed some of the Bing Crosby and Bob Hope road pictures, as well as *Mr. Blandings Builds His Dream House.* He wrote a very funny script that took place on the Barbary Coast near San Francisco during the wild-west days. George Segal played a gambler, con man, and thief in his charming inimitable style. Goldie Hawn played a sweet, lovable dance hall floozy with a lot of edge. They got hooked up together, with George's character having stolen a satchel of money from a gang of bad guys, who in turn had stolen the money from a bank. George is being chased by the gang of bad guys when his path crosses Goldie's, and for the rest of the picture, the two of them are running for their lives. It's a very funny picture, and the chemistry between these two loveable scoundrels was delightful to watch. Normally, I wouldn't be involved with a film until after shooting was finished and a rough cut of the picture was assembled, although I would sometimes go to the set now and then of a film I was going to score, just to say hello to the people I would work with. With *The Duchess and the Dirtwater Fox* there were several scenes where we'd see Goldie performing on a stage of some saloon, so it was like working on a musical where we'd record the songs before the beginning of filming and later the performance on-screen would be lip-synced to the track. Sammy Cahn, the great lyricist of so many standards, was hired to write the lyrics along with Mel Frank. They had been friends, and Mel brought Sammy in to work with me.

Cover of *Songwriter* magazine, June 1979. *Courtesy of the author.*

Family photo from article in *Songwriter* magazine. Left to right: David, Robbie, Charles, Lisa, Joan, and Byron the dog. *Courtesy of the author.*

The style of the musical numbers would be very much in the turn-of-the-century English music hall tradition, filled with sexual innuendo and cute and obvious double entendres, and I knew that this would certainly be a happy experience. The first lyric that Sammy gave me was for Goldie's solo number with the cute provocative title "Please Don't Touch Me Plums," in which Goldie would sing with an English accent while wearing an outrageous costume decorated with fruit in all the obvious places, taunting the cowboy audience with her wares. This was the first of several songs that we would write for the film, and Mel was anxious for Goldie to hear the song so she could start learning it as it had to be choreographed as well for the production. Mel's offices at 20th Century Fox didn't have a piano, so when we all got together, he made a call to find a piano that was available somewhere on the lot. It turned out that Mel Brooks had a piano in his office down the hall from where we were, and it was available to us. We walked down the hall together, Mel, Sammy, Goldie, and I, and into Mel Brooks's private office. I sat down at the piano, and just as I was about to start to sing the song, after a brief piano introduction, I happened to notice a framed photograph of a woman on the piano with the inscription, "Dear Mel, Without you I'd be a piece of shit," and signed "Madeline Kahn." With that I started laughing so hard that it took me a minute to stop long enough to tell everyone else why I was laughing. Now they all read the inscription and they started laughing as well. If nothing else, it put everyone in a proper mood to hear a comedy song. I repeated this story later that day to a friend of mine who knew Mel Brooks, and he said that Mel wrote that inscription himself. I love zany people.

Goldie was a delight to work with, and she was adorable doing the numbers we wrote for her as she danced and sang with that wonderful Goldie Hawn smile. When we had written a few more songs we met again in Lionel Newman's office at Fox. He had a nice grand piano in his office. I sat down at the piano and proceeded to play and sing the new songs. I'm not a singer by any means, but I'd gotten used to singing my songs to singers and directors and producers because most of the lyricists I'd worked with didn't sing at all, so it never occurred to me to ask Sammy Cahn if he wanted that pleasure, which I would have gladly given to him. Everyone loved the new songs and felt that they would work very well in the film. As we were leaving Lionel's office, I put my arm around Sammy's shoulder, as an expression of camaraderie and feeling good about everyone's reaction to our songs and said in the vernacular of Tin Pan Alley, "Well, we sold some songs."

Sammy looked at me, and with a very straight, unsmiling face said, "I always give the first demonstration of my songs." I realized that he was serious, and as it was too late to change anything that day, I said he could certainly have that pleasure in the future. I found out later that Sammy was famous for performing his songs, and "demonstrating his songs" as he called it, and he even had a show in which he performed his songs and told stories about his life in the music business.

We wrote a lovely, very unlikely for a "cowboy picture," a Jewish-sounding song, that was sung over a scene of an equally unlikely Hassidic wedding in a hotel, attended by gritty-looking cowboys who looked like they were straight out of a B Western. Who's to say that wasn't possible in real life?

I wrote a love theme for the film, and everyone felt that if lyrics were added, it could be sung and used over a romantic montage. This now became a chance to have a hit recording artist singing a song for our film with a commercial record release as well.

Sammy and Mel went to work on creating a lyric. When they had something they liked, they brought me in to hear what they'd done. It was a nice, sweet song with a bit too many sugary metaphors to attract a contemporary recording artist. It was hard for me to be as enthusiastic as I would have liked, because the song and lyric needed a little contemporary edge that they didn't have. I had to be honest with them about my reaction, and they took it well and said they would work on it some more. The next time I came back to Mel's office, for some reason that I've forgotten, Mel was in his underwear, and Sammy was sitting at the piano that was now installed in the office. They showed me the changes they made in the lyric, and I wanted so much to say,

"Great, that made the difference," but it didn't. The song still felt somewhat old-fashioned. It was hard to find the words to say beyond those I had already expressed to them without being hurtful, and especially to Sammy Cahn, one of the greatest and most successful lyricists.

"What are you looking for," Mel asked me. All I could say was that the language and images weren't contemporary enough, and when I hesitated for a second, Mel jumped in and said, "God damn it Charlie, we're two old men, we can't write like kids!"

I loved working with Mel Frank and realizing that perhaps I had pushed too hard, I said to them, "Let's send this out to a singer just as it is." They both agreed quickly to that suggestion.

We decided that Frankie Valli would be a good choice. He had many hits as the lead singer with the Four Seasons and had a giant record as a solo artist with "Can't Take My Eyes Off of You." We sent the song to him, and we got word back that he would do it but wanted to talk to me first. I called him, and he suggested meeting for lunch at the Beverly Hills Hotel. I had never met Frankie before, but he was a good friend of my friend Bob Crewe, who produced all of his hit records, which were so familiar to me, that it felt to me as though we had been friends as well. He was such a nice, unassuming man considering all the hit records he'd made. He said that he liked our song very much and would love to sing it, but he had a problem with some of the imagery in the lyrics and wanted to talk to me about making some changes. I had a feeling that that was the reason for his wanting to get together. I told him that I agreed with him, and that I already had been through that several times with Sammy and Mel, but that I was sure that if he called Sammy, that Sammy would respect that and reapproach the parts of the lyric that were a problem for him. Frankie said that he was in awe of Sammy Cahn and was uncomfortable asking him to make changes, that he would prefer it if I would speak to Sammy.

It was a little difficult for me to report this to Sammy and Mel, but they both took it in good enough spirits and said they would try again.

We sent the yet again revised version to Frankie, and he let us know that he would not be doing the song.

Next, we sent the song to Bobby Vinton, as his records were not as driven by contemporary market tastes and he was still very popular. He agreed to sing it in the film and release it as a single, but with the stipulation that he wanted to talk to me first. When I heard that, I thought to myself that if this song is too sugary for Bobby Vinton, we are really in trouble. He did express his concern about that to me over the phone and asked me if I would speak to Sammy about making a few changes. I said that honestly, we'd been down that road and really, the song was not going to change, and that I hoped he would sing it as is. Fortunately for us, he did.

Bobby couldn't have been any nicer. My father came to that recording session, and when Bobby found out that my father was from Poland, he waltzed my father around the control booth, with my father smiling ear to ear.

The difficulties with that song aside, I had a joyful experience working on the film, and that Jewish-sounding theme that I wrote was made into a song with the addition of a lyric by Sammy and Mel, and became "Touch Me Tenderly, Love," which was then sung over the Hassidic wedding scene with a chorus. It has also, since that time, been played at many real-life Jewish weddings, including those of my own children.

Fred Astaire was as charming and nice to know and work with as anyone might expect having known him from his screen and stage persona for so many years.

I was scoring a television film for my friend Sam Strangis, who had been, for years, the head of postproduction at Paramount TV. One of the first films he made for his own production company was a bittersweet comedy about the people living in a retirement community overseen by a tough and unpleasant nurse played by Tyne Daly—think Nurse Ratchet. The film was called *Better Late Than Never*. The newest addition to this world of the retiree, forced to live there because his grown children thought he'd do better in this environment, was Harold Gould. He became the chief instigator to rally the retired troops into doing something exciting in their lives. They decided to hijack a train to show that there was still life in them. Of course it was all in good fun, and when they were stopped, they used their actions as a protest against the mean nurse, and then knowing that their ability to do something different, if not reckless, was still there, they also became more content with their living environment as they enjoyed the thought of the powers they still had.

Norman and I wrote a song to be played over the montage where the hijackers are rolling down the countryside on the hijacked train, feeling full of life and spirit. The song was called "You're Never Too Young," and we wrote it for Fred Astaire, who agreed to sing it for the film. I first met Fred at his home on Tower Road in Beverly Hills. He had a spinet piano in his bedroom, and that's where we had our meeting. I imagine that there must have been a grand piano in the house somewhere, where I could picture George Gershwin playing a new song for him, or perhaps performing at a party, which he was known to do very often, but I never saw it. Or perhaps this was the only piano he had. He sat on the edge of his bed while I was at the piano, and we rehearsed the song. He liked it very much, and was very enthusiastic about singing it and our working together on it. I was really enjoying the whole experience.

I wrote an arrangement for the up-tempo song that included a strong pop beat, and I used three girl chorus singers as backup for his vocals. It was not a typical Fred Astaire song in any way, but he seemed to be having a good time with it, and certainly put all his care and talent into it. Here was this icon, this living legend of the golden era of film musicals in Hollywood, who gave birth to more song standards through his original interpretations in film than probably anyone, and he was singing my song in a gentle but lively voice, sitting on the edge of his bed as I was accompanying him.

On the day of the recording, Norman picked him up at his home and drove him to United Western Studios, where we had done so much recording in the past. Even in his early eighties at that time, he was clearly the best-dressed, most dapper man in the studio that day, wearing an ascot and blue blazer. I stood next to him in the studio as he was rehearsing to the prerecorded track, until we could find a proper balance in his headphones for him to hear his own voice against the track. At some point, I went into the control booth when he was ready to start recording. His voice was clearly softer and more fragile than it was in his youth, and he never had a strong voice, that I heard, to begin with. But he had such style and charm in his performance, even at that time and even at that age, that he still sounded like the Fred Astaire of his younger days, and it was magic. He asked us for a change of balance with the background vocals, and again with the orchestral track. After recording a few takes, to the point where I was very happy with the performance, he asked me in a halting sort of way, which seemed to be a regular part of his speech pattern at that time of his life, if he could do yet another take. I said, "Fred, we'll do it as many times as you'd like, until you're satisfied." I was so much in awe of him. After yet another take or two, he admonished himself and said, "Oh, Fred, you can do better than that. Can I do it once more, Charlie? I know I can do better than that." And he did, and it was. He was a joy to work with, and I will always remember this eighty-years-young legend, who was still pushing himself to be better, when there was really no one ever better.

About a year later, I was walking on Beverly Drive in Beverly Hills with my son David, and we passed Fred and his wife walking past us in the opposite direction. We saw each other and stopped to talk, and he introduced me to his wife, and I introduced them to my son. He was so friendly, and so chatty in his halting way, and we were having a very nice recollection of the film that we worked on together. His wife, who was quite a bit younger than he, seemed to be anxious to end our conversation, and when I became aware of that, I too tried to conclude our conversation. He was holding on to

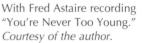

With Fred Astaire recording
"You're Never Too Young."
Courtesy of the author.

her arm, probably for balance, and clearly wanted to continue our little talk, so he kept the conversation flowing. I could see that she was getting more and more irritated at that, so I tried to bring our brief encounter to an end by interjecting, "Well, Fred, it's great to see you again," and, "Well, Fred, I know you and your wife have to leave," but to no avail. He wasn't responding to his wife's growing annoyance. Finally, as he was in the middle of saying something, she simply detached his arm from hers and proceeded to continue walking up the block without him. I saw this as a minicrisis because he was clearly in need of assistance to walk, and here I was the cause of him being left without his wife. So I finally interrupted him and said, "Fred, your wife . . ." and pointed to her, now about twenty feet farther up the block and still walking at a brisk and agitated pace.

With that, he looked up and realized that she had left him and continued on her own, and he pointed to her and said, "Oh, my wife . . ." Now concerned for him, I held him gently by his arm and proceeded to walk with him in her direction, and when I thought he was close enough to her, I sort of gently nudged his arm forward and wished him well, and told him how happy I was to see him again. He continued by himself to catch up with his wife, and they walked away together. I didn't really understand the dynamics between the two of them, but I had a little guilt because of it, even though I knew it was not my fault. But he was Fred Astaire, and frail, and he shouldn't have been left alone to walk by himself.

I never saw him again after that, but I cherish the memory of having that brief friendship and the recording that remains from it.

One time Mademoiselle told me that George Gershwin had come to her house in Paris to ask her if she would teach him. She told me that because he was already so well set in his musical ways and so talented, and so successful, that she felt that she could hurt his music. So she declined to teach him. Years later I read this same version of the story in Edward Jablonsky's biography of Gershwin.

When I received a call from Allen Carr asking me if I would like to work on the motion picture of the hit Broadway show *Grease*, I told him I'd be thrilled to be involved with it. Movie musicals were the rarest of breeds in Hollywood, and I was happy to be asked to be involved in this one. There was of course a golden era of screen musicals, long since past, but now, in the seventies, even the most successful Broadway musicals were seldom made into movies. I would be working with the songs already written for the show, but I also knew that it would be a huge production and a lot of fun being part of this fifties-era musical, with singers, dancers, and big production numbers. I was hired to be the musical director, to adapt the existing songs for the film, to produce and oversee all aspects of the music in the film, and finally, when the film was shot and edited, I would compose the background score, which of course would also make use of the song material where applicable. In addition, and making this job still more attractive for me, Alan said that there would be at least two new songs needed for the film, which he would like me to write, and finally, when the picture was completed, I would produce the soundtrack album for the record release.

I hired a small staff of people including musical and administrative assistants. I had some experience with film musicals, having written the songs with Norman Gimbel, and having been the musical director of *Pufnstuf*, as well as composing the score for that film. In addition, portions of dramatic films that I scored had scenes with "on-screen" musical performances, such as *The Duchess and the Dirtwater Fox*. I knew that this would be a monumental task in recording all the songs with all the various actors and singers, and balancing my needs to make that happen with the director's schedule to use the same people when he needed them for filming, which would naturally take precedent.

The recording facilities on the Paramount lot, Stage M, was a very impressive-looking, large stage with an equally impressive-looking control booth, but neither was set up to handle a 1950s style rock and roll score very well. Along with the engineer, we had to revamp the moveable panel walls to create a more sympathetic acoustical environment for this type of music, which included reworking the drum booth to better handle the drum sound as well. We were all working in unfamiliar territory, but all were very compatible and excited to be on this project.

John Travolta had completed *Saturday Night Fever*, and it had just been released, so he had not yet become the huge star that he was about to become as a result of the success of that film. The female lead had not yet been chosen, and I was among those who thought that Olivia Newton John, who I worked with on *The Other Side of the Mountain*, would make a great Sandy.

We had meeting after meeting with the various people in production who were responsible for their areas of the film to work out all the logistics of scheduling and basic needs.

The director was Randal Kleiser, and the choreographer, whom I would be working especially closely with, was Patricia Birch, who also choreographed the Broadway show. Allan Carr was always setting up and leading those meetings.

One problem appeared almost immediately for me, which would turn out to be a harbinger of things to come. Pat Birch was pushing for Louis St. Louis, who was the musical director of the Broadway show, to be my musical assistant on the film. This struck me as a very bad idea as he had no experience with film and film synchronization. I was also concerned that the people who had been involved with the Broadway production would feel that they "got it right" musically speaking, and that cliché-ridden phrase "Hollywood would screw it up" would infiltrate into my work in trying to get the music done in a manner that I felt necessary for the film. I simply said no, I'd rather choose my own assistant. Pat was quite insistent and very aggressively pushing for her way, to the point where Allan Carr started to call me to see if there was any way that I would accept St. Louis as my assistant. I knew that it would be a problem for me from the beginning, and I held firm. Finally, Pat agreed to hire St. Louis as her dance assistant, although he was neither a dancer nor choreographer as far as I knew, but simply to get him onto the project. That was just fine for me as I had nothing against him, other than that he was not who I wanted to be my assistant. Johnny Oliver had a lot of experience and was an easy guy to work with, and he was my choice, as it should have been.

Everything about doing a musical should be wonderful. In preparation for it, there is an excitement in the air that you can feel. In addition to the normal preparations for shooting a film, there's all the activity surrounding the music; the vocal rehearsals around the piano, the choreographing of the dancers, the production numbers. There's a sense of it being a real throwback to a time long since gone in Hollywood that carries with it a feeling of doing something that's a permanent part of film history, and there's a exuberant sense of bonding with everyone involved as a result. That's of course true in theater as well, but new musicals open all the time on Broadway and else-where, and Hollywood musicals are practically in name only.

I asked Paul Williams to write the new songs with me, as we had just concluded our work together on *One on One*, which was a very happy col-laboration, and we became good friends as well. We were going to write a new main title song called "Grease," as surprisingly enough, there had been no song called "Grease" in the stage show. We would also write a new solo number for John Travolta, who would have a reflective moment alone on the screen with this song.

One day during a production meeting, when the discussion turned to the music, Allan said that he had received two songs from the original songwriters, which they had the right to "submit" for this film version of their show. I knew that they did not have a noninterpolation clause in their agreement for new songs, and as a result, the authors only had the right to "submit" new songs. Obviously, that was the case, because I was hired to write the new songs as part of my contract, along with Paul Williams, who was subsequently hired to write the lyrics. I would later learn that this clause did not appear in my contract, as the written contract would not actually be completed for months, which is not at all uncommon, and a "deal memo" in Hollywood is usually sufficient to begin one's work. This omission would ultimately lead to my leaving the film when Allan Carr wouldn't live up to our understanding. At this moment, however, and at this particular production meeting, Allan was holding a sealed manila envelope with the two songs by the original authors. He threw the envelope across the table toward me and said, "Here, I don't know what you want to do with this, but I'm giving it to you." I had no genuine interest in listening to those songs, as I was already involved writing the new ones, but I made a note to myself at that moment, that if I was ever in the position of those two authors, I would ensure that my work would not be thrown so casually across a table with no chance of it getting a proper hearing.

We were approaching the time to begin prerecording the songs, and everything was falling smoothly into place. Normally, when one prerecords the music tracks to songs where the vocals will the filmed, it's less complicated and more efficient to record with a small combo of musicians, perhaps with just a rhythm section or even just a piano, and fill out whatever orchestration is needed in postproduction when the film is shot and edited. That way, if the director decides to cut away from the on-screen vocal for whatever reason, or even to add additional footage, or compress the footage, we would not be hampered by having a completed orchestra track to deal with. And similarly, it's easier for the composer, after the fact, to make it all work and tie in musically when he has a completed picture in front of him. The most important aspect is to make sure that the time code is intact in order to synchronize any on-screen lip movements or choreographic movement. And that is when my musical assistant Johnny Oliver's work became so important, to ensure that when those scenes were filmed, the lip-sync was accurate.

However, in spite of that, I decided that for the very first recording of the first song, "Summer Nights," I would forego that convention, and bring in the full orchestra with rhythm section as well as the chorus in addition to John and Olivia's duet, which I felt would kick off a tremendous sense of excitement to everyone working on the film by hearing the song fully produced. That worked splendidly, and we were off to a great start. Everyone was on a high, and it set the tone for the shooting that was about to begin.

At the same time, it was troubling, a bit, to me that Robert Stigwood, who was the executive producer, and owner of RSO Records, which was going to release the soundtrack, didn't seem to know me and would continually remark that it was nice to meet me, every time we met. I preferred to take it that he was preoccupied, but I wouldn't know until later that at the same time that Paul Williams and I were working on our two songs, so was Robert Stigwood having other people from within his record and publishing companies writing their versions of the songs for the same scenes.

That particular summer that we began work on the film, my son David was twelve years old and really enjoyed being around the studio and watching all the action surrounding the film. The cast members all were so friendly to David and made him feel like a part of the group. One day, while I was recording Olivia, John Travolta was in the control booth with us, waiting for Olivia to finish her recording so that he would then begin his. At one point, he took a comb out of his back pocket—where we all kept ours in the fifties—and combed his hair back. David was sitting next to him, and when John finished with the comb, he handed it to David and said,

"Here David, you keep it. It'll make you a big man with the girls."

It was really a sweet gesture. David took the comb, looked at it for a moment, and then handed it back to John and said, "Thanks John, but nobody will believe that it's yours anyway."

Jeff Conaway, Didi Conn, Stockard Channing, Olivia, and John were all so talented and terrific to work with.

Louis St. Louis however, became a growing problem for me. As I suspected, he found many faults with my handling of the music and was increasingly vocal to me about his concepts, and to the producers and director as well, and he began to cause a real divide between Pat Birch and me. Normally, I work very closely with choreographers to create a bond between us, but here, that never happened. One day, in the middle of a recording session, St. Louis's comments were getting so obstructive and interfering with our recording to such a point that I actually had to ask him to leave the stage and told him that he would not be welcome to attend future recordings.

Paul and I finished our two songs, and we made a demo of the fifties-style main title called "Grease." We felt that we had nailed the song and that it would lead to a very upbeat fifties rock and roll group sound, that when combined with the animation that was being created for the main title, it would jump out at the beginning of the film. And we felt that we had a song that could be a hit as well, as "Happy Days," my other fifties-style song, had been a few years earlier. For the song we wrote for John Travolta, I simply played and sang it for him at the piano, and he and Allan and Randall Kleiser all thought that it was perfect for the film and said they loved it. But my problems with the external strife didn't diminish. Other people were still submitting songs in place of ours. That I learned only later on.

One day, I received a phone call at home from Allen Carr, who said to me, "Well, the good news is that we're still considering your 'Grease' song, but we have another song for John Travolta." I was taken aback by his nonchalant manner in bringing me this news, and more so by the fact that this was an integral part of my agreement. I told him so, and he answered that that part never got into my contract, which I hadn't even been given yet, in either case.

I said to him, "Allan, what about our understanding?" He only repeated that we still had a chance with our "Grease" song. Allan Carr was Marvin Hamlisch's manager at that time, and I asked him if he would let anyone speak to Marvin the way he was speaking to me.

Then I heard a click over the phone. That was my last conversation with Allan Carr.

Ten minutes later I received a phone call from Neil Maffeo, who was the production manager on the film.

"I heard about your phone conversation," he said, in an empathetic, friendly manner. "If I were you, I'd quit the film. I wouldn't work under these circumstances."

The conversation had "good cop, bad cop" written all over it.

I realized immediately that Allan had put him up to this in order to get me to quit the film so he wouldn't have to fire me. I responded to Neil that I had already done my work by producing most of the songs for the film, and there was no way I would quit, realizing that he was goading me into it. Before the end of the day, I heard from my attorney, Bob Gordon, that they wanted to buy me off the film immediately. I, of course, was very upset and angry with all that had transpired and was not too unhappy to leave the film under those circumstances, even though I had so much of myself invested in the work in the film. My attorney worked out a deal for me to be compensated for my work that I had done and for the scoring part of the film, which I would now not do.

I was, I admit, happy to be out of that unhappy, rancorous situation, and free of all the strife. However, since I actually had already produced most of the entire soundtrack, I should have been smart enough to recognize the value of my work already completed and to insist on retaining my credit and royalty as the producer of the album. I wasn't thinking clearly. I just wanted "out" of a bad situation. As it turned out, the *Grease* soundtrack would become the most successful, biggest-selling soundtrack album of all time, up to that point, selling over twenty million albums.

During my whole career of more than forty years of working in film and television, that was the only gut-wrenching experience I ever had. I had become so accustomed to everything going well and smoothly with my work and professional relationships, and leaving films with nice friendships and a feeling of warmth and camaraderie with the producers and directors I worked with, that I was completely unprepared for the battle that I experienced with *Grease*.

On the positive side, it left me with a gaping hole in my schedule, and I finally had the time to devote all my attention to my ballet, *A Song for Dead Warriors*, which I had been commissioned by the San Francisco Ballet to compose, and had been working on between film assignments. In terms of my determination to get back to composing concert music, this then became the catalyst for putting my work in perspective.

I never forgot the experience I had with that film, of course, nor did I become cynical as a result and let it change my outlook on this business of filmmaking that I had come to love to be part of. I simply moved on.

❧

Colin Higgins's death at the young age of forty-seven was a great loss to the film world. He wrote the wonderful, quirky *Harold and Maude* for his master's degree as a student. Little known is that it was translated into French and performed as a play at the Comédie Française in Paris, directed by Jean Louis Barrault, long before being made into the classic film that it became. He was a friend of Tom Miller and Eddie Milkis, and through them, he and I became friends. I did two very successful and popular films with him, *Foul Play* and *Nine to Five*. He wrote a trilogy of films that was his homage to Alfred Hitchcock, *The Silver Streak* being the first. *Foul Play* came next, and the third film in his planned trilogy, *The Man Who Lost Tuesday*, was never made, even though the prior two were very successful.

The Silver Streak was directed by Arthur Hiller, produced by Miller and Milkis, and was a big hit. That was Tom and Eddie's first motion picture. For their next picture together, *Foul Play*, Colin made his directing debut, and I was asked to do the music. That was the start of an albeit too short but wonderful collaboration before he passed away.

Foul Play was truly one of the best and most memorable experiences I've had working in film. It involved some enormous challenges, and gave me some unique opportunities musically, by incorporating extremely suspenseful, dramatic, operatic scale, and romantic music that could turn on a dime and also underscore this comedy starring Goldie Hawn and Chevy Chase in his first starring role. Dudley Moore had to be talked into playing a seemingly minor role in this film, but as a result, in his next picture, *10*, he had the starring role, with Bo Derek as his costar.

For my part, I had to write a full score with many layers, produce the recording of scenes from the Mikado with the New York City Opera Company, and compose the main title song, which was supposed to sound like the big hit of the day. All that came to pass, along with Oscar and Golden Globe nominations and a song that became a standard.

Going back to the beginning of this adventure, I met with Colin in his office at Paramount, along with Tom and Eddie, to discuss the film before shooting began.

"This is going to be a great opportunity for you musically. You're going to have a lot of fun," Colin said. I knew that as well from having read the script.

The film starts off with a cocktail party in progress. Chevy Chase is a glib outsider to the goings on, and Goldie Hawn is a guest at the party. Chevy approaches Goldie, who's trying to get over a failed relationship, engages her in a bit of glib repartee, and finally suggests that since "you're a nice girl, and I'm a nice guy, why don't we take a shower together?" One of the great approach lines of all time. Goldie passes the line off with the shake of her head and a twist of her mouth, and the scene is over.

Next, the main title, a high shot with Goldie driving her yellow Volkswagen convertible along the magnificent San Francisco coastline, with a song playing full screen as though this is the song that Goldie is listening to on her car radio. The script calls for a song called "Taking Chances," which she sings along with as she is driving. The idea of the song is to plant a seed in her mind, so that when she drives past a nice-looking man who is hitchhiking, she is singing about "taking chances," and stops her car, thinks for a moment, and backs up to pick up the man. That's where the story and intrigue begin.

I asked Norman to write the lyric for this song. We all, songwriters, producers, and director, decided in advance that the best recording artist that we could hope to get would be Barry Manilow. At that moment, there was no one bigger in the record field, and we all agreed that his would be the perfect voice to plant the seed in Goldie's ear, with his recording of this song. None of us knew Barry at that point, but we felt that if we wrote a good song for him, hopefully he would want to do it.

Norman came up with a perfect lyric with the title "Ready to Take a Chance Again." Goldie's character had already been in a failed relationship, so the sense of this song would be perfect for her. I heard Barry's voice in my ear when I was writing the melody to Norman's words. The song would begin simply and plaintively in a comfortable part of his vocal range with the words:

> You remind me, I live in a shell
> Safe from the past, and doing okay
> But not very well.
> No jolts, no surprises,
> My life goes along as it should
> It's all very nice but not very good.

At that point, there would be a big orchestral sweep leading into the chorus section:

> And I'm ready to take a chance again,
> Ready to put my love on the line with you.

After the chorus, the song would go back to the beginning melody, only to build again and this time modulate to a higher key. I played the song at the piano for Eddie, Tom, and Colin. They loved it just as we wrote it, and I quickly made a demo to send to Barry. There was nothing new about the form of the song. Barry had several hits with this same song form, but he loved the melody and lyric when we sent it to him and agreed to do it. He felt so strongly about singing this song that he had to persist with Clive Davis, who was the head of Arista Records, who thought that this wasn't a hit song. Barry told us later that it was important for him to prove to Clive, who had strong influence on all of Barry's previous records, that he could pick a hit song. Still it would be tough going for a while for Paramount to make a deal for Barry to sing our song and hopefully release a single record as well.

Tom and Eddie and Colin felt that Barry's performance was more than as a recording artist. They felt that they were casting their film with Barry Manilow. It took a lot of belief and work on both sides, but sometimes things do come together the way we hope and plan, and Barry was set to record our song.

He went into the studio in New York with his producer, Ron Dante, and he called when the record was completed to say that he'd like to play it for all of us and get our reaction. If you can imagine Barry Manilow, who was probably the hottest recording artist in the world at that moment in time, coming into the control booth of Stage M, on the Paramount lot, holding a tape and looking just a little apprehensive as he was about to play the record of our song that he recorded for the film. That was the picture. It's an interesting thing about true artists at every level. They pursue their art and craft to the highest caliber, with the greatest conviction for what they are doing, and yet are sometimes apprehensive about the reaction they'll get because they're insulated in their work until the world receives it.

Well, a moment later we heard his record, and for me, that was one of the great moments in my musical life. Speaking of "musical," his record was so musical, so "on point" with the song's message and intention, and so thrilling in the chorus sections that we could all hardly contain ourselves when we heard it. Barry was so proud and thrilled with our reactions, as we were with his record.

The filming began, and for this main title sequence, Goldie was filmed singing along to Barry's record. Sometimes, all the best laid plans actually do work.

One of the other musical challenges that I had with *Foul Play* was for the score to connect all the links at the end of the film, when Goldie and Chevy are on a madcap chase scene to get to the Opera House on time to stop a murderer before he kills the pope, who is in attendance of a performance of *The Mikado*. The performance of this Gilbert and Sullivan opera was to be at the War Memorial Opera House in San Francisco. Colin and I planned the sequences of the opera that we were to have recorded and filmed, so that it would begin as the opera actually begins, as the pope and his entourage are seen entering the Opera House. After a brief scene we would cut away from the opera in progress to Goldie and Chevy rushing to get to the Opera House as quickly as possible to stop the murder from happening. That was my cue to begin my score, coming out of a particular point in the opera. After that scene with them heading to the Opera House, I would then lead my score into the next scene of opera in progress, and then cut back to Goldie and Chevy after this next moment in the opera. This form continued, back and forth between opera and chase music, many times until the two stars finally arrived at the Opera House.

If I handled this whole scene correctly, the last ten minutes of the score would come off seamlessly as one piece of music, almost as though Arthur Sullivan had intended it that way. That was the challenge, and I love good challenges. The New York City Opera, conducted by Julius Rudell, was contracted to record the scenes from *The Mikado*. I flew to New York to work with them and produce the recording to our needs while Julius conducted. That alone was a thrilling experience. After we finished the recording, at some point the whole New York City Opera Company was flown to Los Angeles to film the scenes in question. Even though the Opera House in San Francisco was the locale for the film on the screen, they actually filmed the opera sequences at the Shrine Auditorium in Los Angeles, and inserted that footage into the stage at the War Memorial Opera House in San Francisco. When it came time to film the audience in the orchestra section of the theater, they had only five hundred extras to fill a two thousand–seat orchestra section, so Colin had the camera secured to the floor with the whole orchestra section visible, and moved the extras around four times to fill up the theater. If you were able to look closely enough, you'd see the same people sitting in the audience four times in different parts of the house.

Garry Marshall, Goldie Hawn, Chevy Chase, Colin Higgins, Tom Miller, Ed Milkis, and Charles backstage at the War Memorial Opera House, San Francisco. *Courtesy of the author.*

I was in San Francisco with Colin and Eddie and Tom before the filming began. We were having lunch in Scoma's Restaurant on the wharf, and the discussion turned to who would play the part of the opera orchestra conductor on-screen. All the other parts were already cast, including Dudley Moore as a sex freak. This was not a part for an actor. It was simply a momentary shot of the conductor in the pit, but Colin and Eddie were going on with the possibilities of whom to cast. I watched this discussion going back and forth as one watches a tennis match.

Ball in Colin's court: "How about this person?"

Ball hit back to Eddie: "How about that person?"

He returns it to Colin: "What do you think about . . . ?"

Finally I chimed in. "What about me? Am I chopped liver?"

Colin stopped in his tracks, looked at me, and thought for a second. I thought it would be quite natural and fun to boot for me to be the conductor on-screen, for posterity and for my children to see.

Colin looked at me, deep in thought.

Finally he said . . .

"What a good idea. Let's get Dudley Moore to play the conductor. It'll be funny when the sex freak turns out to be the conductor of the orchestra. He could have a lot of fun with that. He's actually a great pianist. I'm sure he could conduct as well."

"Hey Colin, that wasn't my suggestion at all," I thought to myself. But to no avail. So much for stardom.

Colin and Eddie loved the idea of this sex freak–type person turning out to be the opera conductor.

My screen debut would have to wait until I worked with Jackie Cooper, who wanted me to play the conductor for the young Judy Garland in the film he directed, *Rainbow*.

When the scene with Dudley Moore conducting the orchestra, to a playback of the New York City Opera Company, was being shot, Joan and I were in San Francisco for a few days as I wanted to be there for the shooting. Colin asked Joan if she'd like to be an extra and sit in the orchestra watching the performance on stage. He said she could sit with his family right behind Dudley Moore and be on-screen every time they cut to him. She thought that would be fun, but Tom Miller also suggested he get her a car and driver for the day, if she'd rather go shopping and sightseeing. She liked the idea of being part of the filming, but I guess I convinced her that being at the Opera House at 7:00 AM dressed in an evening gown and sitting for hours wouldn't be as much fun as having a car and driver at her disposal for a day of shopping. She took my suggestion, but when we went to the opening of the film, and that scene came up, with Colin's family large as life on the screen behind Dudley Moore, she looked at me and said, "I shouldn't have listened to you."

The picture shot and edited, I began my work, and as Colin predicted, I had a great time writing the score. For a comedic film, I wrote some of the most intense, dissonant, and dramatic music I had ever written, as Goldie's character was constantly being threatened on-screen.

I had a large and wonderful orchestra to record the score on Paramount's Stage M. Tom, Eddie, and Colin were enthusiastic and supportive of everything I wrote. Michael Eisner came down briefly to watch one of the recording sessions. He was the president of Paramount Pictures before taking over as CEO of Disney, and remarked that he had never seen music being recorded before.

It's always an exciting experience, certainly for me, to see the music coming together with the film when it ties together all the emotions in a visceral way and adds another dimension to the movie.

The premiere of *Foul Play* was in San Francisco, and Paramount threw a lavish party there after a private screening. A chartered plane took all the

Scoring *Foul Play,* Charles conducting, at Paramount Pictures Stage M. Goldie Hawn on-screen. *Courtesy of the author.*

invited guests to San Francisco, and Chevy Chase played cabin steward, serving drinks and doing impromptu stand-up comedy. There was a lineup of limos right on the runway as we got off the plane to whisk us all to the screening and party afterward, accompanied by a motorcycle escort of policemen to cut through the traffic.

What a way to earn a living!

Barry Manilow's record of our song was released just prior to the film's release and became an instant hit and was all over the radio. Barry performed the song for the first time live in concert at the Greek Theater in LA. He introduced this new song that he was about to sing and told the audience he was nervous because he had never sung it live before, and he was concerned about the song's range. He finally picked up the sheet music from the piano as though that would give him more confidence, and the orchestra began. The capacity audience of more than five thousand people at the Greek Theater all started to applaud when they heard the piano begin the introduction. From a songwriter's point of view, that represents immediate acknowledgement of the record and is as exciting as a round of bravos at the end.

Barry sang the song magnificently, and always has, and I've heard him do it many times over the years. For a while it was his opening number as it was for one of his TV specials. Barry is such a wonderful singer, performer, songwriter, and all around great guy, and Norman and I were so fortunate in the way it all worked out. I last heard Barry perform "Ready to Take a Chance Again" in his Las Vegas show in 2005, almost thirty years later. Joan and I flew to Vegas with several friends to see Barry's show, and he had the best seats set aside for us. What I didn't know was that in this particular show he was not performing all of his hits, and my song was not in the show at all. But because he knew I would be there for that performance, he put the song in the show for me. He introduced the song he was about to sing and spoke about me and Norman Gimbel and how lucky he was to be the one to get to sing this song, and then proceeded to sing the song passionately and brilliantly as always. We saw Barry backstage after the show, and he was as enthusiastic and excited being on the stage in Vegas as the audience was in being there. And they were ecstatic, as we all were.

I mention this story lest someone think that this is an everyday occurrence in a songwriter's life. It's not, and I never take it for granted. Any songwriter, even with a lot of hits in his catalogue, will tell you that for all the songs that people know, there are many more, maybe just as good or better, that never had a chance, and it's nothing short of miraculous that a song ever emerges and remains in the public's mind. Thanks again, Barry.

The film was a big hit and had a number of classic scenes in it, including Dudley Moore doing a striptease to the Bee Gees' "Staying Alive." We used Barry's new record of his song "Copacabana" as source music in the film, and so it was included on the soundtrack record along with "Ready to Take a Chance Again" and my orchestral score.

After the release and success of the soundtrack, I had another thought that I brought to Clive Davis, the head of Arista Records, who released the album. I flew to New York to meet with Clive about this idea. As part of the score, I wrote a symphonic disco around some themes in *The Mikado*. This was during the height of the disco era. I thought that it could possibly be a hit on its own, and even though it was already on the album, I wanted Clive to hear it with the thought that it could be pulled out as a single.

Clive greeted me very cordially, and after chatting a bit, he put the record on to listen. Moments into the record, his phone rang and he picked it up. The record continued to play as he began his conversation, so he turned the volume down, as apparently it was interfering with his call. I stood up to reach the record and shut it off while he was on the phone because he obviously couldn't concentrate on the music, but he waved me away miming the expression "it's okay, I can still listen." His conversation continued, my record sinking into oblivion with the volume turned down and no one listening. I made one more gesture to stop the record while he was on the phone, and again, he waved me away, assuring me that it was not a problem for him to continue listening to it even while on the phone.

I thought to myself, "I flew to New York to hear my record underscoring Clive Davis's phone conversation."

He finally concluded the call just before the record ended, sat back, and listened to the last fifteen seconds. Then he looked up at me and with a very earnest look on his face said, "I don't think it's a hit." And that was that.

✑

It was a particularly cold winter that year on the East Coast. In California, where it was beautiful and warm, we kept hearing about snow storms and freezing weather in New York. Normally, my parents would come to Los Angeles in the winter, to visit us and our children for a few weeks or a month, and get a reprieve from the cold of winter at the same time. Joan's parent had moved to LA a few years after us. This year, however, my mother was in one of her unexplainably stubborn moods and kept insisting that New York was fine even though my father, who was now retired, was ready to come out at the drop of a hat.

A typical conversation with my parents was, "Dad, why don't you come to California for a few weeks? It's so cold in New York and so beautiful here."

"I'd like to come, but Momma doesn't want to."

"Why not? The kids would love to see you, and really, it's too cold there."

"I know, but Momma says New York is not too cold."

"It's freezing there. How's the heat in the apartment?"

"Not working too well, but she has two sweaters on so she says that it's fine."

"She has to wear two sweaters in the house just to keep warm?"

"And a hat!"

"Dad, let me talk to Mom."

Then I'd have the same conversation with my mother, where she'd assure me that with two sweaters and a hat on in the house she was not cold.

"But Mom, Dad would really like to come."

"He can go. No one's stopping him."

There was no earthly explanation as to why she didn't want to come. She loved us all very much, and our children were all her darlings, but when she set her mind to something, wild horses, as they say, couldn't change her mind. I am also rather persevering and would call often and try to find an opening to turn her around.

One day she told me that her brother, Uncle Dave, had just come back from a cruise on the Love Boat to Mexico and had a wonderful time. Sensing an opportunity, I asked her if that sounded like something she'd like to do.

"A Love Boat Cruise? Of course I would."

"To Mexico?" I asked.

"Of course to Mexico. I'd love to see Mexico."

I said, "Let me talk to the producers of the show, I'll see what they can do," knowing full well that my mother would not enjoy the trip, if even she would go, if she knew that it cost me a lot of money.

I hung up the phone and called my mother-in-law, Blanche Redman, who was a travel agent.

"Blanche, can you book a trip for my parents on the Love Boat, sometime soon. It's very cold in New York and I'd love to get them out of there for a while."

Princess Cruise Line was commonly referred to as the "Love Boat," as it was the ship line actually used on the show.

Blanche called me back in a short while to tell me of the available dates.

I called my mother. "Mom, I spoke to the producer of the show, and he said he would love you and Dad to come on a Love Boat Cruise to Mexico!"

"For free?" she asked.

"Of course for free. The producer invited you."

"What about Uncle Dave?"

"Not for Uncle Dave. The invitation is just for you and Dad." My mother was always looking out for everyone else, never mind that Uncle Dave just came back from the same cruise.

"What do you say, Mom? The boat leaves in three weeks."

So finally, I found a way to get my parents out of New York during a particularly brutal winter. They would come to us in two weeks, spend a week with us, ten days cruising, and then another week with us. By that time the weather in New York would surely improve.

They came to Los Angeles, and I took my father out shopping to buy him cruise wear. His dark, woolen winter suits would just not work on a cruise ship where the temperature was summer-like. It was another moment I remember with smiles about my father. My father was a lovely, sweet, unassuming man, now retired from his window cleaning business and enjoying himself and his new unpressured life. The salesman brought out white pants and beige pants and light color print shirts, with white shoes and belts to match.

The salesman asked him, "What do you think Mr. Fox?"

My father, in his inimitable manner simply said, "Whatever my son thinks I should have is good for me."

"Do you like the way the clothes look on you, for your cruise?"

"What do I know about cruising on a boat? My son knows. If he says it's good, it's good."

I think that I gave him a harder time when as a little boy he would take me to Howard's Clothes in the Bronx for my yearly suit.

The pièce de résistance was a white captain's hat, which he liked very much. And now he was ready for a cruise. He said to me that before they left on the cruise, he would like to meet the producer of the show and thank him personally for his kindness and generosity.

I called Henry Coleman, who was the producer and a very nice man, and a friend, and arranged for a day that I would come down to the set with my father, that would have some interesting scenes to watch being filmed. Then I told Henry that if my father said anything that sounded strange or even weird, let it pass and I'd explain later.

On the appointed day, my father and I went to the 20th Century Fox lot to the sound stage where *Love Boat* was being shot. It was a fabulous indoor set, complete with a swimming pool, a mock-up of a ship with its deck, and many actors and extras in bathing suits and all sorts of shipwear. You would think for a moment that you were already sailing on the ocean. My father was amazed to see all this inside a building, and when I introduced him to

Henry Coleman, his comment to Henry was, "Boy, this must cost a pretty penny, Mr. Coleman," to which Henry replied, "I'm sure you're right about that, Mr. Fox."

Then my father said, "I want to thank you very much, Mr. Coleman, and tell you how much my wife and I appreciate what you've done for us with your kindness and generosity."

Henry, looking a little nonplussed, turned to me with a "what do I say now?" look, and I just gave him a little gesture indicating that I would explain later.

The cruise was one of the highlights of my parents' life. They loved every minute of it and talked about it for years after. As they walked up the gangplank onto the ship, the band was playing my *Love Boat* theme. Our family all came to give them a big sendoff. This was my parents' only experience on a big boat since they'd come over on "the boat," the one that brought all the immigrants to America, more than fifty years earlier.

My father, wearing his cruise outfits and white captain's hat, and my mother with her bright, summer colors and boater's hat, had the time of their lives. They let everyone on the ship know whose son wrote the *Love Boat* music, and even the captain, the one with the real captain's hat, invited them to have dinner with him.

My parents never knew that we paid for their trip although I suspect that maybe my mother had a feeling about it. But if she knew how much a trip like that cost, she never would have gone. There were not many times that I could put one over on my mother.

Sometime during the winter of 1978, Norman Gimbel and I were asked if we would do a musical version of *A Midsummer's Night's Dream* that would play all that summer at the John Anson Ford Theater in Los Angeles. Peg Yorkin was the producer of the Los Angeles Free Shakespeare Festival, which was the West Coast counterpart of the New York Shakespeare Festival in Central Park, headed by Joseph Papp, which was free theater as well. This was to be their first musical production as all the others in the past were the Shakespeare plays as written. The play would be adapted and directed by a young director, Kim Friedman. We met with Kim, and she had a very wild and fun take on a contemporary approach to this classic. It would take place at a resort in Atlantic City, and the fairies would be replaced by sea creatures and an alligator. The players would be the same, and we would be rather faithful to the Shakespearean verse, but it was the attitude and setting and costumes and of course the songs that would give it this novel approach. As Kim was describing what the piece would be, with sea monsters and alligators and a load of fun and lunacy, all the while keeping Shakespeare's writing and play intact, Norman and I were totally lost picturing it, but we liked Kim

Mom and Dad on Love Boat Cruise. *Courtesy of the author.*

very much, and her larger-than-life enthusiasm for her vision won us over, and we agreed to do it.

There was no actual finished script to work from, other than the original play, from which Kim took scenes and embellished on them, and had fun with them, as Norman and I looked for scenes that could be turned into songs to define the characters and their relationships and underline the story and move it forward. We were under a tremendous strain right from the beginning as we had an opening date just a few months away before we had written a note or a word. The score would have a strong rock beat to it, yet be tuneful and character driven. The first song we wrote was for King Oberon, who would be played by the wonderful Cleavon Little. Michael Peters, the talented choreographer of the Michael Jackson videos "Beat It" and "Thriller," created a sinewy, slithering dance number for the chorus dancers while Oberon declared his rule over the kingdom singing "I've got the pow-wow-wer."

The show opened with an Elizabethan-sounding refrain that established the period of the original play, and then turned suddenly into an up-tempo rock version of that same melody, and it brought you into the world of this show that we were establishing a style for. After the opening number, the scene begins with the guests checking in to an otherworldly-looking lobby of a hotel in Atlantic City. A character looking a lot like Will Shakespeare himself, however, wearing dark shades, enters the scene, goes to the front desk and asks for a room, announcing that his name is Shakespeare. The reply came from the desk manager, "I'm sorry, we have no room for Shakespeare tonight." That set the tone for the evening and got a big laugh. We wrote a ballad for Hermia, who was played by Mare Winningham doing her first stage starring role. She sang a song called "Lysander"—"If I ever needed you Lysander, I need you now"—after he left her.

Norman gave me an upbeat lyric for the company to sing as they went to frolic in the ocean: "Let's go to the beach, beach, it's better at the beach beach . . . whah-oh."

And we wrote a quartet for the star-crossed lovers called "What's Going On" as Lysander, Hermia, Demetrius, and Helena each try to figure out how their roles as lovers got reversed. The four characters would bring down the house with that number every performance. For the queen, we all wanted Susan Tyrell, who couldn't take the job for the money that the Shakespeare Festival offered, so we three authors and director gave our modest fees back to the company to help to make it possible for her to do the show with us, which she did. I love live theater, and the heart that goes into it. There is so much heart and soul and energy and hopes and excitement in working before a live audience. There is such a strong bond when everything is working between the creative team, the cast, and the backstage people. Of course, it makes the heartache greater when things don't work well. In this case, we were all walking on a tightrope without a net. We all had to be adventurous with no time to try things out. Norman and I would write a song, rehearse it with the actors, Michael would choreograph, Kim would stage it and set it, and finished, on to the next. We had an amazingly beautiful and huge set that looked like no other, representing this fantasy world. I was in good hands with the music as my friend Ben Lanzarone, who had just moved out from New York, agreed to be the musical director of the twelve-piece orchestra and help with the orchestrations as well.

The John Anson Ford Theater is a wonderful outdoor theater on a hillside in Hollywood, across the freeway from the Hollywood Bowl, and holds about twelve hundred people when packed. We must have had good word of mouth because right from the previews, the audience was filled to capacity every night, and additionally, people sat on top of the wall on the sides, and even sat on the hillside surrounding the theater. It didn't hurt that this was free theater. No one paid for a ticket, which was supported by the festival.

The show was my first experience with theater, and it was like nothing I'd ever known before, and I became quickly enamored with the whole process.

The show wasn't yet completed even as we began performing for an audience. Certain key characters were still missing their numbers, and they would continually ask me and Norman, "Where's my song?"

"It's coming . . . we're working on it," was the usual answer. It was most unusual to be on a stage with an audience every night, and us trying to finish the show. We had originally planned a few previews and then opening night. We needed to push the opening back by a week or so, just to try to complete the creative work. The drama critic for the *Los Angeles Times*, Sylvie Drake, let it be known that she would give us two extra days, and then she'd have to attend a performance and write a review. Peg Yorkin explained to her that we were still trying to complete the show, to please hold off, but Sylvie Drake was unmoved. "I have to write a review to report to the people of Los Angeles."

This was my first experience with a theater reviewer, and I thought, "Is she protecting the Los Angeles audience from the scourge of . . . what? Free musical theater?" In the end she came anyway, and the review was not bad at all. The show played for that entire summer to a packed audience every night.

But before the actual opening night, and before I was able to complete the music for a lyric that Norman gave me, which was to be sung by a wonderful actress, Anne De Salvo, who played Helena, and who was desperate to have a solo to perform in the show, my life was changed by a personal tragedy.

Telephones, which had brought such good news to me in the past, now brought me the worst news I'd ever had. I was woken one morning by a phone call from my mother in New York. Through her sobbing, I could barely make out that my father had died suddenly of a heart attack. I was in shock and disbelief. He was seventy-five years old and wasn't sick for a minute, and had no previous heart condition that I was aware of. It was a hot, humid summer day in the Bronx, and my father and another man stood watch in the lobby of their apartment house, which was kept locked for safety, as men in the building, mostly old-timers, would take turns as vigilantes, protecting the front door to the lobby, because there had been a recent rash of robberies in the building. Nothing specific happened to cause my father's heart attack; he just died with no warning.

I was on a plane with Joan later that morning to New York. My parents had long ago made all the funeral arrangements, in an old New York Orthodox Jewish Cemetery in Queens, to be buried along with my mother's side of the family starting with her own mother. My cousin Matt and my

Uncle Zalmon, both cantors who had married Joan and me, would officiate, and I had nothing to think about other than just to be there with my mother and brothers. Everyone was so kind and thoughtful and helpful to me, as I was beside myself with grief, as were my mother and brothers. After sitting shiva at my mother's house with the family for a few days, I returned to Los Angeles and to the show, which had consumed so much of me before this personal loss, but for the moment, I was removed from the same sense of urgency that I felt before to finish the show. Poor Anne De Salvo begged me to finish her song for the show, and for the first time in my life, I couldn't find my way to the piano. I started feeling chest pains myself, and ended up with a cardiologist recommending that I take an angiogram. I did and was fine. I was thirty-eight years old and healthy. It was all stress. But little by little, my sense of purpose returned, and I was back on board the show.

Producers came from New York to see the show, as there was a lot of heat on it. Joseph Papp came and said he liked it very much, but didn't get to around to offering to bring it to New York. The producer of *Best Little Whorehouse in Texas*, Stevie Phillips, did, however, and we signed a contract with her to take the show into New York the following season. Unfortunately, it never happened. Stevie suggested book writers, and we met with them, but somehow, after the energy and excitement of that summer died down, it never picked up again, and the show went into a sort of limbo state, never to emerge. It remained for me, however, a marvelous experience and only whetted my appetite to do more writing for the theater.

⁗⧽⧽⧿

By this time, I was already involved with the San Francisco Ballet, as I had accepted a commission from them to compose the music for a ballet that would be choreographed by Michael Smuin, the director of that company. My good friend and a wonderful composer, Paul Chihara, who had been the composer in residence with that ballet company, introduced me to Michael Smuin, who was wanting to do a new work based on a Native American theme. I was enthralled by the idea of getting back to the classical world, and with a story ballet, and Michael Smuin, whose work I thought was fantastic, and a great ballet company, it was all the more exciting, and I happily accepted a commission. This was the start of a long and wonderful collaboration and friendship with one of the great choreographers in America.

Michael wanted initially to do a ballet based on the true story of a Native American named Richard Oakes. Oakes was a Mohawk Indian and was the leader of the Indians who took over Alcatraz Island in 1969 as a protest against the impoverished conditions that American Indians lived under. They took over the abandoned Alcatraz Island Prison and claimed it in name of Native Americans everywhere, and stayed on the island for several months until they were finally evicted by the San Francisco police. Richard lived there during this period with his wife, Anna, and their young son. Tragically, his son fell off a cliff on the island and was killed. Sometime after that the Indians were forced off the island, and Richard, unable to contain or control his grief, became an alcoholic and was killed in a bar fight one night by a group of young white men.

Michael and I agreed that we'd tell his story in a one-act ballet and call it *Richard Oakes*. The San Francisco Ballet board thought that this story was still too hot a political issue, nearly ten years after the actual events in San Francisco, and would not let us call the ballet by that name. But we proceeded with thinking of the lead character as being Richard, and that of his wife, Anna, his actual wife's name. I would fly up to San Francisco for a day or two at a time and spend time watching rehearsals and the various ballets the company was doing. The company did an incredible *Romeo and Juliette* that Michael choreographed, as well as Paul Chihara's ballet *Shinju*, based on a Japanese legend, a beautiful and very moving work.

I was very happy to be involved with the world of ballet, and enjoyed the time spent with Michael in devising a libretto that would be the basis for our work. I listened for hours on end to Indian records and read many books dealing with Native American history, culture, and their spirituality. I attended a meeting one night in Los Angeles of the American Indian Movement with Russell Means as the spokesman. It was a moving event for me. I was taken by the beauty and spirituality of the Native Americans and how they've survived in spite of the everyday hardships and cruelty they've endured. At that meeting, a short documentary film was shown called *A Song for Dead Warriors*. It started with an extreme close-up of an ancient-looking Indian woman, whose face looked beautiful but craggy and weathered with age. She was chanting in a voice to match, a very sad-sounding lament to her people. I knew immediately that if we could get the rights to use this footage and her chanting, and hopefully even the title, we would have the start of the ballet and a new title.

Michael loved the idea, and we were successful in getting all those rights. The story that was developing was loosely based on events in Richard Oakes's life, but we made it about the birth, life, and violent death of an Indian at the hands of the oppressors, here in the form of a bullying, sadistic sheriff and his two deputies. It would be dramatic and spiritual and would focus on the romantic relationship between Richard and Anna. We would begin the ballet with a lifeless Richard, connected to four long ropes, each attached to a limb, symbolic of an umbilical cord. At the end of each rope was an Indian chief, each one modeled after a great and actual chief, and each chief was known for a different quality of greatness: Chief Joseph for spirituality, Geronimo for strength, Red Cloud for wisdom, and Sitting Bull for power. We would follow the young Richard's life from his birth, as his umbilical cords are tugged by the chiefs giving him life, and as each man danced a solo for him, they were endowing him with their accomplishments and traits. We would see him as a young man running free in the forest, and on the reservation, dancing with the young Indians, and then in a love-making pas de deux with Anna after he gives her an engagement ring. The sheriff and his men taunt the youngsters and later on that night return to rape Anna, who dies from the treatment, and all in front of Richard. Richard, in pain and grief, becomes an alcoholic and wanders into a bar with a pool game in progress. In his drunkenness he confronts the pool players and gets badly beaten. In his unconscious state he dreams of a return to the time of peace, when buffalo roamed the free land of his ancestors, and through the mist, Anna returns to him in his dream. After the dream, returning to the reality of the pool room floor, where he has been lying unconscious, he awakens with the evil sheriff standing over him. In a violent fight, Richard climbs on top of the sheriff and scalps him, only to be shot dead by two shotgun-wielding deputies.

In the final scene, the curtain comes down with Richard lying dead, while the opening tape of the old woman chanting is repeated.

I didn't want in any way to emulate Indian music, but I studied that music and the people and their history so that I could feel free to write the music that I heard in my mind, while being free at the same time to be influenced by what I had learned in my research and in feeling for those people.

Michael and I traveled to Missoula, Montana, where he was born and raised, and where his mother and father still lived. There was going to be a pow-wow on the Flathead Indian Reservation, and we wanted to be there for it. We spent two days on the reservation, where Indian dancers came from all over the country to vie for prizes while teams of Indian drummers sat in the center of a large circle, and individual groups of four or five drummers beat in unison on one drum while one of them chanted and sang and the others repeated in unison. It's a beautiful and colorful and moving event, with dancers of all ages, from very young to very old, dancing in the circle around the drummers, and each of them wearing their finest ancestral costumes, and colorful feathers and headdresses, and handmade jewelry. It's a sight and experience that I've never forgotten, and with all that combined with the humanity I felt emanated from those people and the story Michael and I had devised, I was ready to begin my work.

I wrote to my teacher in Paris about the ballet and how excited I was to be working on it. Here is a part of the letter that I received in return:

My Dear Charles,

Indeed, your letter retains my attention for it is full of love, of news, of thoughts. . . . So, understand how appreciated is your letter, the picture, the name of the children, their age—well—all what I feel so deeply. Here is also a small picture, and expression of my moved interest for your ballet. You touch there such a breaking-heart subject.

Read between the lines, and realize that I remain,

Most faithfully yours,
Nadia Boulanger

The music that I began writing was not atonal, but dissonant, and lyrical at the same time, and angular to reflect the sudden changes in the story. I worked on the composition for over a year, and the last six months prior to the premiere performance I worked on nothing else.

I loved being consumed by this world that afforded me such freedom even though there was a storyline. I divided the ballet into thirteen scenes. One of the scenes, that of the young dancers having a good time together on the reservation, I rewrote completely after Michael heard my original interpretation and felt that there should be a much more spirited, up-tempo beat to that dance scene. Michael choreographed to everything else exactly as I wrote it, except that he asked me to extend one scene a bit to accommodate a costume change.

Willa Kim, one of the great costume designers, came on board, and Ronald Chase was hired to design the backdrop, photographically. He came up with the idea of using a scrim in front of the stage, with front projections of different real-life pictures, thereby seeming to put the dancers right into those scenes. And with the artful lighting design of Sara Linnie Slocum, it really did look like the dancers were in the scenes. There was a minimum of set pieces used such as a light over the pool table and a bar sign. The buffalos that Willa designed were extraordinary and huge and imposing, and when they came through the stage fog, you would almost believe they were real.

We set May 1, 1979, as the ballet premiere, and for me it became sleepless nights again, even though I had been working on it for a long time. Michael began to develop the ballet, choreographing his dancers while a piano accompanist played a reduction of the score. I think that seeing the dancers for the very first time, starting to learn their movements, as Michael showed them by doing it for them, while a pianist played my music, was again one of the most memorable moments of my musical life. The simple purity of the developing movement to my music, even just in solo piano form, was breathtaking to me.

One night, as we were getting close to the deadline, it was late, but I was still at my desk working on the orchestrations. The first rehearsal with the orchestra and the premiere performance was looming only weeks away. The composition was long finished, and the dancers had been working for months learning Michael's choreography, but I still had much work to complete, and after I'd finish each scene, the copyists would first begin to do their work to copy the individual parts for the orchestra.

It was 1:00 in the morning, and the phone rang. At 1:00 AM I never expect a telephone call, even though my friends know that I'm usually up working at that hour. It was Gary Lemel, the head of music at First Artists Pictures. He apologized for calling so late but said it was urgent. For most people in most professions, to call someone at that hour, it would be preposterous if not unthinkable to find someone awake and working. But among my colleagues who write music for film and TV, who are constantly up against impossible deadlines, you'd probably stand better than an even chance of finding someone still working. In my case, he would have found me working at that hour, and much later, 90 percent of the time. But still, it was a late hour to receive a business call.

"I've just hung up the phone with Barbra Streisand. She wants you to do the music for *The Main Event*."

"Gary," I said. "I'm very flattered and would surely love to work with her on her film, but my agent has already asked me if I could do the film, and I said that I really couldn't because of the deadline with my ballet."

"Then Barbra wants to know if you'll just write a song for her to sing in the film."

Getting a phone call to write a song for Barbra Streisand for her to sing in her new film is just not something that happens every day, so of course, I really was flattered, and even tempted, but I still couldn't take the time away from my already committed work.

"Could you at least meet with her tomorrow morning at 9:00 at MGM and look at the scene the song is meant for and talk to her about it?"

I said, "Gary, its 1:00 in the morning. Is Barbra Streisand waiting by her phone to hear back from you even now?"

"Yes, she is."

I started thinking about my schedule and deadline.

The composition for the ballet was finished, which meant that in my mind and to a great extent on paper, so was the orchestration. It was just left to finish putting it all on score paper, to have a completed score in time for the copyist to copy all the individual parts for the orchestra. My sketches are pretty complete in the details of the orchestration, but it's in the details of the orchestration that the work is finally completed. This was the time to make the most minute changes and additions that would finish the work. Could I take the time away from my work to even meet with Barbra, much less work on a song for a film that would have its own needs? It didn't seem possible. Still, it was very tempting.

"Could I think about it Gary, and call you back?"

"Sure," he said. "Call me in twenty minutes."

"Barbra will still be waiting by the phone?"

"Yes," he said. "Call me back."

The next morning at 9:00 AM I met Barbra at the cutting room for the film on the MGM lot. She was at the Kem table with the film's editor and the director, Howard Zieff, when I walked in. They all greeted me warmly and thanked me for coming. She told me how much she liked my song "Ready to Take a Chance Again"—which was a hit for Barry Manilow and at that point in time had just been nominated for an Oscar—and asked me if I could write a song like that for her. I said that I'd love to try. "Marilyn and Alan Bergman will write the lyrics after you've written the melody," she added.

It's kind of unusual for me to write the melody first for a song that grows out of a visual moment on the screen that has to define a character, a relationship, an expression, or an event. I'm used to working on a song for a film as though it's a "book song," and at the same time can hopefully be a single record release. But obviously, in this case, she wanted to hear a song with the melody that she wanted to sing, even before there was a lyric. She added that it would be wonderful if the song could start as a ballad, then segue into an up-tempo beat.

"Could you do that?" she asked. Already my interest was starting to be piqued with that challenge, and I told her that that sounded like something I could do.

She then asked Howard to show me the scene that the song would be featured in. "What do think?" she asked, after seeing that scene. I said that I would need to see the whole film to see how this scene fit in with the rest of the picture, and to know the character I was writing for. So they made a call to book the main theater at MGM to show me the film.

Barbra and Howard and I walked over to the theater together. She and I sat shoulder to shoulder in the empty theater as Howard excused himself from sitting through the film yet again, saying that he'd be back after it was over. Before the film started, Barbra said to me that if I thought it was funny she hoped I wasn't inhibited to laugh by myself in the theater. I told her that I was a good audience, and if it's funny, I wouldn't feel inhibited at all to laugh.

The theater darkened, the movie started. I'm sure that I must have laughed a little more and a little louder than I would have if I had not been sitting next to the star of the film, although sometimes you can think something is funny and enjoy it without actually laughing out loud. At some point, and through no fault of the film, but just by being in a darkened theater at 9:00 in the morning after working halfway through the night, I was fighting to keep from falling asleep. I can't really say for sure, but I had the horrible feeling that at one point, I nodded off for a moment, as I was leaning on my right elbow, and suddenly it slipped off the armrest, along with my face, which was resting in my cupped right hand. I really didn't know if I had fallen asleep or just slipped off the armrest, but Barbra reacted to that by giving me a very quizzical look. After that moment, I no longer had a problem for the rest of the screening. I left her and Howard later, saying that I would call when I had something to play for her.

I worked on the song for about a week even while I was finishing my ballet. The song took an interesting form, as I found a way for this ballad to move very naturally into an up-tempo number, and back again through a few pivotal chords that I liked very much and thought she might too. It's much easier to write for someone when you know their voice and capabilities. Barbra Streisand's voice rang so clearly in my mind, that I could actually hear her singing the melody in my ear as I wrote it. I worked to the point that I felt that I had the basis of a good song that fit the needs of the picture and that scene in particular. I felt that the melody and the form of the song were clear enough, that Alan and Marilyn Bergman would know what I was going for, and that they would find the right words to grow out of the melody and capture the significance for the film.

I called Barbra and arranged to meet her at her house in Malibu. She gave me her gate code number, and I let myself past the gates, and onto the long driveway on her property after announcing that I was there. She had several houses in a compound on a hill overlooking the ocean. She gave me a tour of the houses before we went to work. One of them was being remodeled to have a fifties architectural look and furnishings to match. She said that one day she would probably donate the whole compound and the houses to the California Conservancy. Several years later, I read that she did just that. She and Jon Peters, who was the film's producer, were living in the beautiful country ranch–style home, which is where we had our meeting.

Barbra and I sat at the piano together, she next to me, as I played my song and sang la-la-la's in place of a lyric not yet written. I did sing a word or phrase here or there of a lyrical thought that seemed to flow from the melody. She said she liked it very much, and I could see from her reactions to what I was playing that she really did, and we ran a cassette tape of her la-la-la-ing along with me, and now and then, she came up with a spontaneous line of lyric that seemed to have just the right expression for the melody. Here was Barbra Streisand, just singing la-la-la's to my melody in learning it, and already it sounded wonderful. We worked for a couple of hours until Jon Peters came into the room where we were.

"Come over here, Jon, I want you to meet someone," she said. What struck me immediately is that through his body language, as he walked over to meet me, it seemed as if he really had no interest in doing so, which would be extremely unusual for a producer of a film when asked to listen to a new song for his picture. I would later learn that she had already recorded a song for the film called "The Main Event/Fight," and Columbia Records felt that they had a hit record, which it turned out to be, and that Barbra, who is a complete perfectionist about her work and her career, continuously searches for whatever could be an improvement on what she already has. In this case a finished record. Jon seemed to dutifully walk over to where we were, shook my hand, and without asking me if he could hear the song, excused himself and left.

I've always loved Barbra Streisand, and think that she is among the very few of the truly great artists in the world, certainly with one of the best and most beautiful voices of our time, and really, a gift to all of us, musicians and audiences alike. However, even though I was paid very well to write this song for her, after all is said and done, I would have preferred not having this seemingly futile opportunity, because it really did eat into my timetable with my ballet, and was ultimately very unsatisfying. It's always been a regret to me that I never heard Barbra sing that song with a lyric by the Bergmans, fully, and in a performance.

That same night, after I left Barbra still feeling very exhilarated, I received a call from Gary Lemel at my house again at about 1:00 in the morning. He was sorry to tell me that Barbra was not going to do my song and explained why to me at that time. The next day I received a call from Alan Bergman saying that he heard the news, but he and Marilyn would still love to hear what I had written for Barbra anyway. I did stop at their house later that day. After I played what I had written, Alan said that he knew that Barbra must have liked it, especially pointing to certain parts of the song and chord changes that he knew she would have loved. But it was not to be, and

I put that song away and got back to my other work, now with a little more pressure because of time.

I never stop feeling how remarkable and fortunate it is to have written songs that have found their way to a worldwide audience when it is so easy for a song to get lost and never find its way. There are so many factors mitigating against it.

⤬

Now, with the first orchestra rehearsals only weeks away, I turned all my attention back completely to the ballet. The San Francisco Ballet had two conductors, Jean Louis LeRoux and Dennis DeCouteau, but it was Dennis who would conduct the premiere. He was a wonderful conductor and a delightful man, and my music was in very good and cheerful hands with him, as he always had a smile and a knowing wink about what was needed from the orchestra. The rehearsals went very smoothly, and as we normally rehearsed from 11:00 AM to 2:00 or 3:00 in the afternoon, I chose to fly up to San Francisco and back to Los Angeles every day, rather than camp out there.

The night before the premiere, as the final dress and technical rehearsals stretched into the late evening hours, it came down to shooting the shotgun blanks that would be used by the deputies to shoot Richard Oakes at the end of the ballet. Michael wanted the effect to be startling and asked for the 100-millimeter blank casings to be used, not knowing how loud that was. My family was in San Francisco for the premiere, of course, and my son David, who was twelve years old and wanted to watch all the rehearsals, finally fell asleep in the first row of the orchestra of the War Memorial Opera House, as it was probably close to midnight. When the two 100-millimeter shotguns went off, one after the other, the noise in the theater was so deafening and startling that David jumped up from his sleep in reaction and proceeded to run out of the theater at breakneck speed. I had to run after him to catch up with him and explain what had happened. It's a moment I'll never forget. Michael finally settled on 50-millimeter shotgun blanks, and we all agreed that it certainly was loud enough.

The premiere performance starred Evelyn Cisneros as Anna, in her first starring role. She would go on to become the prima ballerina of the San Francisco Ballet, and was beautiful and elegant in her portrayal. Antonio Lopez played the young Richard Oakes brilliantly; and the chiefs, featuring Attila Ficzere, were simply dazzling; and finally Vane West, who played the menacing sheriff, was as villainous and wonderful as could be hoped for and received all the appropriate boos for his character in the ballet when he took his bows.

The whole experience with *Warriors* was the most meaningful and satisfying and enriching in my musical career. Shortly after the opening, Michael suggested that we do another ballet together, based on St. Joan, that would include a chorus of singers on the stage.

I loved the idea, and still do, but every ballet company, even major ones such as San Francisco, is limited in budget for doing many new works, and

Antonio Lopez in *A Song for Dead Warriors,* San Francisco Ballet. *Courtesy of the author.*

this project never got started as a result. It would take years, until Michael had his own ballet company, the Smuin Ballet, for us to do our next collaboration, the ballet *Zorro!*

A Song for Dead Warriors was a major hit for the company, and they performed it many times over a period of years around the United States and in other countries as well. Joan and I went to Edinburgh, Scotland, when the company performed it there for the Edinburgh Festival. It was very exciting to see a European audience react to this very American work. My only regret, if that's possible, is that I planned a trip to Paris to give Nadia Boulanger a copy of the score, which I dedicated to her, and unfortunately, she died just a few days before I arrived to see her.

Five years later, in 1984, I went to London for the recording of the ballet score with the National Philharmonic Orchestra. That would be the basis for a taping of the ballet for a television special, this time conducted by Jean-Louis Le Roux. The ballet was shown on PBS for their *Great Performances* series, *Ballet in America*, and my appreciation of the dancing went up even more, as I could see close-ups of the dancers' faces and movement that are not possible to see in a theater. The ballet was awarded an Emmy for best classical programming, and Michael also received an Emmy for choreography for his work.

In 1993, fourteen years after the premiere with the San Francisco Ballet, the Dance Theater of Harlem, led by Arthur Mitchell, added the work to their repertoire and premiered their production of the ballet. Joan and I went to New York for the opening at the New York State Theater in Lincoln Center, and shortly after that, to the Kennedy Center in Washington for a performance that was supposed to be attended by the president and Mrs. Clinton, where they would host a reception for the company afterward. Sadly, that was the weekend that Hillary Clinton's father died, so the evening was hosted by Colin Powell instead.

For ten years, the Dance Theatre of Harlem continued to perform the work on a regular basis on their world tours. Joan and I last saw it in London at Sadler's Wells in 2003, as they featured it on their last tour of the British Isles. Sadly, after that tour, the Dance Theater had such financial strain that they couldn't keep the company going any longer. The dancers were all wonderful, and it remains a great ballet company, and hopefully they will find their way back again. For me, the work has accomplished more and has survived longer that I could have imagined.

⟨≫⟩

Colin Higgins's next picture was *Nine to Five* starring Jane Fonda, Dolly Parton, and Lily Tomlin. In the film, these three women meet and become

White House visit, January 2000, Colin Ebeling, Charles, President Clinton, and Joan. *Courtesy of the author.*

friends working as secretaries in a large urban office for a misogynistic boss played by Dabney Coleman. It was produced by Jane's company for 20th Century Fox.

It was a wonderful, off-the-wall comedy dealing with the abuse these women suffer and their striking back. Colin asked me to score the film, explaining that Dolly had already written the title song, "9 to 5." He knew that I normally worked only on films where I wrote the songs as well, but he really wanted me to do this with him. I was delighted to do another picture with Colin, and since Dolly was the star of the film and the song was already written and recorded, I had no problem saying yes.

I was having a very good time working on this film that again gave me many musical opportunities. In particular, there was a fantasy scene, where the three women sit together after work, partying and smoking grass, and in their drunken stupor, each one tells her fantasy of how she would kill the boss. Jane's and Dolly's scenes follow, and the music that I wrote accompanying these scenes was different for each and fun to write.

Finally, Lily Tomlin tells the others that in her fantasy, she would kill the boss but it would be "kind of cute." In her fantasy, she is Snow White, and she has a small army of animated characters to help her, and suddenly it looks like a Disney movie. At the conclusion of the scene, when she ejects her boss out the window with the help of an ejection seat, as in the Disney movies where the evil witch is killed, peace and prosperity are restored to the kingdom, and the office workers who have been chained to their typewriters are now free. I scored the scene very much in an animated Disney film manner, catching all the silliness with musical stings and a lilting tune, and when the workers are freed from their chains, I brought in a chorus of singers to sing a triumphant refrain of ahhhhs.

Back to reality the next day, Dabney leans back in his chair so far that it falls backward all the way to the floor, causing him to strike his head, and he is knocked unconscious. Lily enters the office and sees him lying unconscious on the floor and believes that she has accidentally poisoned his coffee and he's dead, as she had fantasized in the previous scene, and the fun begins. And it was all fun for me, until the Musicians Union suddenly called a strike, and we could no longer record in this country.

I used an English composer and orchestrator, Ken Thorne, at Lionel Newman's suggestion, to help orchestrate the score. Lionel told me that I should pick up and go to London for a month, finish the score there, and record in London as well. He said to me, "I know it's your anniversary coming up, why don't you get two first-class tickets and take your wife? We'll get you a very nice apartment." So far, this was not exactly a punishment. That plan also changed suddenly as the English musicians went along with the strike of the American musicians. The plan now shifted to recording in Munich. This was now going downhill. The German musicians were having a field day doing the scores for American pictures. My friend Larry Marks, who was head of music at Warner Bros. and in years later became my agent, was in Germany at that moment to record the score for a Warner Bros. film. I called him in Munich to ask him what the situation was for my participating in the recording.

"Don't come here," he said. "You'll jeopardize your relationship with the Musicians Union."

I clearly had no intention of doing that, but at the same time I had a lot of pressure from the producers of the film and Fox executives to get my score done. Lionel suggested that Ken Thorne conduct the score with the German musicians, and I stay in a hotel room in Munich, and after each take of each cue, they would rush the tape to me for my approval. Hiding out in a hotel room in Munich and listening secretly to my music was not exactly what I had in mind in my life. I told Lionel and Colin that I couldn't do that and that I would finish the score in LA with Ken working after me to complete the orchestration. When the work was done, Ken, Lionel, Colin, and the music editor went to Munich for the scoring sessions. I stayed home. I really had no choice, even though it was more than frustrating not being able to conduct or even be present at the recording of my music for an important film.

Ken is a fine musician and I'm sure a very good conductor as well, but through no fault of his, the sessions did not go well. I wasn't there, so I really can't describe exactly how the sessions went, but I got daily reports that the musicians were having a difficult time. One day I actually received an angry call from Lionel accusing me of writing music that was unplayable. To me that meant that they hired the wrong musicians. My score was filled with contemporary rhythmic syncopations and was somewhat "rangey" for the brass. It would have been no problem at all with the musicians in LA or London. To add to it, the studio in Munich had so much echo, or natural delay, in the room that there was no definition of individual instruments or even individual orchestral sections. Everything played was swimming into each other when I remixed the tapes in Los Angeles. That was immediately apparent to me when they returned from Germany and I heard the tapes. Still, when dubbed into the film, the music, as it was recorded in Munich, worked well, and most importantly for me, Colin and even Lionel were finally pleased and happy.

For the release of the soundtrack album, I insisted on rerecording half of the most offensively recorded and played cues with my wonderful LA musicians. The strike was still going on, but since I was recording the music for the album only, not for use in the film, that was permitted, as the strike affected only music recorded to be used in films. It didn't surprise me in the least that the LA musicians played my music brilliantly and effortlessly, and I was completely vindicated in Colin's and Lionel's minds.

The soundtrack that was released had half the score recorded in Germany and half the score in LA. It never affected me again, as once my music is recorded and released on record, I have very little interest in ever hearing it again. My mind is filled with the new music I'm writing that has yet to be recorded and heard. Still, even with all the problems with *Nine to Five*, it remains a significant score for me in my body of work and led to a Grammy nomination for best score for a motion picture, which I share with Dolly Parton for her writing the main title song ("9 to 5"), which became an instant hit record.

Colin Higgins's next film, and as it turned out, tragically, his last, was the film version of the Broadway musical *Best Little Whorehouse in Texas*. He did ask me if I would consider doing the post score after the film and musical scenes were shot, but he really didn't expect that I'd want to do it, as it involved using a lot of material from the original musical score. He was right and thoughtful about that, and in spite of my enjoying working with Colin, Tom, and Eddie, who were again the producers of this film, I did decline, and my friends all understood.

However, they wanted me to write a new song for the film that Burt Reynolds would sing as a solo during a reflective moment on the screen. That I was happy to do.

I met with Burt at his house, and my friend and our temple's cantor, Nate Lam, who is a wonderful vocal coach, was there working with Burt. After an hour or so of us working together, I had a good grasp on what Burt's capabilities were vocally, and I left to discuss the song with Norman Gimbel. The song that we wrote gave Burt's character a moment alone on the screen as he reflected on his relationship with Dolly Parton's character, and it was called "Then There's This Lady." I heard from Colin as well as Tom and Eddie how much they liked the song and felt it was perfect for Burt and that moment in the picture. I rehearsed with Burt again at the piano at his home, and he sounded very natural and comfortable singing it.

Then Dolly Parton heard that Burt had a new song to sing in the film that she hadn't been asked to write. What was told to me was that she was unhappy that she was not asked to write the new song for a picture that she starred in. Apparently, even with all her other successes, she had a need to win her point and replace our song with one of her own. I heard that she went back to Nashville to write a song for Burt for that same scene, and recorded an elaborate demo, with an orchestra of Nashville musicians that she paid for herself. The story that was told to me was that she came back to LA, went out for dinner with Burt, and let him hear her demo, and he agreed to sing her song in place of the one that Norman and I had written. Colin told me that he really had no choice; they had to go with her song, or it would have been too disruptive to the good will on the set. I certainly understood and just chalked this up to another hiccup in the music business.

I think Dolly is a really fine songwriter, and apparently it was important to her to write the new song for her picture. She wrote a song without being asked to do it, paid for the demo recording herself, and Burt liked it enough to sing it in the film. I have to respect that.

As it turned out, that entire scene including Dolly's song was eventually cut out of the film after it was recorded and shot. So it goes.

❦

Working in television can be even more unpredictable as most pilots never get picked up as a series and most series don't survive beyond the first year. For all the shows that I did that were long-running series, there were many more that weren't. I wonder how many people remember the television series *Aloha Paradise* with a terrific vocal of a song by the same name that I wrote with Carole Bayer Sager, which was sung by Steve Lawrence, or *Blansky's Beauties*, with Cindi Grecco singing the title song, after our hit with her on the *Laverne & Shirley* theme song, or *The Shirley Jones Show* with Maureen McGovern singing the theme song, or *A Family for Joe* starring

Robert Mitchum, or *Me and the Chimp, Foul Play* the series, *The Bugaloos, Out of the Blue, The George Burns Comedy Week, $weepstakes, The Joan Rivers Show, The Joe Namath Show,* or *Conan* the series?

And the TV pilots that I did that never made it to series at all, including the *Happy Days* spinoffs "The Potsie & Ralphie Show" and "Pinky Tuscadero." Then there were *The Goodtime Girls, Walking Walter, It's Not Easy, Boomtown Band and Cattle Company, The Natural Look, Newman's Drugstore, Mars: Base One, At Ease, Sisters,* with a song that I wrote with Hal David featuring the on-screen sisters Sally Kellerman and Gail Strickland, sitting at a piano playing and singing a song, and my personal favorite, "The Bobby and Larry Show," which was a Warner Bros. pilot, written by my son Robbie and his college roommate, Billy Ray, and directed by Robbie.

I also had the pleasure of scoring a short film that Rob wrote and directed for Columbia Pictures that was a tender, touching little spoof about a sports legend, *The Great O'Grady,* the world's champion spitter. While my wordless on-screen role as a doctor ended up on the proverbial cutting room floor, fortunately my music remained in this delightful film.

❦

When you're a part of the music world, it's hard not to be involved with protecting the rights that composers and creators have enjoyed when there's always some group trying to legislate changes that would impact our lives negatively. It seems that there's a constant battle regarding performing rights, and with all the digital technology available and growing exponentially, it's more challenging than ever to protect the value of one's work.

I was asked one day by Frances Preston, who was the CEO and head of BMI, if I would consider going on a lobbying effort to Washington on behalf of an important bill that would affect the future of performance payments for music in this country. There was a bill in the subcommittee of the Senate and another in the subcommittee of the House that many senators and congressional representatives had already agreed to sponsor. So of course I said I was happy to be part of that.

Soon after that, I flew to Washington, and over dinner with Frances, our lobbyist, Jim Free, Barry Manilow, lyricist Bruce Sussman, and composer and saxophonist Tom Scott, all of us there for the same purpose, we discussed what we would try to accomplish over the next two days as a group, visiting members of the subcommittee and Congress.

We were briefed on the particulars of the bills in question. The bills were still in subcommittee in both houses, but there were many senators and congressional representatives who had already signed on in support of the bills, which were spurned by the Broadcasters Association, who were trying to decrease the performance royalties that were paid to the licensing organizations, BMI, ASCAP, and SEESAC. There was a real danger that our ability to earn money from our music as it was played over the airwaves would be greatly diminished.

Jim Free was a gem. He knew everyone in Washington and was well liked and had a delightful personality. He set up two days of meetings with congressmen and senators, and we walked the halls of Congress to impart our views on this situation to them, hoping that they would respond and side with our cause. In some instances they had already signed on to these bills, and we tried to get them to change their minds. In some cases they were still undecided, but we met as well with those members of Congress who were actively supporting our position. It was a fascinating learning experience in how our government works, filled with intrigue, personalities, and private as well as public concerns.

Having Barry Manilow as part of our group was the extra magic that opened a lot of doors and created a lot of interest in our cause. As we walked the halls, four composers and Jim Free, very often the senators' and congressmen's staff would come out of their offices to greet us in the halls, excited that we were coming. We posed for pictures together with the representatives and their assistants, and in some cases, listened to demo tapes of hopeful songwriters who used their connections with the representatives and senators to get us to hear their songs. The four of us had a little routine worked out to approach the representatives with. I believe I started by introducing why we were there, and then one by one, the others developed our reasons for asking the representative to side with our positions.

The best and easiest meeting that I recall was with a congressman from Georgia, Doug Barnard. After our initial hellos, we all sat down and I began my brief spiel, as we had rehearsed. Before I could finish stating our position, Congressman Barnard interrupted me and said simply, "Okay, fellas, I'm convinced. I'm off the bill."

I was very happy but a little nonplussed that he was convinced so quickly, so I continued talking, thanking him for having changed his mind, and continued telling him why this was the right decision. He continued listening to me, but I did notice him catch the eye of Jim Free and indicate something to him. With that, Jim stood up, and interrupting my story, said, "Charlie, there's an old expression here in Washington, when you make a sale, stand up, say thank you, and leave."

Another meeting was just the opposite and very frustrating dealing with a harsh reality. Republican senator Alan Simpson of Wyoming greeted us cordially in his office and explained the system of seniority for senators to choose the particular office they want. In his case, he had a fireplace and the view from his window that showed the beautiful Capitol Building in the background. All well and good, but then we started talking about the issues that had brought us all there. He listened carefully and courteously and then said something that I still find hard to believe to this day. He said, "Fellas, I feel very much for your cause. I like music and I would like to side with you, but as it happens, I have an old friend, a college roommate, who owns a radio station in Wyoming, and he asked me to sign on to this bill. Now this radio station gives me a lot of airtime, and as much as I'd like to, I can't go against my old friend."

I thought to myself, this is really the dark side of politics, with quid pro quo and self-serving friendships and Senator Simpson having no qualms in stating his reasons. I responded to him by saying that right in his own home state, at the University of Wyoming, there is a very active musicology department and music library, dedicated to keeping and displaying the musical works of composers as well as their papers, photos, and other memorabilia. I said, "I know this because Gene Gressley, who is head of that department, came to my home in California and asked me, among others I presume, if I would commit my papers and manuscripts to the university for their safekeeping. I agreed to do it, and in the interim, when I bought a new grand piano, I donated my older grand piano to that university for use by their music school." And furthermore, "since your leading university has such an active plan to preserve the work of contemporary American composers, your being on this bill will help to destroy music by taking away a composer's ability to earn a living."

"I'm sorry, fellas," he said. "What can I do? I can't go against my college roommate."

As of this writing, Alan Simpson is no longer a senator.

Orrin Hatch, Republican senator from Utah, and a songwriter himself, who is personally affiliated with ASCAP, was our ally and one of the chief voices against the bill, and he invited us to lunch in the Senate dining room, where among others Strom Thurmond came by our table to tell us he was on our side and to thank us for coming to Washington. The ironies in Washington are certainly true, that politics makes for strange bedfellows, as I've found very little else that I've agreed with these senators about through the years! We did the same the next day with Los Angeles congressmen, Democrats Mel Levine and Howard Berman, who invited us to lunch at the congressional dining room.

I received a note from Jim Free when I got back home informing me that the bill never got out of the Senate and congressional subcommittees and was effectively dead. I knew that there were other groups of concerned people in the music business who also made trips to Washington. I'm sure they felt as good as we did to participate in helping to end a bad legislative action that would have hurt the music community.

I was in Washington another time at the request of Frances Preston, to serve as a witness in a federal trial that was brought by the Disney Channel and the Black Entertainment Television (BET) against BMI.

Only BMI was named as a defendant, but the outcome would certainly have affected ASCAP and SEESAC as well and would have had far-reaching consequences on composers and publishers and the music world in general. This was a lawsuit brought by the broadcasters, who claimed that they were being treated unfairly because they could not deal directly with composers and publishers when they wanted their music performed on the air, and instead, were forced to pay for the whole catalogues of ASCAP and BMI songs, which, they claimed, caused them to pay for titles they never used. On the surface, it sounded like their case had merit, but effectively, it was the first step in destroying performance royalties on the airwaves.

After a trial that lasted several months, in which testimony was heard from many executives on both sides of the issue, I was the first of three composers to give testimony on behalf of the music industry. The others were composers Pat Williams and Richard Sherman.

The day of my testimony was one of the worst days of my professional life. I had had meetings in LA with members of the counsel, and on the morning of my being called as a witness in Washington, I had a preparatory meeting with six attorneys representing BMI to prepare me for the questions that I would be asked. I must have used three towels in mopping the perspiration from my face, and that was prior to going to the courthouse.

It was a large federal court house in Washington. The stakes were enormous because the main issue was whether we as composers had colluded with the performance rights societies, BMI and ASCAP, to keep the users of our music, the TV and radio stations, from dealing directly with us on an individual basis, and therefore we'd be labeled as a monopoly. The byproduct of a loss of this suit would be a challenge to the performance societies' right to exist, and ultimately the broadcasters would be looking to buy out our rights on a one-time basis, eliminating future royalties. It was sure to be disastrous for music writers.

The time I spent on the witness stand was at least as bad as the time we spent preparing for it, but I was able to cut down on the perspiration once I got comfortable with the setting. The large courtroom was sparsely attended. Frances Preston and Thea Zavin of BMI were there, and my wife, Joan, sat alongside them. At one point Frances made the comment to Joan about me that I was starting to get comfortable now as I was busy arranging the pens and pencils and note pads and water cups around me, as well as anything else in my reach.

I spent more than six hours on the witness stand that day, breaking for lunch halfway. The judge admonished me not to discuss the case with anyone during the lunch break. During the afternoon court session, I was able to relax a bit and was almost able to appreciate the setting I was in and my participation in it. I'm sure that neither Pat Williams nor Dick Sherman had a very comfortable time during their testimony either, as it's so far afield from what we do.

After the trial ended that day, I was excused, and thanked by the judge, and later by the BMI folks and all our counsel as being very helpful to the case and shedding light on the issues from a composer's point of view.

Joan and I left immediately for the airport. Waiting at the Dulles airport for the plane that would take us to Florida for a badly needed respite with good friends, I had a vodka on ice in one hand and a hot dog in the other hand that I treated myself to, and I was back in comfortable territory.

Several weeks later I received a phone call that the judge had just ruled in our favor, and the news of that completely made up for my experience.

❦

Boulanger's Thursday Keyboard Harmony class was four hours long, with no break, and I was so fortunate to be in this class. There were only five or six of us in the class, all men except for Claude Françaix, the daughter of the French composer Jean Françaix, who had been a student of Mlle in his youth. This was basically a class for pianists because everything we did was at the piano. It was also the most intense, taxing, and ultimately exhilarating four hours of each week.

Mlle's two little students who lived in the apartment along with their parents, who took care of the house and cooked for Mlle, were named Giovanni and Paolo, and they were probably no more than six and eight years old. Their lessons started at 7:00 AM each morning. Our keyboard harmony class started at 9:00 AM. We all came early because no one would dare take a chance and come late, so we all heard the end of Giovanni's and Paolo's lessons through the walls, and we could predict the difficulty in our class based on hearing the volume of her voice through the walls.

If Giovanni and Paolo left their lessons in the living room, where she taught, wiping away tears, we knew we were in for a rough ride that day.

Mlle's living room had two grand pianos that faced each other on opposite walls of the large room. At the far end of the room was a full pipe organ that looked like it could be in a large cathedral. She was an accomplished organist.

She might start the class with transposition and ask us one by one to sight-read the piano part of one of the songs from Schubert's Die Wintereise *or* Die Shöne Müllerin *or some other piano accompaniment, and then she'd add, to transpose it up a major 2nd, down a minor 3rd or to some other key, and she expected to hear the whole piano part as Schubert wrote it, with nuances, just in a different key. There was really no magic or secret to how to do this. We had to learn seven clefs so that you could change virtually any note to any other note simply by changing the clef in your mind as you sight-read the work. There would be of course changes of accidentals depending on what the transposition was. I used to practice this at home for hours at a time to be prepared for this class. And of course, you would sometimes hear the most bizarre sounds coming from the piano when someone was having a problem. Oddly enough, Boulanger didn't have a problem with wrong notes so much as stopping the tempo. That was sacrilege.*

She would say, "The time does not stop. You must continue counting the measures even if you play nothing, then come back in when you can. But the time must not stop."

That meant that the unlucky person at the piano having a problem with transposition would be counting the beats and trying to find his way back into the music. The rest of us were all grouped around the piano, pointing to the measures as they flew by and counting along with that poor person.

Sometimes Mlle would take a page from Bach's Art of the Fugue *and ask us to invent all sorts of musical exercises, such as taking a single melody and playing it with the left hand while playing the same melody starting on the last note and playing it backward with the right hand. That wasn't hard until your eyes crossed somewhere in the middle.*

She would ask us to make canons by playing a melody as written, and two bars later begin the same melody an octave lower in the left hand, beginning at the first measure, while the right hand continued its part, two measures ahead of the left hand. And to make it more difficult, she might ask you to invert the countermelody so that if a note as written went up, you'd invert it and play that same interval down.

She had an apron-like cloth that would go over your head and reach out to cover the piano keys so you could not see your hands on the keyboard, and then ask you to sight-read something. Suddenly one was like a blind person, having to find the starting notes and continue with no reference to the keyboard.

We would have to reduce the score of a Mozart string quartet or a Haydn symphony to make it sound as though it was a piano solo, sight-reading all the instrument parts and finding the lead lines, the accompaniment to the melody, or contrapuntal parts. All the while . . . Never stopping.

It was grueling while you were the person in the hot seat. But then you went home and practiced the same thing and little by little it became easier. At that point she would find something more to challenge us.

We were all young, and we were not above fooling around to release some of the tension from time to time. If someone was at the piano sight-reading a solo part in a concerto or a two-piano reduction of an orchestral work, Mlle was at the other piano playing the orchestra part. There were times when the piano solo had a certain number of measures of rest before coming in again, and God help you if you came in at the wrong place. Well, the rest of us not at the piano would normally be helping the poor soul at the piano by conducting or counting out loud and pointing to the orchestra part as Mlle played it, and if the soloist had an eight-measure rest, for example, we would help that person count the beats until the next entrance.

"Un, deux, trois, quatre.

"Un, deux, trois, quatre.

"Un, deux, trois, quatre.

"Un, deux, trois, quatre."

And then sometimes just for the fun of it, when we came to the last measure before the piano's next entrance, we'd catch each other's eyes and as if on cue we'd all say,

"Un, deux, QUATRE!" (purposely leaving out a beat).

And the poor soloist now had to make a quick decision: listen to our prompting (did he lose a beat?) or have confidence in his own count. And if that person lost confidence and went with the unruly crowd and came in a beat early . . . poor soul.

"Mais non! Mais non!" Mademoiselle would scream. "Why can't you count!?"

And that person would look at us like we were traitors . . . which we were.

Later on after the class, we would all go together to the café across the street from 36 Rue Ballu and unwind with a beer or café. It was only then that the humiliated soloist could finally laugh at what had happened.

It was, all in all, the most taxing, but most exhilarating and wonderful class one could imagine. We all felt as though we had gone through the war and come out better for it.

❧

I was asked to do a film called *Six Pack* starring Kenny Rogers making his acting debut in a major motion picture. He was at the height of his fame, having made so many hit records. His warm personality and beautiful voice came through in his records, and this was the story of a loner, a racing car driver in the South who by a twist of fate gets involved with six orphaned siblings. Kenny becomes their father figure, and they get involved with his racing career. It was a warm, rollicking film, and he was perfect to play the role.

When I was first asked to score this 20th Century Fox film, it was left in the air whether I would write the main title song as well, so I declined. However, a short time later my agent called to say that Fox agreed to have me write the song as well.

In the film world that I've known, there's never a guarantee that they'll use your work, as scores and songs do sometimes get replaced. It's only guaranteed that you'll be paid for you work. Still and all, when you're hired to score a film and write a song, you're now in collaboration with the filmmakers, and if some part of your work doesn't work for them, you can always make changes or rewrite it completely. That's part of the collaborative process, but needless to say, the challenge is to get it right the first time.

My plane landed in Atlanta, where *Six Pack* was being shot, one blustery winter afternoon with wet snow falling lightly. A driver was waiting to take me to the motel about thirty minutes from Atlanta that served as the production office for the film, and where the cast and crew stayed.

Dan Petrie was a wonderful director and as nice a man as I've ever worked with. This would be the only film I would do with Dan, but I always felt a warm friendship from him over the years, and in fact, I did several pictures with his wife, producer Dorothea Petrie. I met with Dan for the first time at the production office. He was most concerned to talk to me about the song that I was supposed to write for Kenny, who was insistent that he would not sing a song in this picture, that he wanted to be known as an actor, independent of his being a recording artist. This must have been the reason why Fox was reluctant to commit to my writing a song in the first place. I said to him that I was surprised to hear that, because I was asked to come to Atlanta to get started writing a song for him. Dan said he hoped that would happen, but he left it up to me to handle it carefully with Kenny, and to convince him that he should sing a song. I had never met him before, but I couldn't imagine that he needed convincing to sing a song in his own picture.

The next day, the rain and snow over, Kenny flew down from his ranch outside Atlanta in his own jet helicopter. Dan and I met with him in a dimly lit motel room with two beds and chair. Kenny and I sat on the two beds facing each other and Dan sat on the wooden chair at the end of the beds. We had some friendly conversation getting to know each other. We both had the same business manager, although I'm certain that he had a lot more business to take care of than I did.

He said he heard a story about me from our mutual friend that he thought was so funny that he repeated it to other people. The story began that I owned a condominium in Mammoth, California, next to the ski mountain. One time I sent a check for my telephone bill for more money than was actually billed, by mistake obviously. We did not go back to Mammoth for a while, but the next month my statement from the phone company indicated a credit, which, without looking at it carefully, I assumed was a bill, and just paid it. The following month the credit was double what it was the month before, and again, I paid the higher amount without looking carefully at the bill. Now my credit balance was doubling each month, and without realizing what was happening, I mentioned to Joan that our telephone bill was outrageous in Mammoth, considering we hadn't been there in months. Finally, the last of what I thought was a bill was so high that I called the phone company to complain, and the woman in the billing department simply said to me, "Mr. Fox, would you please stop paying your credit balance?"

That was a true story, but I never expected that it would reach Kenny Rogers's ears and keep him chuckling.

We had a nice meeting, and after a while, Kenny asked me what I thought he should do regarding a song. He said that 20th Century Fox wanted him to sing a main title song for the picture, but he really didn't want to detract from his being recognized as an actor. He said that he had gotten a lot of pressure from Fox to do a song, but so far he was resisting.

"What do you think I should do?" he asked me. "Should I sing a song for my picture?"

I said honestly and directly that he should absolutely do a song. "Who should we get to sing a song in your picture, Barbra Streisand?"

He laughed and said he had been bombarded with tapes, all unsolicited, from people hoping he would listen to their songs. And then he said, furthermore, that he hates a title song that gives away what the picture is about before the picture unfolds. I said I agreed with him completely. I hate that too.

It occurred to me at that moment that the song that Norman Gimbel and I devised for *The Last American Hero*, "I Got a Name," which Jim Croce sang, was closer to what I thought we could do for his picture. Over the main title, just introduce the character that Kenny plays as someone who was ready and open for new things in his life. That would set the stage for his meeting these orphaned kids, when he is ready to accept something new in his life. Then I said we could develop the song so that for a montage in the middle of the film we'd learn more about the character, when he was having doubts about his direction, and finally at the end, the character in the song would conclude with his life having been changed.

He had an immediate and positive response to this thought and asked me if we could do that for him. I simply said, "I know we can. Just let me out of here, and I'll call Norman, and be back in a week or two with a song for you to hear."

Now he seemed genuinely excited. I know I was, and Dan certainly was, that our meeting had gone this well.

On my way out the door, Kenny called after me and said, "I have a new album being released. I'll tell the record company to hold up the release, and we'll call the album whatever the song title is."

I said, "Great. See you in a week or two."

I had several phone calls that night from the execs at Fox telling me how happy they were that Kenny had changed his mind and would now do a song.

I called Norman before I got on the plane back to LA so he could get started thinking about the direction the song would take. Within two weeks, as promised, I was back in Atlanta with a finished demo of our song called "Nothing But the Sky and Me." It was about an unencumbered person enjoying the freedom of his life, moving down life's sweet road and having nothing between him and the sky. It set up the character in a completely unpredictable setting for what was about to change in his life.

This time I met with Kenny in his very elaborate tour bus, which also served as his dressing room. The bus was filled with people, his manager, the producer, Kenny's wife, and of course Dan Petrie and me. The bus had an equally elaborate sound system, and the song sounded great when it was played for everyone. And it was played it several times in a row.

It sounded like it would be a hit for sure with Kenny singing. I didn't have to spend long. Everyone was ecstatic, and Kenny loved the song. I left the bus and headed back to Los Angeles the same day. There was going to be a wrap party for the film at Kenny's ranch the following day, but I was more interested in getting home.

That was the end of the good part. Now reality set in.

When I came home, I had congratulatory messages from many people. The next day I started to hear rumblings that Kenny liked our approach to the song so much that he was thinking of writing one himself. By the end of the week, ours was out, and Kenny was going to sing his own song. Dan Petrie asked me to meet him for lunch in LA to explain what had happened. In the commissary at 20th Century Fox, Dan had a cassette machine with him with earphones, and he wanted me to hear Kenny's version then and there. "How can I compete with Kenny Rogers in writing a song that he's going to sing in his picture?" I thought to myself. I listened to his song and made the comment to Dan that "this song does exactly what Kenny didn't want to do; it gives away the story of the picture before we're introduced to the characters."

"I know," he said, "He'll have to change a few things." But Kenny was now so enthusiastic about tying in a song with the picture's release that he promised that on his upcoming tour, he would promote the film by showing clips of the film while he was singing his song live. That was all that Fox could hope for in getting him to help in promoting the film.

The outcome of that was a foregone conclusion. I had no say in the matter. The only say that I had was whether I would agree to go back into the studio and rescore some of the scenes using the melody of Kenny's song. Everyone was very happy with my whole score, but that suggestion came from Sherry Lansing, the head of Fox studios, and perhaps originated with Kenny himself. This, I said, I couldn't do. I had already scored the film, and everyone loved my work. I wasn't going to start to make changes to interpolate a tune that had no bearing on the design of the score. If they wanted that done, they'd have to get someone other than me to do it. Dan said that he understood, and would explain to Sherry that we should leave the score as is. "It works great and the picture is finished," he said. I appreciated that very much.

There really was no one to blame from my point of view. Things are what they are in the business, and one has to keep his life in focus. But needless to say, I was very disappointed. For the record, Kenny's song did become a hit, but not one of his really big hits.

It's easy to remember the successes when it comes to songwriting; they're still part of the landscape. But you also remember the ones that got away. Norman Gimbel used to say that every song is a business, that if it doesn't happen today, it can always happen tomorrow. I do agree with that, but in reality it seems like there is a moment in time when the stars align, and everything goes as planned and hoped for, especially when one is writing songs to be part of a film where the record will be released in conjunction with the release of that film. And once that moment passes, it doesn't seem to have a chance again. "Nothing But the Sky and Me" remains unrecorded.

❧

The Gods Must Be Crazy II was the sequel to that delightful and very successful film about an African bushman in the Kalahari Desert who sees an empty coke bottle that is dropped by a careless pilot and believes that this is a signal from the heavens, and he has the self-made position of spreading the word.

I was asked to do the sequel and to travel to Sandton, just outside of Johannesburg, to meet with the director, Jamie Uys. He was South Africa's leading film director but had a reputation of being notoriously slow in delivering his films to the studios. In this case it was Columbia Pictures, produced by the Jerry Weintraub Company. Before I left for Johannesburg, Jerry called me and asked me to try to assess how long it would really be before the film was finished and if I could get Jamie to move it along a little more quickly. That's kind of an odd position for a composer to be in, but I said that I would do what I could and let him know. It's about twenty-four hours of actual flying time from LA to Johannesburg through London, so I was exhausted after a long flight, but at my hotel in Sandton there was a message waiting for me from Jamie, welcoming me, and asking me to call him after I've had a nap, that he was anxious to get together.

After I slept for a few hours, I had a driver waiting for me downstairs in front of the hotel, who would be my personal driver for the week that I would be in South Africa. He was a nice young fellow whose wife and children lived in Soweto. He was able to live in Johannesburg because he had a work permit, but that privilege did not extend to his wife and family, so it was only on weekends that he would see his family when he'd return to Soweto. This was 1989, and although Pieter Botha was the prime minister of South Africa, and many things had improved for the black people in that country, and apartheid would be dead with the election of Nelson Mandela, and things would turn around completely, it was still under the rule of apartheid at that time.

Sandton is a suburb of Johannesburg, and the production company operated out of a private house with a garden. Jamie was probably in his midseventies and was a lovely man with a very cheerful, if overworked, presence about him. Because he had worked on many films with animals in their natural habitat, he was used to taking months, if not years, to shoot all his footage. And because he told his stories on film by using so much wild footage of these animals, and with several stories interconnecting within a film, he would also take months to edit a film, if not years, as well. I could see immediately the problems that were caused as a result and why he wasn't able to deliver a finished print anywhere near on schedule. Jamie showed me around the production offices. He had six or seven editing rooms going full time cutting the film. He worked seven days a week, and for the week I was there, he didn't even have the time for us to have a social dinner. He asked me right away, how long did I think it would take to spot the picture? I answered that it should take a us a day to spot it together. "Oh my goodness," he responded. "I thought it would take a week!" That gave me a pretty good idea of why the film was so far behind schedule.

We screened the film together. It was really a sweet and fun picture about a native bushman, Xixo (pronounced Ziso) who becomes separated from his two children in the Kalahari Desert and spends the rest of the picture searching for them, as he passes through several subplot stories of the Angolan-Cuban war, downed pilots and stranded newspaper reporters, love interests and angry ostriches. It was all very farfetched and silly, but fun, and in the end touching when Xixo is reunited with his children, who were actually played by his own children in real life. It was also a mess, and far from being finished editorially. The storytelling process with the several stories that were interwoven was anything but clear.

I asked Jamie how much time he would need to work on the film before turning over a finished picture to the studio so that I could begin my work. I told him at that time how anxious the studio was to be able to plan the postproduction schedule and release date. He said that he'd be finished in two to three weeks. I knew there was no way that he'd have a final cut that really was "final" in three weeks. I said to him that I'd rather that he take all the time he needed to get it right, because with all the intercutting between stories, my music would have to be devised to make all those transitions work smoothly, and I didn't want to have to make a lot of changes once I got it right. He agreed, and said there'd be no problem. That the film that he would send would be locked.

For the rest of the week that I was there I made use of my time by going to concerts to get ingrained with South African music, which I loved and found both fresh and uplifting. With my driver accompanying me, I went to a concert at the famous Mayfair theater with Hugh Masakela and his band performing. It was only a few years before that time when blacks could perform on that stage, but they could not sit in the theater. At this time, they also didn't have to carry identity cards with them at all times.

My hotel was connected to a huge shopping plaza, mostly underground, with movie theaters and all sorts of shops. But along the walls of the shopping plaza there were emergency boxes that informed you of what to do in case of a bombing. In 2006 we are sadly used to being checked for bombs or weapons as we board a plane. In 1989, in Sandton, South Africa, people were frisked just entering the Hyatt Hotel where I stayed. Terrorism was the concern, even though the issues that brought it on were completely different than they are today.

There was an all-day concert in an outdoor amphitheater featuring many of the leading South African groups, and I was excited to go to this concert. As we approached the amphitheater, we noticed one small police car about a block away, just sitting parked, I guess in case there were any problems to report, but far enough away not to interfere. Entering the concert grounds, my driver was looking for a place to park amid a sea of cars, and as we passed by the gates for the artists' entrance, the guards, seeing me, the only white face among five thousand or more, opened the gates for us, I guess assuming that I was the concert promoter or someone important, but he wouldn't let my driver in, so we continued to look for a space. Finally, he had the thought of dropping me off at the entrance so I wouldn't have to walk while he parked far away. I got out of the car, feeling somewhat conspicuous among all the staring eyes. However, I really was not uncomfortable to be there. I loved their music and was happy to get the chance to listen to so much of it. All the while, the music from the concert was blaring out from the loudspeakers over the walls of the amphitheater, and I was anxious to get inside.

Waiting for my driver to return, and without being aware of it, my space was being encroached upon, little by little, by men all around me, asking questions of me, innocent questions, seemingly friendly questions, but still, I was clearly out of place. All I wanted to say was, "Hey guys, I love the music too. I'm only here to listen to the music. Great day for a concert, huh?" But I must admit that I was starting to feel a little concerned.

With that, I felt an arm on my shoulder as my driver returned to take me back to the car. He said that he was feeling uncomfortable leaving me alone, and thought that the wise thing would be to leave quickly. He was probably right, but I always regretted missing that concert.

Before leaving for Los Angeles, which happened to be on the day of Yom Kippur, I went to services at a Conservative synagogue in Sandton. It was only half filled or less on the holiest day of the year in the Jewish religion. I was very moved to be there, and was welcomed very warmly by the people all around me where I sat. I couldn't stay for the whole service as I was departing that day, but as I walked out of the synagogue, I asked a man if he knew where there was a telephone so that I could call my driver to pick me up. He said that he could drive me to my hotel, it wasn't far away. I asked him how he knew who I was and where I was staying. He answered, "It's a small synagogue and we don't have many strangers. The whole synagogue knows who you are." I guess word travels fast in religious circles.

Jamie had asked me if I would consider recording the score in Johannesburg or perhaps halfway between us in London, but I felt that for this score, which would require so much native-sounding percussion and "feel," played by excellent sight-readers, that I was much more in control by recording with the musicians I knew so well in Los Angeles.

Back home in LA, when the finished film arrived, I began my work. My music editor "broke down" the film for me and gave me the timings for the individual cues. I asked the music editor to keep in touch with the film editor in Sandton to make sure there were no changes in the film that would affect my work. Several times I called Jamie Uys personally to let him know how my work was coming along and to ask him the same question:

"Any changes?"

"Oh no, no changes at all," was his steady response.

I had an orchestra contracted, which included four full synthesizer setups for all the electronics and unusual sounds, along with all the African percussive instruments. I hired a chorus of South African students living in

LA to sing part of the score that I wrote, and the chorus members themselves added the words in their own language.

The night before my first recording session, which was to take place at my own studio, Evergreen, the music editor called me to say that he received a new print of the film that we should score to. He reported that unfortunately, 90 percent of the film had been changed. Exactly what I was hoping to avoid. Now, and for the most part, my music, which was timed carefully to the action, would be out of sync and wouldn't work. It was a nightmare. I called Jamie and asked him why he hadn't let me know sooner. I could have postponed the recording sessions to give me the time to make the changes in my music that would be necessary.

"Oh, I didn't realize it would affect you so much," was his answer.

I informed the people at the Weintraub Organization, and they were very understanding and supportive of my situation. It was too late to cancel the first two days of recording. They said to make the best of those two days with the orchestra, making changes on the spot, right from the podium, and we'd put off the other sessions as long as necessary.

I reworked the score to accommodate the changed film and rewrote everything that needed to be rewritten, and recorded the balance of the score a week later, and everything now worked fine again. I remixed the music at Evergreen and sent the completed mix to South Africa. The music was cut into the film in South Africa, and the dubbing was completed there as well.

Jamie called me to congratulate me and tell me how much he loved the score. All's well that ends well. . . .

NOT! . . .

Jamie treated my score as he did all the other film footage. He disassembled it from the film as I had written it and used and reused my music in places I never intended, in ways that made no sense, and cut portions of the music at will. He totally destroyed my sense of cohesiveness that I had worked for, for so long.

I didn't know any of this until I sat in a screening room with a hundred other people, watching the completed film for the first time. I was in shock. This had never happened to me before, and I didn't expect it at all. It was unbearable for me to watch the film, and although I stayed to the end, I never saw it again, and never will. Fortunately there is a CD of the music as I wrote it for the film. That, for me at least, is the proper musical legacy that remains from this picture.

❦

A film made for Turner Cable, *Christmas in Connecticut*, was the only film that Arnold Schwarzenegger ever directed. It was an upbeat comedy centering around a Martha Stewart–type person, played by Dyan Cannon, who had a popular TV cooking show but didn't know how to cook at all. Tony Curtis played her show's producer, and Kris Kristofferson played a local hero who was invited to stay at Dyan's house in Connecticut and be part of the show to help boost the ratings. What followed was fun to farce to romance. I was asked to do the music. My cousin Cyrus Yavneh, who produced many movies as well as the *24* TV series several years later, was the producer, and that was the only time we ever worked together.

Cy and I grew up together in New York. Our mothers were sisters who were born in Israel and remained very close forever. So the two of us have also been closest friends as cousins, and it was wonderful and special working together.

I met with Arnold Schwarzenegger for the first time in his office, on the top floor of the building and shopping center that he owned on Main Street in Venice. He was very warm and friendly immediately, and as my work on the film progressed, he was always very easy to work with.

We began to talk about the film and the overall design for the score. He said that he wasn't sure how he could contribute his feelings about the music, that he never worked with music before. I said that was great, we didn't have to discuss any technical aspects of the score or the recording of it, we could just discuss the film and what it needed, and let me worry about the music. That opened the door for him, and he proved to have a lot of insight as to

With Arnold Schwarzenegger in Charles's studio at home. *Courtesy of the author.*

what he was feeling about the film's needs. To me, that translates into a musical concept. He impressed me right away as being very smart as well as nice and genuinely warm.

One day I went to the location where they were shooting a big dance sequence that was supposed to take place in Connecticut in the middle of winter. Of course, this scene was actually filmed in San Marino, just outside Pasadena, which would normally not ever be covered with snow. Snow was brought in to cover the grounds surrounding the house, and as you stood in front of the house, you'd swear that you were back East in the middle of winter. There were a lot of actors and many extras involved in this dance number, which Cyrus's wife, Lynn Taylor, a well-known choreographer, was choreographing. After she had worked with the dancers and they were ready to start filming, Arnold let Lynn handle the technical aspects of the filming as well, knowing that she had much more experience in filming a big dance number, and he was smart enough to let her take over. One of the attributes to me of a good director is someone who lets everyone do their best work, and this is an example of that.

When I finished composing the score, I asked Arnold to come to my house to hear the musical cues one by one in sync with the film. I created a mock-up of the orchestral score with a synthesized orchestra that made it easier for him to hear what it would sound like, roughly, with a real orchestra. When Arnold came into my studio, he spent quite a bit of time looking at all the photos and memorabilia that I had on my walls and on the shelves of my bookcase, just as I had done in his office that first day I met him.

He came to a picture of me with his brother-in-law, Ted Kennedy, and asked me in his often imitated accented voice, "You like hanging around with Democrats?"

I said I did.

He said, "I'm married to one."

Arnold listened carefully to all the cues, and responded to each one as I hoped he would. We were in sync musically, and he saw what I was going for, and he liked it.

He had never worked with a composer before, but he understood and reacted intuitively to what the music was contributing.

In one scene, Kris Kristofferson was walking up a flight of stairs, but before he started to ascend the staircase, there was a funny piece of business, and I had the music responding to his reaction at the foot of the stairs. Arnold said that he could see what I was going for, but he thought the comedy should pay off a few beats later, when Kristofferson gets to the top of the stairs. I understood what his sense of the payoff for that scene was, and what I needed to do to make it work, and it was easy for me to make an adjustment in the music. For someone who never worked with music before, he had a keen awareness of its impact.

I flew to Salt Lake City along with the executive producer, Stan Brooks, to record the score with an orchestra comprising members of the Utah Symphony. Arnold loved the score I wrote, and it dubbed easily into the film. We all spent a lot of time together on the dubbing stage in finishing the film. As we neared the end of the dub, on the final day, Arnold and Cy and I were sitting together and making small talk. Arnold asked Cy what project he was doing next, and then asked me the same. We both told him.

Then I asked Arnold what he was going to do next, and he said, "I don't know yet."

So I put my hand on his shoulder and said, "Don't worry, I'm sure something will come along."

He loved that. He has a terrific sense of humor and laughed a lot. Little did I know that one day, what would come along is that he would become our governor.

Robbie, Lisa, Joan, and David with Charles receiving BMI's Richard Kirk Award for Lifetime Achievement in 1993. *Courtesy of the author.*

For the film *The Last Married Couple in America*, my friend and the film's producer, Ed Feldman, wanted to introduce me to the director, Gil Cates, because he thought we'd hit it off. Was he right. Gil was born and raised in the Bronx, as Ed was, and in fact, Gil and I went to the same junior high school, he a few years earlier than I. Gil lived across the street from that school on Creston Ave., and who's to say our paths didn't cross even then? *The Last Married Couple in America* was great fun to work on, and Gil remains one of my closest friends, and one of the people I truly love and admire from all my years in films.

When I was on the podium recording the music for that film on the Universal soundstage, he was sitting next to Joan in the control booth, and at one point Natalie Wood and her daughter Natasha came into the studio unbeknownst to me to watch the recording of the music for this film, in which she was a costar. Joan said to Gil that I would die if I knew that Natalie was there watching me, because I've always loved her. Gil said, "Who doesn't? Every guy has loved Natalie Wood."

That film was the first of many that I did with Gil. The next film was *Oh God, Book II* with George Burns, another wonderful experience for me, and it was followed by another nine or ten television films over the years.

Gil always said that he loves when I start to work on his pictures, because he can stop worrying about the music. I worry enough for both of us.

Over the years, Gil and his wonderful wife, Judy, Dr. Judith Reichman, and Joan and I have gone on vacations together and had some great times together, although never, we lament, enough. Thinking about my friend Gil, and the work we've done together along with his producing partner Dennis Doty and his wife, Jeralyn, who are also dear friends, always puts a smile on my face. And that's saying a lot in this business I've been so privileged to be part of.

❦

Norman Gimbel wrote some of the classic songs of the bossa nova era with Antonio Carlos Jobim, such as "Girl from Ipanema," "So Nice," and "Summer Samba." With Michel Legrand, he wrote the songs from *The Umbrellas of Cherbourg*, which included "Watch What Happens" and "I Will Wait for You," the most beautiful songs, all. I was very happy when Ron Anton of BMI suggested that we work together on the film *Pufnstuf* and introduced us over the phone when I was in New York in Ron's office and Norman was in Los Angeles.

Norman Gimbel has been my principal collaborator for over thirty years, and we've written more than 150 songs together. Norman's lyrics have extraordinary beauty and sensitivity and understanding of the human condition. There's never a wasted or excessive word with his lyrics. I would sometimes drive him crazy when I would expand musically on a lyric he gave me, causing him to have to double up on his thoughts or simply have to repeat an expression that worked perfectly in a similar way without repeating his words. But I guess that's part of collaboration, and we've had a good one. As friends, we helped to dust off many cars over the years as we'd lean against them discussing the work at hand or our lives and families, or chasing the dreams in our work together.

Most of the songs we wrote together were recorded for films, television, and records, and we've enjoyed seeing our songs climbing up the charts many times with some of the great singers of the day. We had two stage musical shows produced, *Midsummer Night's Dream* with Cleavon Little and Mare Winningham at the John Anson Ford Theater in Los Angeles, and *The Eleventh*, starring Shelley Berman at the Off Broadway theater in Ft. Lauderdale. We wrote several other shows together that didn't reach a full production stage.

We wrote and produced about forty songs for Lori Lieberman on four albums for Capitol Records. The only big hit that emerged from those songs was the Roberta Flack recording of "Killing Me Softly," which years later

Charles Fox Songbook Concert, Gindi Auditorium, Los Angeles. Charles at the piano.
Courtesy of the author.

became a big hit for the Fugees as well. If you were to ask Norman or me which ten of our songs together we liked the best, we might each have a completely different list, but I think those songs that we wrote for Lori were our best, and those records we made together with Lori stand as those we're most proud of.

❧

Hal David is one of my favorite people, and along with his lovely wife, Eunice, Joan and I count them among our closest friends. Hal is a brilliant lyricist whose work with Burt Bacharach produced the songs that along with those by the Beatles and Paul Simon I most admire from every vantage point. Their songs are the soundtrack to our lives, through most of the second half of the twentieth century.

I first called Hal in the midseventies to ask him to write a song with me for a TV pilot that ultimately did not sell. But I was so happy to work with him and get to know him. He's such a gentle man, with the warmest smile and the best sense of humor, and he is an extraordinary conveyer of feelings

Paul Williams presenting Hal David and Charles with the Humanitarian Award from American Friends of Tel Aviv's Assaf Harofeh Medical Center, 1993. *Courtesy of the author.*

Joan and Charles—induction
to the Songwriters Hall of
Fame, New York, June 2004.
Courtesy of the author.

through the poetry in his lyrics. Hal and I collaborated many times over the years, and we've written many songs together for television, film, and theater. We never had a hit record together, or at least haven't yet, but some of my proudest work is with Hal, particularly in the two musicals that we wrote together, *The Chosen* with Chaim Potok, and *The Turning Point*, based on the film. Unfortunately, these shows have yet to be produced. But that is the business, and that we don't control. However, the songwriting we do control, and that we're both very proud of.

❧

Jerry Goldsmith and his beautiful wife, Carol, and Joan and I had a wonderful friendship, and it continues with Carol now that Jerry's gone. We had known each other and had been friendly for many years, but in the last five years of Jerry's life, our friendship together really blossomed. I truly miss

Jerry. We had a lot of laughs together, but also a lot of talks about music, and I miss that. It might sound strange to say, but there have been very few people that I discuss music with. Long before we became friends, I admired his work so much and really was a fan. For me, his was the ultimate voice in music for film. He had an extraordinary sense of uniting drama and music, and always with his own personal, unique approach. I think he created some of the best, most beautiful, and most profound music while artfully bringing out the soul of each film he worked on.

Jerry and Carol had two grand pianos in their living room, and we had many great musical evenings together. They were great hosts, and after wonderful dinners that often included composers David Newman and his wife, Krys, and at different times the composers James Newton Howard, Sandy Courage, Leonard Rosenman, Jack Elliot, pianist Mike Lang, and others, with two people at each piano, we'd sight-read through eight-hand reductions of symphonies and all sorts of orchestral works. Between the dinners, friendship, laughs, and music, we had some of the most memorable evenings.

Once, after a superb dinner at Carol and Jerry's house, where the other guests were Carole King and director Phil Alden Robinson, we got into a discussion of song collaboration. Carole had just returned from a trip to France, where she collaborated on songs with different songwriters every day for a week, and each day they would produce at least one song. Jerry asked Carole how she could sit in a room with someone and write a song without any work being done individually in preparation. I was somewhat more used to that way of collaborating than Jerry, but it still was not my preferred way of writing songs either.

"Easy," Carole said. "C'mon, let's go to the piano, the three of us composers, and write a song right now."

As we left the dining room, Joan said that this would be our last night out for a while as I was about to get very busy with a deadline.

"That." Carole said. "Last Night Out. Great title." And with that, she asked me to sit at one piano and Jerry at the other.

"Play a phrase, any phrase to start the beginning of a song."

I did, and in an instant Jerry picked up a second musical phrase as a continuation of mine. Carole came up with some words to go with the developing melody. Then she took over at my piano and started to embellish on the direction of the music. All the while Joan, Phil, and Carol Goldsmith, who were sitting on the other side of the room on the sofas, were hurling lyric suggestions as one would toss a baseball in practice. Before long, through all the fun in getting there, a song started to emerge that we all agreed wasn't a bad start. We called it a night with that and left that incomplete song dangling in the memory of a wonderful evening. It was enough, and proved that it could

James Newton Howard, Jerry Goldsmith, David Newman, and Charles at Carol and Jerry Goldsmith's house. *Courtesy of the author.*

be fun to collaborate on a song from scratch in a room together, at least after a great dinner and a lot of wine. It still is not my preference to write songs that way, but it was surely a great night.

Jerry was diagnosed with colon cancer and fought bravely for several years to keep his musical life intact until nearly the end. He was extraordinarily courageous and dedicated. He continued to compose and conduct as well right through his last score, *The Looney Tunes Movie.* During that period, he also continued to teach his graduate course in film composition at UCLA, and one day asked me if I could take over his class when he wasn't feeling well. I said that I would gladly, but I had never taught before. He said that shouldn't be a problem, that he gave his class an assignment to do a theme and variations, and all I'd have to do for the three-hour class was to critique the student's work and help them to develop it. That, I said, I could do, and I found that I really enjoyed working with the students, who were already somewhat accomplished. I ended up finishing that quarter for Jerry, and UCLA asked me to continue with the class the following year as a visiting professor. Not in my wildest dreams did I imagine myself one day teaching composition in a university, but I have done it now for the past five years, and am very happy to be able to help young composers in their work, and I have Jerry to thank for that. I also feel in some small way that I'm finally able to give back what I received from my dear Mlle Boulanger.

One time during that period, Jerry was scheduled to conduct a concert of his works with the Young Musicians Foundation Orchestra in LA, in an evening honoring him given by the Jewish Federation. He wasn't feeling up to it, and about a week before the concert, he asked me if I would conduct it for him. I said I'd be proud to, and spent the next week studying his scores. It's one thing to listen to someone's music and another to study his work as he wrote it in score form. I became even more taken with his work as a result. The concert went very well, and I enjoyed it thoroughly. He did continue conducting concerts that he had long been scheduled to do with orchestras around the world. As time went by, occasionally he was not feeling well enough to do a particular concert and had to cancel.

About a year before he passed away, he had concerts back to back in Japan and London. He loved working with the London Symphony Orchestra but felt it would be too much to do the Japan concerts as well, and he asked me if I would conduct those concerts for him. I said of course I would immediately when he called me. I couldn't say no to Jerry even though I was deeply immersed finishing the orchestration on my ballet, *Zorro!* I had a deadline looming for the premiere in San Francisco, and I was coming down to the wire before having to leave for Prague to record the music in advance of the premiere. But I was so glad that he asked me, even though that meant that I would have less time to do my own work.

I had just two weeks to study Jerry's scores, which included some of his best and most challenging work. I orchestrated my ballet during the day and studied his music at night. I would have the hundred-member Kanagawa Philharmonic to conduct along with an eighty-voice chorus for the suite from *The Omen*, Jerry's brilliant, Oscar-winning score, which hadn't been performed in many years.

The Omen is a great and intricate score that produced some of the most intense, beautifully written music. The orchestra would also perform a thirty-minute suite from *Star Trek* that was extremely detailed in its orchestration and coloration, and Jerry's wonderful music from *Patton* in addition to others. Conducting the two concerts in Yokohama and Tokyo were very rewarding experiences, and the orchestra and chorus were a pleasure to work with, and played and sang their hearts out for me. The director of the Kanagawa asked me if I would perform a piece of mine as well for the Tokyo concert and "Killing Me Softly" additionally as an encore piece. At that concert, some of the leading Japanese composers were there, and during the concert they made a presentation to me, inviting me into the Japanese Composers Society. I was very honored and touched by this. In the Tokyo concert, I performed my *Cut to the Chase Suite*, which includes chase scenes from seven or eight of my films, and I wrote a symphonic arrangement of "Killing Me Softly" specifically for that concert. The welcoming we had from the people involved with the Kanagawa Philharmonic and the friendships that Joan and I made as a result were heartwarming and touching, and the reception from the audiences for both concerts was resounding and quite memorable. We spent a great week in Japan, which I'll never forget.

Jerry's music is so appreciated by film and concert audiences around the world, and I felt proud to bring his music to Japan, played by such a fine orchestra and chorus. After Jerry died, the Belgium Philharmonic performed a tribute concert of his works that also included his great *Planet of the Apes* score. Joan

Charles conducting the Kanagawa Philharmonic and Chorus in Yokohama. *Courtesy of the author.*

and I were in Paris at that time, and we went from there to Ghent, Belgium, to join Carol for the concert at the Opera House along with a few other good friends of Carol and Jerry who came from Los Angeles. It was a very moving concert and fitting tribute. I was so glad we could be there for it.

In the summer after Jerry died, the composer Pat Williams asked me to conduct a tribute to Jerry during one of his concerts with the Henry Mancini

Institute Orchestra. It was very exciting for me because the orchestra of young musicians from around the world played Jerry's "Motion Picture Medley" so beautifully, and the audience gave them a standing ovation. For an encore I announced to the audience that we would play his wonderful *Star Trek* theme that we had prepared. That too was rousing and exhilarating, and when it ended it brought the audience back to its feet again. It was a lovely tribute to Jerry.

With his passing, the world lost one of the premier composers of the second half of the twentieth century, and I lost a good friend.

⌘

The world of Paris circa 1959 is long gone, with its buses that were open in the back that you could hop on even while they were moving, when the market at Les Halles was still a market, flooded with fresh foods brought in from the environs of Paris, and a soupe a l'onion *at Au Pied de Cochon, which was filled with workers who were starting their day after 3:00 AM downstairs at the bar in their white coveralls and berets, having their morning* vin rouge, *while the accordion player upstairs was playing for a crowded, noisy restaurant filled with patrons who were milking everything out of a night of revelry. When the Latin Quarter was populated with students from the Sorbonne and elsewhere, more so than with tourists. When it was still possible to catch a glimpse of Camus or Sartre at Café Flore, or Pierre Boulez surrounded by students in a café, one of whom I happened to be one day, while he discussed music that really was avant garde.*

Every now and then, I would have dinner in a little family restaurant on the Left Bank. Normally, at that time, the restaurants that I could afford to eat in had a small cover charge for a paper napkin and silverware. There would be a basket of bread on the table, and at the end of dinner, the waiter would write the bill directly on each diner's paper table cloth and ask, "Combien de pains?" *("How many pieces of bread did you eat?") and charge you accordingly.*

The working-class people who ate at these restaurants would sometimes pay a little extra to have a cloth napkin, and since some of these people usually ate in the same restaurant each night, they would fold up their napkins very neatly, leaving an unused portion of the napkin as the exposed side, and put it into a little wooden cubicle with their names in each box so that it could be reused the next night. If they managed carefully, they could use that same napkin for an entire week. The Parisian working class didn't earn much money and simply got by.

⌘

Many years later when Joan and I were visiting Paris, long after Mlle had passed away, our daughter Lisa met us there to spend a week with us. She wanted to see the places that were important to me when I lived there. We had a taxi drop us off at the Place Clichy, and we walked the two blocks to 36 Rue Ballu. It's now called Place Lili Boulanger, named for Mlle's sister, who was a great composer but died at a very early age. There is a small plaque on the right side of the door of the entranceway that states that Nadia and Lili Boulanger had lived here.

I stepped inside the doorway, and my mind rushed to moments long gone. A young woman was coming down the stairs and saw us standing there, looking, I guess, out of place, and she asked if she could help. I explained why we were there and asked her if she knew who Mlle Boulanger was.

"*Non. Pas de tous.*"

Other people appeared, but they didn't know of Mlle either, except that they were aware of the plaque.

How could they not have known that the most prominent people in the arts for many years had made their way to the third floor to visit Mlle Boulanger? That Stravinsky, Copland, Hindemith, Gershwin, Yehudi Menuhin, Marc Chagall, Leonard Bernstein, the poet Paul Valéry, and countless others had been there, as well as even Prince Rainier, her godson. It was now all a long-forgotten memory.

After a week in Paris, we drove to Fontainebleau on the way to the South of France, and the little village that we love so, Mougins. When we parked our car outside the palace gates and walked down the long, regal cobblestoned entranceway, toward the grand horseshoe staircase, my heart rose with sweet memories, as it always has.

The right side of the palace was our music wing, the Conservatoire de Musique, where we had our classes and where Mlle lived, on the second floor at the end of the long hallway. The school had been closed for many years, and now it was just back to being part of the museum in the palace. Our concert hall, the Salle Jeu de Paume, was converted back to its original purpose of being an indoor tennis court and was now used by the local inhabitants of Fontainebleau.

I asked several docents or workers in the museum if they knew that this had been a school at one time. "*Non, je ne le savais pas.*" They had no idea.

So I showed them around the building as though I was the docent, and they seemed to enjoy that, but still, it had no significance for them, just a passing curiosity.

We then went to the street where our school restaurant had been, in a courtyard behind gates, and where adjacent to that building was a small house that I lived in one summer, along with some of the other students. The heavy wooden gate covering the entrance was locked, but I could peek through it and see that the buildings were in total disrepair, a relic of some bygone era.

And even our main student residence, where most of the students lived my first summer in Fontainebleau, with its magnificent gardens in the back, was now a private home. The house was set back from the street, with a garden and walkway in front, and with a high stone wall protecting the privacy of the people who lived there, as most of the houses in Fontainebleau were designed that way. I rang the doorbell on the wooden gate, and a young woman who lived there with her parents came out and said she had no idea of what this building was in 1959.

There have been many books written on the subject "you can't go back." This was that real-life experience for me. Such an important time in my life, such meaning that I carry with me, disappeared in a changing world. I don't suppose I'll ever look for those places again in Paris or Fontainebleau. In my mind, they have not changed at all. Better to leave it that way.

❧

Michael Smuin and I had remained friends all those years since working on *A Song for Dead Warriors*. At least once or twice a year, Joan and I went to San Francisco to visit Michael and usually to see a premiere of a new work of his.

One evening, while we were having dinner together with Michael after seeing a performance his ballet company, Michael asked me, "What do you think of 'Zorro' as a ballet?"

I said simply, "That's my name in Spanish."

He took that as I intended, as a "Yes, I think that's a really good idea, and I'd love to do it with you."

Michael then and for ten years before that had had his own ballet company that he started when he left the San Francisco Ballet. It was a wonderful company that toured the United States and Europe. Michael was a great talent and an original voice in the world of classical ballet, and I was thrilled to do another ballet with him.

He brought Matthew Robbins into the project to devise the libretto. Matthew is a well-known screenwriter and film director who had written, among other films, *The Sugarland Express*, the Steven Spielberg film that I did not get to do.

For me, composing the music for a ballet is very different from working on a film, although there are certainly a lot of similarities such as telling a story musically and accompanying a range of emotions as well as story points. But that's where it ends.

Ballet is about music and dance. Whereas in my two ballets there are definitely stories being told, the music has a much freer sense of composition, as it does not take a back seat to the dance. They are one. And of course, there don't have to be specific timings as in film. That means that while I'm developing the music around the story, I can develop it for its own internal needs in advancing the composition. The form is dictated by the music itself, and it's wonderfully satisfying and challenging. And ultimately, to see the piece danced to, with costumes, purpose, and drama, all set to brilliant choreography with great dancers, is as satisfying as it gets for me.

Matthew Robbins came up with a fresh and unique idea of doing a movie within a story. The young Emilio is an usher in a movie theater where his heartthrob, a young, beautiful woman, works as a ticket taker. She's constantly being harassed by the evil theater manager. All this, while the film *Zorro* is being shown inside the theater. Zorro eventually comes out of the film to help the young Emilio, and Emilio similarly goes into the film and gets caught up in Zorro's world. It's a fantasy and is charming and done with so much humor in Michael's hands, and of course it's dramatic, as it is Zorro after all, an action hero. The first and most successful and most imitated of all the superheroes.

The three of us met many times to collaborate in San Francisco as Matthew was developing the story and Michael and I were giving him our reaction and our input. We both loved what he was doing. During one of our sessions, Matthew might have a thought about something, and Michael would picture that in his mind and stand up and do some dance movements that illustrated what he was seeing. On occasion, I would go to the piano and improvise something similarly with music to illustrate what I was hearing.

With Michael Smuin and Matthew Robbins in San Francisco. *Courtesy of the author.*

We were all very much in sync. When Matthew had finished the story in libretto form, I worked with it, breaking it down into eleven scenes. That started to give me a sense of musical form. I spent the better part of a year composing the music as the ballet is nearly an hour long. After each scene was completed, I'd go to San Francisco to let them hear it, and eventually, when I didn't have the liberty of time, I simply sent a CD of my music, with a mock-up of the orchestra that I did in my synthesizer studio at my house.

Michael started working with his dancers scene by scene, right behind me, as I'd finish each scene. At that point, I was so busy with my work that I couldn't go to San Francisco and see how it was coming along. But I heard from different people that it was looking fantastic. I never did get to see a rehearsal until my work was finished, and indeed, until the whole ballet was choreographed and finished as well. That was only a day before I was going to leave for Prague to record the music. I flew to San Francisco the day before flying to Prague, because I wanted to have the visual image of the ballet and dancers in my mind while I was conducting.

We had thought of using a live orchestra for the performances, but there really wasn't enough room in the Yerba Buena Center theater for a sizable enough orchestra for this score. The ballet was going to have to be danced to a prerecorded CD. With *A Song for Dead Warriors* I had seen it performed only with live orchestras all these years, both with the San Francisco Ballet and the Dance Theater of Harlem. But many ballet companies do perform to tape, especially when touring.

The Smuin Ballet company had been rehearsing for months to the synthesized version of the score, so in effect, they had gotten used to the fixed tempos. A live orchestra is bound to have some tempo differences from performance to performance, but in this case, for the recording, I told Michael that I would stay as close as possible to what the dancers were used to, because if something was too fast or too slow, it would not be alterable later. During the course of composing the piece, I would get together with Michael from time to time to go over the score with him, note by note, measure by measure. There were lots of meter changes in certain scenes, and he wanted to understand every detail. All the counterpoint, all the sudden changes, every bit of orchestration detail.

He even asked me something that I've never been asked by a choreographer: What did I see the dancers doing at a certain point? What kind of movement did I see? I told him my thoughts of what I imagined at that moment, in my own descriptive but lay language, and he said it was helpful. We were so much on the same wavelength with this work.

In Prague I worked with the Czech Chamber Philharmonic Orchestra, and with musicians added to that group, it brought the total to about eighty-five players. It was a first-rate orchestra, and Pavel Prantl, the orchestra contractor, was a fine violinist and the concertmaster as well. The studio was antiquated, but by using Pro-Tools and having an excellent engineer and a fine Czech composer, Milan Slavicky, as a supervisor to help balance the orchestra as he read the score and called cues out to the engineer, it all worked very well, and I was very pleased overall with the sound. The musicians were wonderful, and it was a pleasure conducting them. I did, however, have one rather uneasy moment during one of the sessions.

For one of the scenes, I wrote a solo part for the first violin chair that incorporated the use of many double stops (two strings played at the same time). Pavel played what I wrote and said it was awkward to play and suggested that it would sound better with two violins playing divisi. I said that I knew it would be difficult to play, but that that produced the sound that I wanted as a result of the double stops. Pavel seemed to be challenging me and offered the part to the violinist on his left, who shared his stand. As he did that, there were a few snickers in the violin section. Sometimes it is a pretty lonely profession standing in front of an orchestra, especially when one is in another country and doesn't speak the same language as the orchestra members.

❧

I was extremely apprehensive about the rehearsals for this first piece that I had written since arriving in Fontainebleau. It was for such an unusual complement of musicians, seven flutes, trumpet, and string quartet, and I had to quickly teach myself to conduct, because Mlle Boulanger said that a composer must conduct his own work.

The Salle Jeu de Paume was originally built as the indoor tennis court in the palace, but it had been converted to a long and narrow concert hall for the benefit of our school. This is where our formal concerts took place during the summer sessions. At one point during the rehearsal of my piece, Mlle Boulanger, who had been standing at my side as I was conducting, stopped me and made a comment about something in the performance of the composition that I really don't recall. She made a suggestion to me on how to improve it. I was suddenly on the spot. I didn't really care for her suggestion, but I certainly didn't want to offend her, so I didn't quite know how to handle the dilemma, on the stage, in front of the musicians.

I thought for a moment about her comments and my feelings about them, and finally turned back to the orchestra and said, "Would you please play it about halfway between the way Mlle suggests and the way I had intended."

With that, Mlle stopped me again and admonished me, saying, "My dear, compromises makes for very nice friendship but for very bad music. Play it the way you wrote it to be played, or the way I suggested, but don't make compromises."

"Very well," I said to the orchestra very firmly. . . . "Play it the way Mlle suggests."

And I got out of a tight spot . . . and I also never forgot her words.

I told Pavel that we'd record that section with two violins playing divisi, as opposed to the way I wrote it, and that we'd listen back afterward.

The part played by two violins was played very smoothly with no problems, and I asked Pavel to listen to a playback with me in the control booth. After hearing it together, I said to him, "Now do you see what I am missing? I need the sound of one violin playing the double stops as I intended, so that forces you to dig into the strings to produce the effect that I'm looking for. Now, this is nice and even sounding, but not rugged and forceful as I need."

He nodded that he understood, and said, "Let's do it again, no problem." He played it once as I wrote it, perfectly, with just the right texture. I thanked him and moved on to the next scene, without making any fanfare about it, happy to proceed. But when we took our lunch break that day, he did not invite me to join him at his table. I had lunch instead with the engineer and Milan. By the end of the day, Pavel was back to his pleasant self.

With Czech Chamber Philharmonic Orchestra in Prague. *Courtesy of the author.*

We mixed the music in Prague, and I sent the finished recording on CD directly to the Smuin Ballet in San Francisco. To ensure that my tempos were exactly what the dancers had gotten used to, I put timings on the score every few measures so I knew that I was as close as possible to the original tempos. All my work in films made that not a difficult task to do. There was no time to make adjustments with the dancers if the tempos didn't work for them, so that way I could be certain that it would not be a problem.

The ballet company had only a day or two to rehearse to the actual recording, but I heard from them that they were thrilled to hear the live orchestra performance, when they had gotten used to the synthesized orchestra.

Zorro! poster. *Photo by Tom Hauck.*

The premiere of the ballet was more than I could have imagined. The costumes by Ann Beck and the spare set décor by Douglas Schmidt and lighting by Sara Linnie Slocum were all superb. There is a filmed sequence at the opening where an animated fox spins around many times quickly, projected on the screen, and finally appears to jump out from the screen to the stage and turns into the live Zorro. The music begins with a trumpet fanfare, with a quasi-Spanish flavor to announce the entrance of Zorro. I used that theme quite a bit in different ways throughout the piece. It seemed from the audience's reaction to that first moment that they were with it and were enjoying it. The ballet looked fantastic, and the dancers were perfect and wonderful, especially the four principals: Zorro, Emilio, Rosa, and the Theater Manager.

The reviews were glowing, and it was clear that the ballet would continue to be performed, which is all I can ever hope for. It played eighteen performances during that month. About a year after that I conducted the premiere of the *Zorro Suite* performed by the Henry Mancini Institute Orchestra at Royce Hall. The suite combines several of the scenes from the ballet as a separate orchestral work.

I have to say that my experiences with ballet have been the most musically rewarding for me of all. Michael and I were hoping one day to do that ballet together based on St. Joan. He already had a drawing of the set with the chorus of singers acting as a jury behind the dancers. We hoped it would not be years before we undertook this work. Tragically, Michael Smuin passed away suddenly in April 2007 while teaching class at his ballet school. Celia Fushille, who worked with Michael for years, has continued brilliantly as the director of the Smuin Ballet, and the company continues to be a driving force in the world of ballet.

⬖

There are moments when my thoughts turn to Mlle Boulanger, and how I wish she could have heard these works. She was always content just to know that I was composing and that music was my life. But a teacher as rare and extraordinary and deeply spiritual and as dedicated as Nadia Boulanger was to generations of composers and musicians should enjoy the fruits of her teaching and influence.

Of course she did with generations of her earlier students, beginning with Aaron Copland, and followed by Virgil Thomson, Walter Piston, and Elliot Carter, among many others who made such a mark on the world of music in the decades following her teaching. She was anything but naïve, and she certainly knew what she had accomplished with her teaching and influence. What is so interesting and moving to me is how much a part of my life she's remained, even beyond music. She has been a very real and cherished

Rodolphe Cassand and Easton Smith, above, and below, an ensemble from *Zorro! Photos by Tom Hauck.*

Fox conducting the Poland National Opera Company chorus and orchestra in Warsaw, in the premiere of his Oratorio *Lament and Prayer*, based on the words of Pope John Paul II. *Courtesy of the author.*

presence in my whole life. That is something I wish that she could know. That all that she gave to me stays with me in my life and my work, and for that alone, there are no words to express my feelings.

Mlle often spoke to me about a housekeeper that she once had who found the most unusual and out-of-the-way places that dust was hiding, but she always found the dust and got rid of it. Boulanger's physical description of this woman as she was searching for dust, and the squeaking sounds she made as she described her finding the dust and doing away with it, always made me laugh. Sometimes I thought that Mlle admired this woman as much as if she had written a great symphony. She admired her work ethic and her determination to do all that she could do. She admired her fortitude

Charles conducting his *Victory at Entebbe Suite* in Ariel, Israel. *Courtesy of the author.*

and simplicity. She did what she did, and she did it with all the care that one could possibly have.

Boulanger would sometimes make a point to me by saying in her rough-textured but lovely voice, which had a sound like no other, and in her somewhat fractured but poetic English, "Have I done all what I could do?" I still hear those words and her voice in my ear as I sometimes ask myself, "Have I done all what I can do?" And the answer is always, "No." There is always more to do.

There are those times in one's work, however, when instinctively you know that the work is finished. The last brush stroke on a canvas, or the last hemi-demi-semi-quaver in a musical composition. That's not to say that more could not be written or changed, but it is time to put the pen down and move on. With that in mind, I conclude this memoir, such as it is, with a brief letter to my beloved teacher.

> *My Dear Mlle Boulanger,*
>
> *I am writing again to you after many years, at a point in time when I am not far away in age from the age that you were when we first met in Fontainebleau. You've been with me these many years, and your voice rings as clearly to me now as ever, and I still find that very comforting and illuminating. Through life's myriad challenges, I still draw strength and inspiration from your words and sometimes even, from your words unspoken. Rest assured that there is still much to do, and much music to write, and as for this book of memories, I dedicate it to you.*
>
> > *Faithfully and lovingly yours,*
> > *Charles Fox*

Nadia Boulanger sent this picture to Charles near the end of her life. Inscription starts "To my dear Charles. . . ." The rest is too blurred to make out. *Courtesy of the author.*

Index

Note: Italic page numbers indicate photographs.

About the Author

Charles Fox was born and raised in the Bronx, where he received his early musical education. He studied composition for several years in Paris with the famed Nadia Boulanger. As a composer, he's written in almost every musical genre from pop songs to ballets. He composed the music for over one hundred motion pictures and television films. His iconic music for such TV series as *Happy Days*, *Laverne & Shirley*, *Wonder Woman*, and *Love Boat*, and songs such as "Killing Me Softly" and "I Got a Name" and "Ready to Take a Chance Again," made him one of the most performed composers in the world. At one point it was estimated that three hundred million people heard his music weekly. His ballets, including *A Song for Dead Warriors*, have toured the world, and he's conducted symphony orchestras performing his music in many countries. He recently conducted his oratorio *Lament and Prayer*, based on the words of Pope John Paul II, with the Poland National Opera company in Warsaw.

Charles has received almost every recognition as a composer and songwriter.

He is the recipient of a Grammy Award for best song, two Emmy Awards, and multiple nominations for "Love, American Style," as well as Oscar and Golden Globe nominations for films such as *Foul Play* and *The Other Side of the Mountain*. He received lifetime achievement awards from Broadcast Music Inc. (BMI) and the Society of Composers and Lyricists and was inducted into the Songwriters Hall of Fame in 2004. He teaches a graduate class in composition at UCLA and is a governor of the Motion Picture Academy. In 2009 he came full cycle to his beginnings when he was inducted into the Bronx Walk of Fame with a permanent plaque high on a lamppost on the Grand Concourse and 161th St. in front of the Federal Court House and across the street from Yankee Stadium.

Fox was inducted into the Bronx Walk of Fame in June 2009. *Courtesy of the author.*

He is currently working on a commission from the Polish government, to compose a new work in honor of the 200th birthday of Chopin, which he will conduct in Gdansk, Poland, in August 2010.

Charles and his wife, Joan, have lived in Los Angeles since 1970.